An Age of Limits

01/06

UNIVERSITY OF
WOLVERHAMPTON

ONE WEEK LOAN

An Age of Limits

Social Theory for the 21st Century

Ralph Schroeder
University of Oxford, UK

First published 2013 by
PALGRAVE MACMILLAN

Palgrave Macmillan in the UK is an imprint of Macmillan Publishers Limited, registered in England, company number 785998, of Houndmills, Basingstoke, Hampshire RG21 6XS.

Palgrave Macmillan in the US is a division of St Martin's Press LLC, 175 Fifth Avenue, New York, NY 10010.

Palgrave Macmillan is the global academic imprint of the above companies and has companies and representatives throughout the world.

Palgrave® and Macmillan® are registered trademarks in the United States, the United Kingdom, Europe and other countries.

ISBN 978–0–230–36060–0   hardback
ISBN 978–0–230–36061–7   paperback

This book is printed on paper suitable for recycling and made from fully managed and sustained forest sources. Logging, pulping and manufacturing processes are expected to conform to the environmental regulations of the country of origin.

A catalogue record for this book is available from the British Library.

A catalog record for this book is available from the Library of Congress.

Typeset by MPS Limited, Chennai, India.

Contents

v

Tables and Figures

Tables

Figures

Acknowledgments

It is a great pleasure to acknowledge a number of debts. Ernest Gellner helped get me started on many of the questions tackled here. Randall Collins, John Hall and Michael Mann were excellent critics along the way and provided extremely useful feedback on the manuscript, as did Richard Swedberg, Mohammad Nafissi, Grant Blank and Sven Steinmo for individual chapters. David Gellner was a source of useful references for India. Jesper Schlaeger commented on China and Atul Kohli made penetrating remarks on the whole of Chapter 8. David Owen kindly gave advice on the philosophical debates in Chapter 9. The usual disclaimers apply. I have also learnt much in conversations with Thomas Heimer, Annika and Thomas Rickne, Marie Arehag, Ann-Sofie Axelsson and Henrik Bjoerck. Eric Meyer helped with the diagrams, and he knows how much visual clarity has helped to crystallize my arguments. Finally, my greatest thanks, as ever, go to my family. Sven and Anja are now off on their own academic adventures: they've been very patient with me, and Jen has been more patient than I could possibly wish.

1
From the Birth of the Modern World to the Age of Limits

Ages and labels

What are the main patterns of contemporary social change? Looking across the landscape of contemporary social theory, it seems that social scientists have given up on this question. Classical sociological theorists are ritually invoked, but without any great faith that Marx, Weber or Durkheim can yield more than the occasional concept or insight. Labels proliferate, but their weakness is indicated by the fact that they are derivative: 'late', 'post-' or 'radicalized' modernity. Totalizing concepts such as 'capitalism' that were once regarded as central are nowadays seen as reductive: is society really driven by an economic logic? In any event, most current thinkers argue that there are no more 'grand narratives', and instead that there is 'agency' in how we socially construct the world, implying a plurality of these constructions without any means to adjudicate between them.

In this book I shall argue that the lack of an overarching theory of social change is an obstacle to advance in social scientific knowledge and that it can be remedied. At the same time, there are good reasons why a lack of coherence has come about. A major one is that the economy, politics and culture are either treated separately, or if they *are* treated jointly, there is little agreement about where to draw the boundaries between them. This has resulted in disciplinary 'turf wars', so that economists, for example, try to explain politics with 'rational choice', or cultural studies argues that states and markets are always already culturally constructed. In fact, this book will argue, these boundaries are much clearer than this disciplinary messiness suggests, especially if we take a long-term comparative-historical perspective. Indeed, from such a perspective, there is much substantive (though not theoretical)

1

agreement about how markets, states and forms of culture have taken separate forms in the modern world, and how they interrelate. There is also a wealth of evidence about these relationships. And, as we shall see in the conclusion, with a systematic social theory in place, it is also possible to inform fundamental philosophical disputes, such as freedom versus equality, or the universality or otherwise of modernity.

This chapter will begin by outlining some key comparative-historical patterns and the concepts that can be derived from the agreement about these. It will start with the question of what contemporary society should be called, and where and when it became 'modern'. Then it will move on to the question of how to separate the economic, political and cultural realms in different periods. The two – ages and labels – are connected. Yet, as we shall see, once ages and labels have been dealt with, the conceptual groundwork will have been laid for a detailed account of contemporary social change.

We can begin by probing how to label the contemporary social world. Use of the Marxist term 'capitalism' in an overarching way has fallen out of favour after the demise of communism and of Marxist sociology. 'Capitalism' has also always been associated with a perspective that reduces the workings of society to an economic dynamic, a perspective that is no longer dominant (though a lot of its tacit assumptions remain in place, as we shall see). The main alternative has been 'modernity', but this term is regarded as vague and empty, and also depends on the ability to specify a break between modernity and what came before. Moreover, 'modernity' is associated with modernization theory, which was popular into the 1960s when the prevailing view was that 'the rest' would catch up with 'the West'. Nowadays, with China the world's second largest economy and poised to become the largest one, such a Western-centric view seems outdated. Other labels, such as the 'risk society' (Beck 1992) or 'liquid time' (Bauman 2007) and the like fall within what Mann has called the 'sociology of the last five minutes', and are soon forgotten.

What is to be done? One idea, to abandon imposing patterns onto history altogether, can be disposed of immediately. As Gellner put it, 'we inevitably assume a pattern of history . . . The only choice we do have is whether we make our vision as explicit, coherent and compatible with the available facts as we can, or whether we employ it more or less unconsciously and incoherently' (1988: 11). If, however, we are to impose a pattern, then we also need concepts for different periods. And the same, as we shall see, applies to defining the relations between the different orders of social life.

A good starting point is to recognize that the two problems are linked – isn't the relation between states and markets different depending on the period we have in view? I will argue that relations between, for example, the political and the economic order can indeed be identified throughout the modern period and distinguished from how they related before then, so that it is also possible to speak of a transition to modernity. As a consequence of this transition, a differentiation took place between the political, economic and cultural orders such that they became dominated by institutions – democratic states, free markets and rapid-discovery science – that have become ever more autonomous. This solves both problems – the transition to a new type of society, and the distinction between different social orders – at once. At the same time, this move puts the burden, of course, onto explaining *how* 'modern' states, markets and science differ from what has gone before, and how they have continued to operate autonomously since. And while the argument will need much further elaboration, it can be noted immediately that it entails that no one single institution characterizes or dominates modern society. Indeed, the argument will be that the tension between the three – their limits vis-à-vis each other – is one defining feature of the current period within modernity, roughly since the 1970s: the Age of Limits.

To understand the break inaugurated by modern institutions, it is necessary to take one step back (literally) in order to move forwards: the major debates about the emergence of capitalism and modernity have often located this break in a big transition in Europe during the 15th or 16th centuries. This made for an account of the 'rise of the West', whereby there was a break between the feudalism of the Middle Ages as against the modernity of capitalism. Yet this way of locating the origins of modernity, shared by Marx and Weber, has recently been challenged by the argument that Chinese levels of economic growth and living standards were similar to European ones up until the 19th century (Pomeranz 2000).[1] There is a related argument made by 'world-systems' thinkers, who want to submerge the early modern European 'rise' within more long-term shifts within a wider capitalist economy, thus making the West interdependent with its subjugation of 'the rest'.

These debates are ongoing, but they can be sidestepped for our purposes since – even on the view which pushes the rise of the West to the 19th century – there was still, even for Pomeranz, a 'great divergence' during the 19th century, with Europe or the West leaping ahead and China falling behind economically (all these issues will be revisited later in this and other chapters). Historians are generally agreed that the industrial revolution (some would say that there were two of them) resulted in a breakthrough to permanent and sustained economic growth, and that this breakthrough took place sometime during the 19th century in Europe and the United States – or perhaps a bit earlier in England. This breakthrough, as we shall see, had as a necessary (if not sufficient) condition the emergence of an autonomous technology-driven science. It only needs to be added that this revolution was self-generated – it did not rest on exploitation and gains from European colonies or empires (a controversial point, evidence will be presented later). If these arguments can be supported in what follows, then we can locate the transition to modernity in the 19th century, and in the democratic revolutions of the late 18th century which caused a rupture similar to the industrial revolution in the political order, even if some of the patterns that will be described reach further back, and were uneven or delayed in places.

Where recent debates nevertheless need to be paid close attention to is insofar as they move away from a Western-centric perspective, or what Hodgson called 'Westernism' (1993). Put differently, the transition to modernity (or any other label for contemporary society) must be placed in a global context since we are nowadays far more aware of possible interconnections between, say, American and Chinese economic power. One advantage in taking a global purview is that the problem of scope can be avoided – after all, society at its largest extent is global. Yet one requirement then is to specify which concepts or patterns apply to the West (the origins of the processes of globalizing modernity, in a global context), and how they subsequently apply throughout what is nowadays also called the global North – and also to take into account wherever necessary the interplay between the West and the non-West during these origins and the global North and South in the later phases, for either of the pair (though again, we have just ruled out or suspended, for the moment at least, the relation between the West and 'the rest' in terms of the West being propelled into modernity via its relations of empire or colonization).

It can be mentioned straight away that widening the context to a global one does not mean accepting the idea of 'globalization', which has become an alternative master concept in social theory (Walby 2009; Martell 2010). 'Global' will be used here only when there are relations that truly encompass or affect all societies. Thus 'globalization' must be applied more sparingly than as another way to refer to 'Americanization' or to the spread of capitalist economic relations, which is how the term is often used.

This brings us to placing the transition to modernity in a global context in the 19th century. Global histories have recently charted how the 19th century marks the 'birth of the modern world' (Bayly 2004) or the 'transformation of the world' (Osterhammel 2009). On these accounts, the long 19th century began with the French and American Revolutions and came to an abrupt end with the First World War.[2] This caesura will provide our starting point in a moment. In the meantime, it will be useful to briefly chart a course from the 19th century to the present: what of the periods thereafter – as seen from a global perspective – the short 20th century which lasted from 1914 until 1989–91? On a global canvas, this was an 'Age of Extremes' (Hobsbawm 1994), which can be further subdivided into a period of World Wars (1914–45) followed by a 'Global Cold War' (Westad 2005), which was at the same time a period of rapid decolonization. The 'Age of Extremes' began with authoritarianisms of the right and left (fascism and communism), but later saw a 'Golden Age' of unprecedented post-war economic growth which tapered off in the 1970s. For the 'Age of Extremes', as we shall see, it is therefore necessary to recognize that global wars play havoc with the autonomy of the political and economic orders, while exceptional economic growth, which also came to characterize some emerging economies, as well as decolonization, also complicate a clear separation between the global North and South.

In any event, the period since then, which can be dated from the mid-1970s and the end of exceptional economic growth in the global West and North, including outside the Western/Northern alliance from 1989–91 onwards which saw the end of the challenge of authoritarianism, provides the label for the period that this book will focus on, the contemporary world which, I argue, is an 'Age of Limits'. Much more will be said about these limits, but in terms of periodization, this period began with economic instability, a retrenchment of political movements, and growing awareness of how the transformation of nature rebounds on society. Arguably, these limits reach even further back: for example, signs of the negative impacts of the transformation of nature could already be seen during the industrial revolution. Yet these limits were not widely recognized until the 1970s, and it is still not universally agreed, to continue with this example, that open-ended growth is unsustainable now. This book argues, however, that these limits are not just characteristic of economies and technological transformation, but also politically, where the origins of limits lie in the narrowing of political options within democratic states, at least in the West or North. Further, the North, and most other parts of the world, are also constrained by giving a free reign to markets – not in an ideological or political sense – but in a structural one. These narrowings have only crystallized with the economic reforms in China and become entrenched globally with the decline of the Soviet Union in the 1980s. The 'Age of Extremes' (and within it, the Golden Age) has thus given way to an 'Age of Limits' beginning during the 1970s–80s, which can be defined as a period of relatively declining economic growth, a narrowing of political options, as well as constraints on the technological transformation of the environment.[3]

We will need to return to this periodization later. For the moment, it is sufficient to note that the global and the modern are not alternatives; indeed, we can speak of a globalizing modernity, whereby modern patterns increasingly take on a global scope. Globalization is thus a way of moving away from a Western-centric perspective to one which specifies the processes of modernity as and when they characterize a Global North. Again, this argument rests on the idea that the rise of the modern Western world was not initially reliant upon the non-Western world or the South. Once this 'reliance' has been ruled out (again, evidence will presented in due course, and caveats introduced for certain periods and processes), we can focus on the modern developed world or simply the North, which consists of Western and other market democracies. These arguments can now be taken further to specify how the transition to modernity led to a differentiation of the political, economic and cultural orders. Again, the argument will be that modernity began not just with industrialization and the emergence of markets, but also with the advent of democratic states in the political order, and of the separation of a technology-driven rapid-discovery science from the rest of culture. These three distinct modern processes began in the long 19th century, and all of them have since become globalized – even if this global spread has varied in depth and scope.

Disciplinary approaches to politics, economics and culture

Before we chart the emergence of uniquely modern institutions in the three orders, a brief excursus is necessary about why they are not typically treated as autonomous – or if they are, why they are treated differently by different disciplines without making the relationship between them explicit in structural terms. To begin with, we can note that in contemporary social thought, the economy is dominated by economists and fellow-travellers in other disciplines whose approach rests on treating people as individuals and their choices as rational. As we shall see, there is some truth in treating economic actions as divisible and the aggregations of these actions as maximizing. Yet in much of the rest of social science, this autonomy is not recognized, and it is argued instead that the economy is subject to political direction, as in the school of 'political economy' (which we shall encounter later).

In the realm of culture, as already mentioned, it has become fashionable to argue that people have 'agency' in their everyday practices, and the idea of science as separate from culture is rejected. Yet while I will agree here that people's everyday life ought to be an anchor for grounding claims about social change, it will also be shown that culture explains little unless it is seen as part of larger structural changes. Moreover, cultural – and political and economic – structures are often only indirectly related to everyday change: science is a good example, because the institutions producing rapid-discovery science are remote from everyday culture, even if science indirectly, via consumer technologies for example, has profoundly reshaped everyday life. In what follows, I will provide a sociological account of science, but draw frequently on anthropology and social history for understandings of culture and everyday life (but argue that, ultimately, much of everyday life can be relegated to history and anthropology as being outside the scope of understanding macro-social changes).

This leads to a further point, which is that macro structural changes are only discernible over longer periods. Science only dominates modern culture at one remove since its abstract worldview must be adhered to only within a specialist realm which leaves large swathes of culture untouched. At the same time, this scientific worldview has come to monopolize – again, over a long period and in a diffuse way – serious knowledge. Similarly, disembedded and atomized economic interactions provide a 'structure' only in the diffuse sense that markets shape our everyday life at an aggregate level of the distribution of resources. Finally, the same indirectness applies to the political realm, where everyday life is transformed only by longer-term changes in the distribution of political power. In the case of politics, however, there is more than the diffuse structure of markets and of science as worldview: modern states concentrate power within a centralized structure with boundaries in which rights and resources are distributed; the nation-state.

It can be seen that the relations between these autonomous spheres or orders and the relations between them are rarely addressed because of an academic disciplinary division of labour. Again, the exceptions are sweeping social theories like Marxism which have tried to reduce social change to underlying economic forces, and these have been swept aside, leaving us with economists and their rational actors, or cultural studies with 'agency'. Other sociological theories such as 'structuration' also rely on actors reflexively shaping social change (Giddens 1990) and thus leave macro-relations rather open-ended in the sense that they are somehow interdependent with this micro-reflexivity. Only a few theories systematically tackle the relations between different macro-social orders (Gellner 1988) or powers (Mann 1986, 1993), and these will be engaged with below. Before embarking on an account of how the economic, political and cultural orders became separated, it is worth pointing out that, whatever autonomy we will ascribe to them, these structures will need to be systematically related to one another in some way – in spite of any disciplinary differences – since otherwise it could indeed be possible that one determines or suffuses the other(s).

My approach, in contrast to theories with a single model of power or a single (economic) approach to institutions, will be to ask three questions simultaneously: which institutions dominate at the macro-level and with what scope? Where are the cleavages between the dominant institution in one order or domain of society as against other orders or domains? And how does power, or how do these dominant institutions, operate in each of these domains or orders? These might seem overly ambitious questions to raise anew, but one advantage that makes it manageable is that I will seek to answer this question only for the modern period – a mere 200–250 years or so (other theories typically address all human societies) – and to focus more specifically within this period on the break within modernity between the Age of Extremes and the Age of Limits. Even so, I will argue that any systematic and structural account which ties these three questions together needs to recognize that different forms of power and different institutions operate in each order.

We will return to this point once we have identified these institutions and powers. It can be anticipated, however, that their different mechanisms also constitute a limit – not insuperable in disciplinary or theoretical terms – but in practice (such that, for example, the freedom of markets constrains states' room for manoeuvre, or science circumscribes the claims of culture). Further, it can be anticipated that, for example, the centralized authority of the state and diffuse relations of markets operate at different geographic scales and within different time horizons. In this respect, the only approach is a global one which sees states operating in world of states and markets operating more globally, and to chart how the trajectories of individual states and of economies intersect, and when and to what extent they have become independent of each other. It is this intersection – or the lack of an intersection – which characterizes the Age of Limits.

Before taking this idea further, it is now time for a sketch of how these orders became autonomous. A final reflection can be added before doing so: a key reason for the lack of coherence of sociological theory is that sociology has not set itself apart from other disciplines. The lack of boundaries, from the point of view of the sociology of knowledge, is a sign of weak organization. It is therefore necessary to produce a clear and unified account of how economies, states and culture operate from a sociological perspective, while also specifying how this account differs from or overlaps with that in other disciplines, in order to strengthen theory within and around sociology: within – because no matter the subdiscipline (say, political or economic sociology), there needs to be both a clear delimitation of what the topic covers but also how the economy and politics interrelate; and around – because it needs to be clear how a sociological account differs from 'economics' or 'political science'. This larger point will not be needed on the way, but again we will need to return to it in the conclusion.

The emergence of free markets, rapid-discovery science, and democratic states

Free markets

There are three terms which have been used to describe the modern economic order: industrial society, capitalism and markets. Industrial society is based on enhanced productive capacity, mainly through the application of energy to production. A problem with putting so much emphasis on this transformation in production is that a necessary condition for industrialization was extrinsic to the economic order – science and technology, and how they made possible the uses of non-human and non-animal energy. As we shall see, this assigns a 'prime mover' role to science and technology which is only partly warranted.[4] The term capitalism, on the other hand, focuses on the commodification of labour, the private ownership of the means of production, and the classes created by both. This, too, is an important characteristic of the 19th century. Yet as we shall see, the classes to which capitalism gave rise played a role for only a limited period, and on their own played only a limited role. Further, I shall argue that class dynamics are no longer central in the Age of Limits.

This leaves 'markets' which, for reasons that will be argued at greater length in Chapter 4, trump both the other concepts. This is because, although markets have existed throughout recorded history, modern 'disembedded' markets, which combine private property (including contractual labour) and formally free exchange, arose as a new and autonomous institution during the 19th century on a mass basis, and the characteristic of disembeddeness has dominated the economic order ever since. The exception is that during mass mobilization warfare, in the first half of the 'Age of Extremes', and among right and left authoritarianisms, markets were partly subordinated to states (the American Civil War could be added as another exception). Apart from this, markets have become increasingly 'disembedded' from other social relations – and since the word 'disembedded' is awkward, I will interchangeably use 'free' to indicate formally free exchanges and freedom from being subject to political and cultural constraints. I should add immediately that there is no implication that 'free' markets are necessarily associated with 'liberal' states, or that they are 'efficient' or operate without monopolies, or that within market economies there may not be asymmetries whereby some gain at the expense of others. In short, the word 'free' is used in the sense of 'unfettered', and has no intrinsic relation to political 'freedom'. As we shall see, economies only partly consist of free markets, since large parts of the economy – typically between a third and a half – are 'unfree'. But it is a mistake, I shall argue, not to recognize that the economy is also *not* part of a 'political economy', and thus to overlook that free markets also impose severe constraints – limits – on societies.

Before elaborating the notion of disembedded markets further, it will be useful to see how this idea relates to industrialization and capitalism. As mentioned, the take-off of industrialization occurred in the 19th century, first in England/Britain and then across the main Western powers. The contrast with China makes this clear (Mann 1993: 261, 262), as does the contrast with pre-industrial societies (Crone 1989). The American 'system' of mass production emerged somewhat later in the course of the 19th century, adding machines to the production process (Hounshell 1984). Certain technological advances were required, however, for *mass* production – and consumption – to take off in the 20th century. What connects mass production to mass consumption, however, were *mass* markets, requiring the logistical means (transport and communication) or infrastructures to tie the two together (Beniger 1986). Put differently, it is only when commodities (including labour) are exchanged on a large scale that free – disembedded – markets become dominant.

Industrialization thus enabled capitalism – or better, markets – to operate on the basis of a leap in scale and scope. Free exchanges of labour and products (their capitalist 'commodification'), in turn, created classes which, as we shall see, resulted in a wave of struggles to gain rights from the state. Yet most social scientists nowadays agree that the role of classes, whatever it may have been during the onset of modern capitalism and perhaps into the post-war period, has since waned. Further, the main impact of classes was not, as Marxists would have it, in class relations shaping society as a whole: instead, classes gained different degrees of political power – rights as citizens – within the state. It is therefore not possible to have a purely economic understanding of power relations which treats the state as epiphenomenal. And even if economic inequalities in some respects nowadays remain as pronounced as they have been in the past, the impact of classes on social change has diminished.[5] We will see later that this capability has become quite restricted in recent decades, and this applies both to change 'from below' as well as to economic elites, which may be more cohesive than lower classes, but which are also relatively uninterested in political power except insofar as it promotes well-functioning markets and thus profit.

Without 'macro-actors' like capitalist or working classes, and with industrial technology relegated to lesser importance than the coupling of mass production to mass consumption, we have arrived at markets as a more incisive concept. What sets modern markets apart from pre-modern ones (as will be documented further below) is that they are dis-embedded or untrammelled or formally free. This is so in several senses: first, modern markets are separated from the state. As Gellner points out, in modern capitalist societies, there is more of a separation between the economy and politics than ever: 'Economic activities become autonomous and can, for once, be governed by purely "economic" considerations' (1979: 285). Second, even if free markets – in the geographical sense of long-distance trade going beyond local subsistence economies – existed in pre-modern societies, they only become large-scale in terms of volume during the 19th century (perhaps somewhat earlier in some countries). Thus Mann (though he prefers 'capitalism') says that 'capitalist property and market forms were thoroughly institutionalized (by 1760 in Britain, by 1860 almost everywhere else in the West)' (1993: 82, cf. 219). Bayly agrees (2004: 174) that a global market for rising industries was created in the course of the 19th century and he points out (2004: 290) that the notion of the hidden hand of the market was also new, though by the mid-19th century it had spread from Britain throughout the West (2004: 300–02). Markets thus became national or transnational in a way that affected the whole of society, not just an elite or individual nation-states.

The modern economy is, to be sure, supported by state-enabled infrastructures (such as transport, public health and education), which also took off in the late 19th century. This is often given as a reason why – then, as now – the political and the economic should not be separated. On this view, the state is seen as providing the necessary preconditions for the rise and maintenance of markets. But the state's promotion of infrastructures such as those just mentioned, or even its championing of national economic strategies as in the late 19th century debates about autochtonous economic policies (associated with Friedrich List; see Bayly 2004: 300–02) are not incompatible with the growth of markets: for example, even though states grew enormously during the late 19th century in terms of the infrastructures they provided, as Mann points out, 'state activities *decreased* as a proportion of national economic activity between the mid-eighteenth and the early twentieth century' (1993: 368).

Hence we have arrived at a single form of how 'capitalism' - in my view, 'free markets' – 'and states cohabit the world', enshrined in the notion of 'laissez-faire' whereby 'the state merely endorses (or is unable to change) existing market terms, and does not try to change them authoritatively' (Mann 1993: 33). As we shall see, the state's role in industrial take-off of growth was central (Chang 2002), but again, the state also simultaneously and deliberately promoted a separate order of free economic activity. Thus the story – to jump ahead – of late-developing countries such as the 'Asian tigers' where the state guides industrialization, sometimes known as an escort-and-release strategy, and discussed by those interested in economic development (Weiss and Hobson 1995), also fits with the notion of disembedded markets: even here, the point is ultimately to strengthen economies so that they can compete internationally and unaided by the state.

'Capitalism' is a useful term insofar as it highlights the open-ended pursuit of profits, but this is also entailed by 'disembedded markets', where profit is subsumed under the more general pursuit of maximizing growth in an open-ended manner. The notion of 'profit' is also misleading: profit is pursued by firms, though those using 'capitalism' want to indicate by using this term that some classes profit at the expense of others. Perhaps; but this is not a structural condition which currently 'drives' capitalism. Indeed, one of the constraints of free markets is that there are no mechanisms to steer growth or channel profits systematically, or to mitigate inequalities (but nor can these inequalities be exploited in a systemic manner). The notion of disembedded markets does not prejudge the stratified outcomes of inequalities which, as we shall see, are growing in some parts of the world and declining in others.

Similarly with the Schumpeterian conception of capitalism and how innovation is financed with venture capital to create fleeting monopolies in competitive niches, and how this process extends to ever greater parts of the economy: this process can also be explained in terms of markets (White 1981), with innovation relegated to being an extra-economic force (Schroeder 2007: 66–9). Whether such fleeting monopolies are crucial, as for Schumpeter, or if other processes are more important or must be added to these 'destructive' processes, is left open by using 'markets' instead.

The extent to which markets have become disembedded from their political (including nation-bound) contexts is a more difficult issue, and we shall see that this waxes and wanes during the modern period. However, again, it will be argued that the separateness of markets has been overridden during the 20th century mainly in two ways; in authoritarian societies, and during war. In any event, apart from these instances, disembedding vis-à-vis the state means that markets are to a large extent excluded from the realm of state control, and the state is thus left with 'economic policy' which shapes the varieties of how markets are governed, but within severe constraints.

Modern markets are characterized by the expectation of open-ended and permanent economic growth, which became part of society's self-image for the first time during the 19th century. Mann says that capitalism and industrialization have been overrated (1993: 726) because they did not change distributive power relations. Similarly, Gellner points out: 'what defines the market is not that people exchange things . . . but that they do so in the spirit of maximizing economic advantage and, above all, that they do it with an almost total disregard of other considerations' (1988: 130). Or again, 'economic advantage is divisible, calculable and negotiable' (1988: 175). A precondition for this calculability and divisibility is the commodification of labour and of products so that exchange can take place via the medium of money (Ingham 2004). The separateness of this money economy became institutionalized, not just in central banks, but also in superordinate financial markets for money itself. Finally, these markets require private property, which must be guaranteed by the state, but this property is also subject to 'contract' outside of – in the sense inviolable to the intrusion by – the state. Thus law guarantees that some property is beyond the state (China is an exception among the developing economies that will be discussed, but as we shall see, whether China is a market or capitalist economy is still subject to debate, and the absence of property guarantees is central to this debate).

Disembeddedness entails homogeneous relations across the economic order, and in this respect the economic order has also become separated or demarcated from others. The autonomy of the economy applies both to a separate theoretical mechanism (unbounded and divisible maximization by means of exchange) and to how this order is organized in practice (across day-to-day practices of work and consumption). As we shall see, a key argument has been that even if markets became disembedded in the course of the industrial revolution, they became reembedded or subject to control after the Second World War (Polanyi). Yet this argument is misleading insofar as, although welfare states were created to counteract the effect of markets on economic security, markets also continued to be disembedded still further.

The main point, for now, is that the concept of capitalism stands or falls without the notion of classes (or, on a global scale, of a core which exploits the periphery), which would thus make economic relations central to social change as a whole. The notion of capitalism further requires, ultimately, a crisis in economic growth for its detractors, or a movement towards greater benefits for all, or global markets 'trumping' national policies, according to its cheerleaders. Neither fits contemporary social change, where the problem lies precisely in the fact that free markets are uncontrollable, thus intensifying (within and between some parts of the world) the inequalities generated by markets, as well as pushing growth towards potential catastrophes for the environment without the ability to control this. In any event, as we shall see, nation-states are not 'trumped' by markets, but neither are class relations from 'above' or from 'below' a driving force: hence 'disembedded' or 'free' captures modern market relations better than the term 'capitalist' market relations.

The notion of industrial society pivots on the industrial revolution, but large-scale industrial manufacturing, too, as we shall see, is no longer a central or defining feature of developed economies. Markets, which include formally free labour and property, do not require classes or crisis or the driving force of a particular economic sector. Disembeddedness has the advantage, however, of pointing to a unique modern characteristic – the autonomy of the economic order – and the open-ended and divisible and atomized relations within it. Free markets

are the dominant institution ordering economic relations, and the economic environment that is being thus ordered consists of the commodities (labour, goods, services) that are exchanged via the mechanism of
money. (This schema, of a dominant institution, ordering an environment, via a distinctive mechanism – characterizes all three social orders,
and will be elaborated shortly.)

Three cultures, one structural

The cultural order is seemingly complex because there are so many
components that can be considered as falling under this rubric. Yet I will
argue that once a fundamental distinction is made between knowledge
on the one hand as against belief and the rest of culture on the other,
this complexity vanishes. Culture can be divided into three main parts:
science, religion and consumption. Only science is structurally essential in modern societies, though consumption is deeply entrenched
in everyday life. The reason why this division within culture has been
overlooked is because this area has been poorly theorized, particularly
since culture was treated for some time in sociology as equivalent to
ideology. With ideology no longer used (we shall see that it plays a useful role in characterizing some periods and regimes and movements, but
under the rubric of the political order), culture in the social sciences has
become highly fragmented without coherent overarching concepts. But
as soon as the role of culture is restricted to the parts that cause macro-
social change, only one remains as playing a structurally essential role.

To begin with then, science must be separated: the distinction
between legitimate knowledge and the rest of culture pre-dates the 19th
century, but it only deepened, intensified and became institutionalized
in the modern world. Collins (1998) calls it 'high-consensus rapid-
discovery science' because only modern science, unlike pre-modern,
science started generating a consistently growing stream of results.
Further, scientific knowledge gained an autonomous institutional footing in the university system of the late 19th century. Before the 19th
century, science was subject to religion and to the state. But in the late
19th century, it not only gained a separate base in universities, but also
started to play a central role in the economy in the shape of separate
research departments in large firms (Osterhammel 2009: 398). In this
period, science became recognized as consisting of a distinct body of
knowledge, and professional expertise and science gained legitimacy
because of the success of industrial production – rather than by recourse
to religious or other cultural sources of legitimacy or authority (Bayly
2004: 313, 318). In the 20th century, this independent base became

solidified and the powerfulness of science was recognized not just in its own right, but as a motor of innovation and prerequisite for growing consumption.

Apart from this institutionalization, science occupies the apex of culture because it represents legitimate claims to an exclusive monopoly of valid knowledge. In this sense, science is separate from the rest of culture, but this very separation also entails that the scientific worldview does not enter into or pervade everyday life. Hence a curious feature of science is that although it is all-powerful – indeed universal – in the realm of cognition or knowledge, it is nevertheless compartmentalized and stays separate from the rest of culture and social life generally. The furthest and most powerful extensions of science into society are technological systems (where, as we shall see, this separation does not quite hold), but even these systems – foremost transport, communication and energy – have mostly faded into the background of everyday life. The relation between science and technology has in any event become closer – as we shall see later – and for this reason the label 'technoscience' has come to be used (Shinn 2007), which reflects not only the role that science plays in innovation, but also that the main role of technoscience in everyday life is via technological artifacts.

And while science also extends into several apparatuses of professional expertise (for example, health, education and social care), unlike the economic and political orders, science does not have powerful elites but needs allies among extra-scientific elites and among the public. The power of expertise or experts is therefore not on par with the power of political and economic elites, though on the other hand scientific knowledge does not need to rest or rely on extra-scientific cultural authority since the products of technoscience – the growing transformation of the environment that it manipulates, nature or the physical world (including humans, as with health and medicine) – and the resulting economic growth, are plain for all to see.

The second component of modern culture, consumerism, also predated the great transformation, but only extended into everyday life on a mass basis in the 20th century. Consumption only became a dominant part of culture after the industrial revolution, even if its roots among elites predate the modern period. Consumerism takes up the largest share of free time and of non-essential spending, and so is far more important in terms of role of culture in everyday life than science or religion. On the other hand, it is not a cohesive or clearly demarcated part of culture so that this role is rather diffuse. In any event, despite its centrality to everyday life, and its role in driving economic growth, it is (perhaps luckily) not an indispensable part of modern society insofar as it has no independent structural source of authority or legitimacy. It can be noted straight away that this 'dispensability' of consumption requires making a distinction between economic growth of products and services for needs as against for wants – with only the latter counting as consumption. This idea is contentious, and perhaps incomprehensible or unacceptable to economists. But as we shall see, in developed societies, growth of spending on consumption or leisure now outstrips other household spending. In any event, the legitimacy of consumer culture lies in its pervasiveness within everyday life, and while the impetus to growing consumption is well-entrenched, it is not clear if this part of everyday culture dictates or necessitates any particular norms or particularly high levels.[6]

Religion, which was the most powerful source of cultural legitimacy in agrarian or traditional societies and accounted for the most pervasive everyday cultural practices in these societies, has become residual. Bayly (2004: 480) argues that although religions did not become more uniform in the 19th century, the idea of what a religion is did. With the separation of religion from its imbrication in social life, the path was paved for its diminishing role. The fact that religion has nevertheless persisted at lower but not insignificant levels has obscured the onward march of secularization as well as the replacement of the exclusive legitimacy of religion by that of science. And there is a further anomaly to deal with, which is that, supposedly, religion still plays a central role in the United States, alone in this respect among developed Western societies. Yet as we shall see, there are also reasons to treat this as an exception that proves the rule, and the alleged strength of religion in the United States also has structural limits.

Apart from these three elements, as mentioned, culture in sociology was previously thought to consist of ideology, or of a public sphere of political discourse. But this has become misleading for periods and places – such as the North after 1989–91 – when political regimes are no longer legitimated by a single overarching ideology. Arguably, the Age of Extremes was an age in which ideology played a stronger role than before, but it has played a lesser one since, in the Age of Limits. Whether science and consumption are on the wane, or how they face limits, is a question that will be pursued later, though religion is not just limited but it has also become excluded from a structural role. Thus culture consists of three parts plus or minus one – two, if religion is excluded, four if ideology is included within culture (as opposed to subsuming ideology under politics, as I argue). In my view it is more accurate to conceive of culture as science versus the rest – as the monopoly of legitimate cognition versus the rest of culture – with this rest lacking dominance or exclusive authority. In this vein, Gellner has argued, partly following Weber, that science (or cognition) will remain in continuing tension with culture apart from science – or with everyday cultural life and ideology (1988: 213–14). As we shall see, however, this tension is only prominent in particular niches. Thus the structural role of the dominant institution of science, resting on the mechanism of its cognitive authority and ability to manipulate – or transform – its environment, nature or the physical world, is generally unchallenged.

Politics: democratic states and citizens

The separateness or autonomy of the modern state predates industrialization (Mann 1988: 1–32). But it was strengthened in a novel way via two processes during the long 19th century: popular legitimation and enhanced state capacity. Both combined so that larger bodies of citizens were incorporated into more pluralist democratic states, though this incorporation was still aspirational in some of the great powers and incomplete for others. Still, in the political order the onset of modernity can be dated to the French and American revolutions, though similar revolutionary impulses were in evidence around the world (Osterhammel 2009: 747). States before the 19th century were controlled by aristocratic regimes with an elite based partly on wealth and partly on religious authority. After the democratic revolutions, they became controlled by 'the people' or their representatives, and the dominant institutions of democratic states, in turn, now exercised control over their environments – 'people', or populations. But there are two versions of how this – democratic – control or increasing state responsiveness to people came about; liberal and radical. Moreover, these two alternatives, as I will argue later in Chapter 3, still constitute the main disagreement in political sociology, though I will argue that these alternatives also overlap, and postpone discussion of their respective normative implications until the concluding chapter (9).

From a liberal perspective, the rise of political mass participation can be seen as the formation of 'civil society', as a push from below against elites. The notion of 'civil society' is unclear, however, because it has been used in two ways: to refer both to a political counterweight against the state – or an economic one. The latter version of the liberal perspective foregrounds the idea that economic rights constitute a sphere of 'free' associations. Arguably (we shall consider these arguments later), this way of thinking about an 'economic' civil society as a counterweight against the state is no longer useful after the collapse of communism in 1989–91 – as practically all societies now have a market 'civil society' which is insulated from the state. (And there is of course a connection here with how I earlier defined modern markets as 'free' or disembedded, though I will distance myself from this way of seeing civil society: nothing hinges on this connection for my argument).

The second version of a liberal perspective is to see civil society more politically, as consisting of voluntaristic associations that provide a counterbalance against the state. As we shall see, this conception of modern politics concentrates on the unfolding of political freedoms in civil society (as opposed to the free contracts and exchanges of property of economic liberalism). However, to regard bourgeois political freedoms as the motor of social or political change is also of limited use: they define a sphere that is free from the state without a positive view of the state. Without such a positive view of the state, it becomes difficult to identify differences between states (as we shall see) since some 'strong' states have freedoms that are as well-established as those where states are 'weak'. Both these (economic and political) perspectives on civil society, however, share a further idea, which is that a growing middle class provides a counterweight against the state, and this idea fits with the overall pattern of economic growth that has marked the modern period (though the question of whether a growing middle class is compatible with growing inequality in parts of the world will need to be considered too). Still, as we shall see, the idea of a growing middle class – 'the people' with increased freedoms and rights and as a cohesive counterweight and input into the state – is a viable way to conceptualize modern democratic states.

The second interpretation, a radical (or leftist) one, is to delineate how citizens or classes struggled for rights within the state, gaining, in the end, ever deeper rights – from civil, to political, to social – though not necessarily everywhere in this order (Marshall 1950; Turner 1986). This process can also be depicted as the granting of citizenship rights by the state to ever widening circles of citizens on the one hand, which has at the same time increased the penetration of the state into the lives of its citizens and populations on the other. There are different paths of how state elites responded to these pressures for inclusion, and also authoritarian variants of this process – whereby authoritarian regimes derived their legitimacy from the 'people' represented via a single elite embodying a 'moral project' (Perez-Diaz 1993). Thus Mann (2011) has divided modern states into pluralist democracies versus single-party states (previously he distinguished between bureaucratic-democratic versus authoritarian ones [1993: 60]). In either case, the state has responded to pressures from below, with one party or (in democracies) several channelling these pressures via competing parties into different directions of pluralist states. Note that, unlike the civil society perspective, which is based on an evolutionist-functionalist idea (differentiation, leading to cohesion), this radical perspective is based on the idea of conflict and social change characterized by ongoing struggle.

In either case, pluralist regimes have become established across most of the North or West, and liberals and (some) radicals would agree that the 'democratic' state is one in which political power is contested – polyarchy – and legitimacy is derived from 'the people'. Note that democracy from a sociological perspective does not mean voting rights or the representation of the electorate as individual voters (as it might for political science). Instead, democracy means, first, the extent to which major interest groups in society share power in the state, and second, how this dominant institution (or power) rules or responds: how do ruling classes or elites engage with other groups in civil society or with classes and citizens? This way of framing the issue – my preference, to be supported later, is to use 'ruling elites' and to hyphenate 'class-citizens' – allows for economic sources of political struggles, as for liberals and radicals. Yet it will also allow me to argue that these economic sources of change no longer play a decisive role in political change: indeed, I will argue that markets play a greater constraining role in the Age of Limits. In any event, sociological accounts of democracy are about the interests of different groups and about state power, and not about individual interests or the provision by the state of public goods – as for many political scientists. Further, the radical and liberal perspectives can be subsumed under the single idea that the dominant institutions of democratic states shape and are shaped by their environments – 'people' and other groups – via a process of incorporation, conceived either as struggle or in terms of the cohesive inputs from a plural but majoritarian body of the population.

There is an additional trajectory to the modern state, which is that the state has extended its bureaucratic or infrastructural capacity, its scale and scope, and thus deepened its penetration into the lives of citizens (Dandeker 1990). State capacity can thus be seen as enhanced capacity via resource extraction (taxes) for the enhancement of administrative capacity (a bureaucratic apparatus) and for the provision of infrastructural services and welfare states. But it is not only more resources (from around 30 per cent to 50 per cent of GDP) which have caused this enhancement: partly this is also a result of organizational-managerial techniques which have expanded the scale and scope of bureaucracies, a feature that states share with large corporations. Further, state capacity consists partly of administration, and partly of infrastructure provision – though the latter is of concern here mainly insofar as it relates to the provision and the distribution of (social) rights (rather than transport and the like). And again, the flipside of (social) rights is an increased ordering of populations.

If we now take these two patterns together, the politics of mass society have occurred in several stages, deepening and becoming more extensive over time. This was generally a unidirectional process across all (modern Northern) nation-states, even if there have been authoritarian and other rights-revoking reversals. Thus ultimately there is a single arc of increasing popular legitimation over the course of modernity. It is a similar case with bureaucratization, which consists of a unidirectional growth throughout the modern period of administrative capacity, even if there have been periods of greater intensity of authoritarian state bureaucracies, and possibly a recent plateauing. It will thus be necessary to ask: with this plateauing of state growth, are there now limits to the extension of social rights, and are these rights perhaps even bound to become more restricted with relative economic decline?

In any event, these processes, of deepening democracy, the extension of citizenship rights and/or the expansion of civil society, and the growth of bureaucracy, are characteristic of all modern states since at least the democratic revolutions of the long 19th century. The key question, as we shall see, is to examine the varieties of democratic states from a sociological perspective: how do plural powers correspond with the reach and depth of rights? In the final analysis, as mentioned, I will argue that while the liberal and radical interpretations of the trajectories of modern states differ (but also overlap on key points), it is the normative implications that can be derived from them that set them apart. And although there are also different types of democratic states – they have diverged – even more important is that they now also face similar constraints. Still, again, democratic states are the dominant institution that orders and derives legitimacy from its environment – 'people' – by extending rights to them and being responsive to the inputs from 'the people'.

Differentiation and macro-social orders

The birth of the modern world was not just an historical caesura. It also created a new type of social structure. Henceforth there was a deeper division or separation between three orders of society, each of which is dominated by a single institution: markets, states and science – each prefixed by 'modern' and by adjectives (disembedded or 'free', democratic and rapid-discovery), and these dominant institutions of a globalizing modernity differ from the macro-social orders and dominant institutions in traditional or agrarian or pre-modern societies (Table 1.1).

These dominant institutions operate with different mechanisms (exchange, incorporation and transformation). *What* they control or exercise power over is their environments – respectively, commodities by which people and organizations meet their needs and wants, 'people' as they aggregate into parties and interest groups and how these shape collective rules and coercion, and the physical or natural world insofar as it lends itself to being known and exploited for human needs and wants. So what we have is that, within each macro-social order, institutions exercise control or power within or over their environments (see Table 1.2).

What is the significance of this differentiation into three separate macro-social orders? To arrive at this, it is worth spelling out how the ideas that I am proposing – deliberately – depart from the terminology of conventional social theory. The conceptual schema put forward here – macro-social orders, in which there is a dominant institution in the modern period which organizes its environment – avoids a lot of the theoretical baggage associated with existing theories. Orders and institutions are more neutral than 'systems', which would prejudge the analysis in favour of an evolutionary-functionalist approach. Similarly with singular conceptions of 'power', which would imply that one type of power operates throughout all social orders or operates in one particular way; such as 'power over' that operates in a zero-sum way. On the other hand, these concepts provide sufficient flexibility so that it is possible to recognize that the three substantive patterns in each order

Table 1.1 From pre-modern societies to globalizing modernity

Macro-social order	Pre-modern societies	Transition	Globalizing modernity
Politics	Traditional legitimacy of states	Democratic revolution	Democratization from below
Economy	Local subsistence, limited trans-local exchange	Industrial revolution	Mass markets for open-ended consumption
Culture	Dominance of religion	Scientific revolution	Disenchantment by science

Table 1.2 Dominant institutions, modes of control or power, environments, and spatial reach

Macro-social order	Dominant institution	Mode of control or power	Environment	Spatial reach
Politics	Democratic state, with a monopoly of legitimate violence and extension of rights	Centralized authority extends and deepens scope, pluralized from below	'People' aggregated into interest groups	Bounded by nation-state
Economy	Free market, with atomistic and divisible exchange for meeting needs and wants	Increasing scale, scope and disembeddedness of commodified exchange	Commodities (labour, goods, services)	Increasingly global networks
Culture	Rapid-discovery science, with an exclusive monopoly on truth and the cumulative extension of certified knowledge	Increasingly intensive exploitation of nature and extensive technological infrastructures	Physical or natural world	Universal, bounded by natural resources

have taken different directions. This flexibility is more important than having a theoretical apparatus which, so to speak, imposes a single patternedness upon social change a priori. This point will emerge fully in the chapters ahead, and conclusions drawn from it at the end, but it must be elaborated briefly here.

Existing social theories implicitly or explicitly favour an analysis based on evolution and function, conflict and power, institutions being shaped by rational choice, or how social change takes place via cultural construction and agency. These approaches overlook, in my view, first, that social change does not take place in the same way as it did before the *modern* period (this has been argued already), but also, secondly, that there are different mechanisms that operate differently in these social orders. I used the terms 'macro-social orders' or simply 'orders' which are not commonly used by social scientists.[7] 'Systems' or 'power' would carry with them certain baggage, but I could have equally used 'spheres' (Weber sometimes used this term) or 'structures' if three structures could be said to sit side by side, or 'powers' if that did not prejudge how power was exercised. But I have argued already – and will pursue further in the substantive chapters below – that in the *modern* period, different dominant institutions gained autonomy from each other (thus separating the orders), which also entails that they operate differently in relation to their 'environments', which are also different.

Thus there is a 'horizontal' differentiation (orders becoming separated) and a 'vertical' distinction between the institutions and the environments they exercise power or control over, but which also shapes them. One implication that should be noted immediately is that this is a thoroughly sociological account: top-down, through how the environment is being shaped, as well as bottom-up, via the environment that shapes and constrains. The term 'environment' I borrow from Luhmann, without accepting any of the baggage of his systems theory, to simply indicate how the dominant institutions relate to different parts of society that they are interacting with or that they are shaping. Thus again, we have social orders, each with a dominant institution that organizes its environment in a particular way.

What are the 'environments' that are being organized? In the modern period, and for democracies, these are 'people' ('civil society' or 'citizen-classes' – we shall see what hangs on the difference in Chapter 3), for markets it consists of 'commodities' (including goods, services and labour), and for science it is the 'natural or physical world'. What is distinctive about the modern period is that these three environments shape dominant institutions 'from below' insofar as they have become politicized, commodified and more amenable to transformation. Second, *how* they are shaped is quite different for each order, but one implication that can be anticipated is that if one order is to affect a second order, the first order (via the mechanism of authority, or money, or knowledge) must be translated into the second. In this respect, as we shall see, there are severe, if not insuperable, limits.

In any event, this terminology allows me to avoid more general questions about social evolution and power throughout history, and also to use 'orders' in what follows as a kind of placeholder – since it is the three dominant institutions themselves that count (and institutions become differentiated substantively, as macro-social orders, which simply indicate separate parts of the social world, cannot). We will need to pin down the substantive patterns of social change of dominant institutions in what follows. And the concepts pertaining to these dominant institutions carry theoretical 'baggage' of their own, and I shall make clear what this baggage is in due course. However, to anticipate, this 'baggage' does not violate value-freedom, or prejudge the analysis in favour of any one political or social course or option, even if it can inform them in a specific and limited way. This highly contentious point will be elaborated in the concluding chapter.

As I will argue later (see also Table 1.3 below), there is also a difference within modernity between the Age of Limits and what comes before. In presenting these three tables and this conceptual schema of social change, I am drawing on theorists such as Mann, Gellner, Turner, Luhmann and Collins – who are, in turn, developing further the ideas of classical sociological theory. These contemporary theorists are quite different: Gellner was a neo-evolutionist and structural functionalist, Mann has a theory of networks of power, Turner combines evolutionism and functionalism, Luhmann is a systems theorist, and Collins is a conflict theorist. What they have in common, however, is that they are committed to the idea that macro-sociological theory should be empirical and testable. These tables can therefore be seen as my attempt to establish the shared ground between them, as well as to improve upon them. We will return in the chapters that follow to provide the comparative-historical evidence underpinning these tables and discuss where any gaps or disagreements lie – and what hangs on them.

Before elaborating the tables further, I need to discuss where I depart from these theorists, a major one being how the mechanisms (others would call them types of power) that operate in the three orders are different in kind. For example, the political order is primarily characterized by conflict, whereas the economic and cultural orders are mainly characterized by cohesion – and thus functionalism. Or again – briefly – in the modern period, the state is centralized, the economy is decentralized, and valid knowledge has gatekeepers but it is universal. My argument is thus that the dominant institutions that I have identified are orthogonal to each other.

On this point I depart from contemporary and classical social thinkers with – as we shall see – major implications. Modern institutions, I will argue, have developed autonomous trajectories which are working themselves out, and as the modern period gives way to an Age of Limits, this autonomy has now become frozen and, combined with the fact that de-differentiation is unlikely, this is precisely one of the novel features that characterizes our age, as indicated in Table 1.3. Thus we not only have a fundamental break between traditional, pre-modern societies (or pre-capitalist ones, if that terminology is preferred) and modern ones, no matter when the transition is precisely dated (Table 1.1), but also a transition between the Age of Extremes and the

Table 1.3 From the Age of Extremes to the Age of Limits

Macro-social order	Age of Extremes	Age of Limits	Differentiation	Limits of interaction between social orders
Politics	Citizen-class struggles to extend and deepen democracy and rights	Constraint on extending the depth and universalism of social rights	Segregation of economic and political struggle	Rights cannot be guaranteed if made divisible Rule-making cannot be straightjacketed by truth
Economy	Growth of disembedded markets for maximizing interests via exchange	Superordinate financial markets and consumer demand are contained	Financial pyramiding creates political instability, constraints on how technology extends human environmental footprint	Exchange cannot be fluid if subject to the constraints of rule-making Exchange cannot open-endedly harness truth or the transformation of nature
Culture	Monopoly of scientific expertise, increasing dependence on large technological systems for high growth	Transformation of the environment encounters rebounding	Scientific knowledge transcends political and economic steering, large technological systems are ossified but require massive social engineering	Knowledge about the natural world cannot be extended, without loss, by rule-making or exchange

Age of Limits (Table 1.3). One of the limits of our age is that there are tensions between three autonomous and orthogonal dominant institutions and how they shape and are shaped by their environments. How these tensions may or may not be resolved will be discussed in the concluding chapter – and previewed briefly shortly.

One implication of this orthogonality – or differentiation between institutions – can be spelled out immediately: while the processes within each social order have taken their course (the last column in Table 1.1), the shift to an Age of Limits entails not only that there are limits within each order (second column in Table 1.3), but also limits to the interaction between them (last two columns in Table 1.3). These limits to the interactions between orders are also represented schematically in Figure 1.1.

Looking at the last column in Table 1.3 and the dashed arrows in Figure 1.1, what these indicate is that in the Age of Limits, the interaction between dominant institutions and orders (including their environments) has become unlikely or more indirect. This is because once the processes of how dominant institutions shape and are shaped by their environments (the solid arrows in Figure 1.1) have become exhausted or run up against buffers in an Age of Limits (second column in Table 1.3), the modes of how power or control operate (dashed ovals in Figure 1.1) can only weakly interact with those of other social orders (dashed arrows between them) because to do so would involve a translation that entails de-differentiation. Yet de-differentiation is problematic,

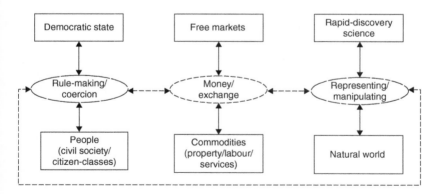

Figure 1.1 Differentiation and interaction within and between macro-social orders

Solid arrows = shaping, via control and power
Dashed arrows = indirect control and power via translation

as Luhmann argued, and this weakness or these limits (or these dashed arrows) can be put into words (see also the last column in Table 1.3): As we have seen, the medium of market exchange is money in overcoming scarcity, of the state it is rule-making concerning citizenship, and of technoscience it is advancing knowledge to manipulate the natural world. Therefore, if translation occurs, it is likely to be re-translated into the medium of the other order and dissolve, as it were, into its dominant institutions. Thus:

- Money exchange can be transformed into rule-making only if it subjects itself to the logic of applying these rules in a binding and consistent way
- Money exchange can be translated into knowledge advance only as long as it adheres to a criterion of validity
- Rule-making or coercion can be transformed into money exchange as long as it subjects itself to the logic of divisible exchange
- Rule-making or coercion can serve knowledge advance inasmuch as its norms support the criterion of validity
- Knowledge can serve rule-making as long as its advances can be adapted to become binding norms
- Knowledge can subject itself to money exchange as long as its advances can be translated into divisible monetary value.

These may seem to be rather mechanical ways to describe the relations between social orders (they are also summarized in the last two columns of Table 1.3), but such simplification is needed to be able to account for processes that can, in fact, take a variety of forms in terms of the 'couplings' (to borrow Luhmannian language again) between the orders that they attempt. Put the other way around, if the orders interrelate, the dominant institution and its environment remains intact, but the means are transformed. Thus while a coupling can be stronger and weaker, it is subject to limits. And while this summary must simplify, what counts, again, is how these processes and limits are detailed and how they fit the substance of, in this case, the changes in social structures of the Age of Limits. Further, as we shall see in the conclusion, the orthogonality of social orders also applies to their temporal horizons and spatial boundedness, reinforcing but also providing openings for different relationships between them (to be discussed shortly). Finally, one way to think of the chapters to follow is that they lead towards a different and more concrete version of Figure 1.1 in Figures 9.1 and 9.2 in the concluding chapter, where the main directions of these arrows will be narrowed further still, to indicate the limits confronting contemporary social change, and the counterforces against these limits.

With this apparatus in place, further departures from other thinkers that are indicated in these tables can be pinpointed: again, these departures, as well as the substantive elaboration of these tables, will come in the chapters to follow. One departure is that although the tables draw extensively on Mann's definitions of power, I have simplified his theory so that rather than four sources of power, I have three orders (as does Gellner). The reason for leaving out military power are explained in the next section: briefly, with the exception of American military power, this source of power is no longer central to social change in the Age of Limits within the global North (though I agree with Mann that it was important up until the end of World War II, and perhaps the end of the Cold War for some sets of nation-states in the North). However, a further simplification is that, unlike Mann, whose different types of power operate in all four of his sources, my argument – again – is that power (or also control in my schema) operates differently in the dominant institutions within each order.[8]

Mann argues that 'capitalism' – or what I call the economic order and disembedded markets – 'is an unusually diffused form of power organization, whereas states are essentially authoritative' (1993: 727). '*Diffused power*,' he says, 'spreads in a more spontaneous, unconscious, decentered way throughout a population, resulting in similar social practices that embody power relations but are not explicitly commanded. It typically comprises, not command or obedience, but an understanding that these practices are natural or moral or result from self-evident common interest' (1986: 8). I agree that this applies to markets. In contrast, '*authoritative power* is actually willed by groups and institutions. It comprises definite commands and conscious obedience' (Mann 1986: 8), which in my view applies to democratic states. As we shall see, the difference between the two is, in my view fundamental: the organization exercised by states (or power of states, in Mann's theory) is coercive and centralized – 'authority' or 'authoritative' – whereas in modern markets, it is difficult to even conceive of this as 'power' because the concentrations of resources (greater power) are fleeting and do not consist of systematic power of A over B (as with authoritative power), but rather in an uneven and stratified distribution arising from exchange (to be discussed shortly). In short, I agree with the distinctions between different types of power, but depart from Mann in arguing that how the two types operate – in modern societies at least – differs as between the political and the economic orders and characterize states and markets respectively. Still, in this case, as the quotes above indicate, for *modern* capitalism, Mann agrees that political power is authoritative and economic power diffused.

Thus I will use both power and control, depending on the substantive processes involved: in the political order, it often seems fitting to speak of 'power over', though in terms of how people express their interests in the state, it also seems appropriate to speak of control. In the case of scientific and technological mastery over the natural world, either control or power over capture this process. For markets, finally, neither power nor control fit entirely, since power in this case is, in Mann's schema, mainly 'diffused power' and 'spontaneous' and 'decentred' (though temporary monopolies of innovations can also be described as exercising control). As we shall see in Chapter 9 (it has already been mentioned), differentiation between the three orders and the autonomy of institutions entail that they fail to overlap and are orthogonal to each other, and this can override the commonalities and intersections between them.

Culture is different again, and here my account departs from other theories, particularly in relation to science, which I regard, as argued earlier, as separate from the rest of culture. Science is a quite diffuse form of power, though it is also intensive in its control over nature, and jealous in its exclusiveness.[9] This account of science and technology is based on a previous book (Schroeder 2007) where I draw heavily on Gellner and Collins and argue for the autonomy of science and technology from society and from culture (Mann thinks that science is not an autonomous power – I disagree). It is an account based on realism in relation to scientific knowledge and makes the case for technological determinism, both deeply unpopular positions in contemporary social science – or more precisely, within the subspecialism of the sociology of science and technology (this will be discussed in Chapters 5 to 7). The implication, however, is that, like economic power, science is a mainly a diffuse form of power, but there is also an (at least partly) zero-sum game between science and other forms of culture such as religion or any other claims to authority. And while technoscience supports the culture of consumerism, there is no necessary connection (again, luckily) between science and consumption from the side of technoscience: one support for this point is that societies that have been successful in terms of technoscientific advance – China and the Soviet Union before the 1980s – have not promoted consumerism. In separating out science as 'cognition', however, and assigning a structural role to it in modern society (rather than to culture or ideology), I follow Gellner (for example, 1988), who, as far as I am aware, is the only other theorist to do this. Hence, so far, my proposal is: Mann, minus the fourth military source of power, divided into two separate and differentiated types of power or control, minus culture/ideology (as in other theories of power) but replaced by science (or cognition).

The dominant institutions or forms of power – or control – in each of these macro-social orders are bounded vis-à-vis each other, though there would be clearly be overlaps if they were represented in a three-circle Venn diagram. But this overlap is an evasion on the part of social science, often expressed in terms of: 'of course social reality is more complex than these concepts imply'. This may be true, but it is possible go further in specifying what the implications of the interrelations between the institutions and orders are, and this will help us to pinpoint what kinds of limits contemporary social change imposes on future social development – or not.

Another immediate reply that can be pre-empted is: 'how could the economy be anything but cultural?' or 'how could culture not be political?', and so on for all the different combinations. However, this reply would also need to put forward a constructive proposal about how the economy is cultural and the like. Again, this (logically!) entails either spelling out reciprocal influences between the economy and culture (but this means they must be separate, and such influences or lack of influences will detailed below), or some kind of 'primacy' must be specified. In the latter case, this must entail the claim (to continue with the example) that the economy is determined by culture. Tackling 'primacy' will also be attempted here, although I will argue in the concluding chapter that one limit to the present age, unlike previous ages, is that there is no primacy, but that the 'stand-off' between social orders and their institutions must be theorized.[10]

As we shall see, a major constant throughout the modern period (including the long 19th century and the Ages of Extremes and of Limits) is the autonomy of the three orders, which has grown with the increasing scale and scope of each order and its powers or means of control, even if there have been exceptions of periods of larger overlaps between them (again, the subordination of economic markets to the political authority of authoritarian states during the great wars and the Cold War provide examples). And again, the evasion entailed by 'everything is political' and likewise for the other two orders is not worth pursuing; instead, how the three orders and their dominant institutions operate differently and interrelate will need to be detailed.

An added complication is that these institutions and orders are also spatially bounded in different ways (Table 1.1, last column). This is clear in the case of political authority because in the modern period, states have become centralized and bounded by nations; Mann says the state is 'a territorially demarcated area' and 'political relations radiate outwards from a centre' (1988: 4). Nation-states, to use Giddens' terminology, have become the main modern 'containers' of political power (1985). The economic order, on the other hand, consists of networks of exchange that are not territorially bounded in the same way and that have expanded spatially over the course of the modern period, even if some of its space-transcending flows like trade and labour migration and foreign direct investment have waxed and waned. Finally, science is universal vis-à-vis nature, even if technological infrastructures, for example, are often bounded by nations and always – given current technological capabilities – by the natural world at the scale of the planet.[11]

Thus there is also no single pattern of conflict or cohesion in modern social change, the two being the main alternatives in social theory. As we shall see – some of this has already been sketched – *within* the modern period, the differentiation of three orders remains and, with exceptions, intensifies. Indeed, I will argue that this differentiation now, in an Age of Limits, takes a different shape from what has gone before. At the same time, I shall argue that alternative interpretations of, for example, the struggle for modern pluralist democracy – more conflictually for the left/radical, and more cohesively for the liberal – can in fact be seen as complementary rather than at odds with each other. And it is possible to go beyond both in specifying how limits confront both interpretations. In the concluding chapter, it will thus be necessary spell out the shifting balance between conflict or cohesion in *contemporary* social change – within and between the three orders – and how this relates to social and political norms or ideals.

In the concluding chapter it will also be necessary to further support the claim that the defining feature of an Age of Limits is the tension between the three orders and their dominant institutions – a key reason to use this label. The tension arises from how the differentiation and its intensification have become stuck: it is not possible – here again I draw on Luhmann without embracing any of the 'baggage' of his theory – for one order to shape the others directly, or overcome the limits within one order by interacting with the others without translation. Instead, this mutual shaping or relieving of tensions is mainly indirect (as we saw in Figure 1.1 and the last columns of Table 1.3) and the mechanism of one order must be filtered into the mechanism of the other. As we shall see, this limit constrains different options for social development that will be presented, and how they can inform addressing urgent social challenges. But these options are thus also exempted from value-ladenness. To take just one example: a Tobin tax on financial transactions (often proposed at the rate of 0.5% or less), which would constitute a statist intervention in markets, could potentially ease the curbs on expenditure for welfare that are due to restrictions on state borrowings. Yet these tax incomes would nevertheless need to be filtered into financial (economic) stability or avoidance of volatility rather than into greater (political) extensions by the state of social rights (welfare spending) – for reasons that will become apparent. Again, this is a highly contentious point, and similar ones apply to other current challenges. These will be addressed in the concluding chapter.

The tension between three orders is one reason for the label 'Age of Limits'. But these limits (as already mentioned) are also due to the different spatial reach of the orders and their institutions: The limits of the transformation of the environment by technoscience, for example, are planetary, whereas the limits of economic growth via financialization and expanding economies are generally confined to the global North (though with ramifications beyond the North), and the limits to deepening democracy and social citizenship are confined within nation-states. A similar point pertains to their differing time horizons: long-term in relation to the transformation of the natural world, shortest for the political order (financial crises complicate this picture, but they take time to percolate into politics), with the economy in between. These limits on all three orders and their interrelationships, however, have only emerged during the Age which they define: what has led up to them in the modern globalizing period, and how they have become resolved (or not) thus far, now needs to be spelled out in detail. One final limit – this time a theoretical one – is that it is not possible to predict how these shapings or tensions or conflict will become resolved (again: or not) in the future, even if it can be shown how they currently impose constraints on social development, and some individual patterns – such as shortages of natural resources available for transformation – can be foreseen. It can also be foreseen that de-differentiation, while it is possible, is problematic.

These limits also relate to the discussion of power above: one reason why I prefer to speak of dominant institutions and how they entail the autonomy of – or differentiation between – different social orders, is that it makes little sense to impose a single dominant institution or idea of power on all social orders and for all periods (at least for the modern period). To use power in an everyday or sociological sense of the word is appropriate when groups dominate each other in an asymmetric relationship or via institutions; Mann's authoritative power. But science dominates universally over nature, and consists of a very diffuse type of authority – or better: control – which is nevertheless intensive or concentrated in its deployment vis-à-vis nature. Similarly, markets nowadays entail a very far-flung and diffuse type of control. Thus there are 'interaction cleavages' between the types of power for Mann (1986: 13), or in Mann's more recent work, powers are at 'non-equivalent' or at 'non-congruent angles' or they are 'orthogonal' (Mann 2012: 5), a term I will borrow. But if the tensions of contemporary social change are unresolved, then we also cannot apply a single model of power or control to all three orders or establish primacy between them in a straightforward way. Nevertheless, sociological knowledge must attempt to understand the interrelations between the three macro-social orders and their dominant institutions and the mechanisms whereby they relate to their environments. As I will avoid a singular usage of 'power' and often speak of control, and also all-determining primacy or asymmetries which drive social change, what I will conclude with instead is that the different orders (and the several asymmetries and instabilities in markets, democracies, and in how science transforms the natural world) strain against each other, with different spatial and time horizons and different forms of translations – and different potential primacies – between them.

Not having a single mechanism which brings the driving forces of social change together obviously has the disadvantage of complexity. The advantage, however, is that I will be able to specify different limits within each order, as well as how the failure of the interrelation – or tension between them – is itself a superordinate mechanism which drives and blocks contemporary social change. This tension or conflict rests on the fact that the mechanisms of power and control are not a single phenomenon within a single dominant institution (as for example 'power' is for analyses of 'capitalism') – but the mechanisms and institutions are also not infinitely complex as applied to the current condition of social development in relation to different environments: the domination over the natural world pulls in one direction, the drive for economic growth in another, and how states exercise plural authority and provide rights to groups of citizens is constrained in yet another manner. How we have arrived at this structural intersection or non-intersection of institutions and environments and the constraints within and between them – that is precisely the question, and one which reductive sociological theories (power and single primacy, evolution and function), or theories which are completely open (agency and choice) in terms of the forces that shape contemporary social change, both overlook.

This final point also allows me to preview a key conclusion of the book. As we have seen, there are three master processes in the modern period: democratization from below, the disembedding of markets and the transformation of nature. All three did not necessarily follow a linear path, and during the Age of Extremes, they suffered partial reversals in wartime, but in the post-war Golden Age they resumed and are still ongoing. But they have become stalled in the Age of Limits. These three processes can therefore be described as following a developmental course, which entails – to return to the introductory paragraphs – an overall theory of social change. A major part of this course of development is that these processes have increasingly subjected the three orders of society to differentiation: these orders, in which different institutions have come to dominate, have grown increasingly separate and gained ever greater autonomy from one another, also in relation to how they have ordered their environments. Since the three processes also have a logic (or 'directional pattern') whereby the dominant institutions within each order have expanded and intensified their processes of exercising power or control (size of the state, market expansion and an enhanced transformation of nature), this differentiation has also taken place in a non-zero sum way – although during the Age of Extremes, this was not an irreversible process.

What, then, about differentiation in the Age of Limits? If patterns of social development can be extracted from the course of a globalizing modernity, then these limits are a result of the exhaustion of this logic of expansion and intensification – and in this way impose limits on this autonomy. Thus while the autonomy of the three dominant institutions remains in place (no de-differentiation is on the horizon), it is also frozen – with specific tensions in the substantive (steering and resource) relations between them. Further social development is possible, but this is no longer fuelled by stable open-ended economic growth, which in turn has rested on the transformation of nature (itself subject to rebound), or by the struggle over the extension of social citizenship which depended on the expansion of the state's economic resources (recalling that the dashed arrows in Figure 1.1 interconnect all three orders, but the solid arrows only connect dominant institutions to their own environments). Thus further social development can only mainly take place, for example, via the redistribution of political authority. Yet as we will see, this political struggle is also exhausted and stalled. Political conflict took various routes before the Age of Limits in two main ways: as democratization from below via an expanding middle class (which lends itself to a functionalist account) or via working classes and their allies (a conflict account). As we shall see in Chapter 3, there is evidence for both, but it remains to be seen whether and how this struggle will continue or resume. Irrespective of these two interpretations, however, the forces which drove them are – again – exhausted.

Of course, this exhaustion does not imply an end to political struggle or social development, an 'end of history'. The process of political redistribution of authority does not have to centre exclusively around the redistribution of social rights (or, in the past, over stratified economic resources): perhaps civil society groups and social movements will also pursue other goals. Yet the expansion and deepening of social citizenship and distribution of economic resources, as I shall argue in the concluding chapter – departing from objective and value-free social theory into the realm of norms and political philosophy – are still at the core of notions of progress in social development. But again, with the extension and deepening of social rights stalled, inequalities in social rights and economic distribution depend not only on economic growth or a greater push for social rights, because they are also enabled by and dependent on advances – and the constraints imposed thereon – in the transformation of nature. Differentiation – put differently: the way that social orders and their dominant institutions interrelate or fail to do so, also in relation to social rights and economic justice – is thus central to contemporary social change and progress or development.

Stratification: elites and people

Differentiation of separate orders has implications for how power is distributed: indeed, different power bases are typically regarded as a sign of a multi-dimensional Weberian perspective on power – as opposed to a Marxist one which centres on economic power and a binary divide between 'capital' and 'labour'. However, a theory whereby power and stratification have several Weberian interrelated dimensions is too open-ended. Instead, it is possible to specify in a more precise and parsimonious way how different forces in stratification relate to each other, as follows: first, I have argued that citizen-classes or a middle class/civil society – henceforth in shorthand simply 'people' – constitute pressure from below or a balance against the state. 'People' are stratified politically in terms of the depth and breadth of social rights, with ramifications for economic inequalities and these, as we shall see, obviously vary across societies. Yet economic inequalities, wealth and income, are also a product of markets, and these are a second form of stratification. Even if, therefore, we see economic and political cleavages as having been conjointly responsible for democratizing the state and redistributing wealth and income in the past, one characteristic of the Age of Limits is that they have now in large part become separated. Thus democratization has reached a steady state whereby different models of the distribution of social rights are now firmly in place: for example, in the fragmented pluralism of the US with its circumscribed and particularistic social rights in contrast to the state-centric corporatism in Sweden with more extensive and universalist social rights. Even if economic and political forces can be seen operating together before the Age of Limits, the primary impetus for social change nowadays comes from social movements rather than from the intertwining of economic and political cleavages. And the possibilities and constraints of these social movements also rest on fragmented pluralism versus state-centric corporatism, leaving existing forms of stratification among 'people', and markets, in place.

It is a similar case with ruling elites. As Gellner argues, 'modern societies do of course possess a "ruling class", but no formal line is drawn around it. Its personnel rotates, to a greater or lesser degree, and its separation from the rest of the population is gradual . . . There may be a distinction between the state and civil society, but there is no clear and formalized separation of a state class from the governed population' (1988: 261). However, within this ruling 'class' (I prefer 'elites' since class could be taken to imply the binary capital/labour division and thus the primacy of economic power), it is possible to distinguish between further between economic and political elites: the main 'interest' of political elites is to perpetuate party power in government (and if parties are in power, they are part of the state, whereas out of power, they are 'parties' trying to obtain power), and the primary interest of economic elites lies in maintaining their wealth and income.

The two nowadays overlap inasmuch as the need to pursue economic growth is common to both; for re-election in the case of political elites and to obtain higher returns in the case of economic elites. Both serve to uphold a hierarchy in society, and arguments about the permeability or otherwise of this hierarchy are bound to continue: in any event, the social background of political elites is skewed, and the concentration of wealth and income among the economic elite (the top 1 per cent or 10 per cent) is now persistent and/or growing – as we shall see. Yet there is no uniform interlock between the two elites; rather, they are also shaped by fragmented pluralism or state-centric corporatism (or other types of regimes, for example, a party regime in China where political elites dominate, and populist fragmentation in India which concentrates power in elites which cater to this populism or dominate because of the absence of a coherent political elite.)

Thus the negative view of 'capitalism', whereby political and economic elites constitute a united front against 'people' on distributional issues, and the positive view of 'capitalism', whereby there are no skewed distributional issues but only the play of free interests, are both misleading: political and economic elites share the aim of 'growth', and that aim is also shared by 'people'. Yet since 'sovereignty is ascribed to "the people"'(Gellner 1988: 261) rather than to ruling elites and they share basic aims or interests, hierarchy (or stratification) has become entrenched, even though the push against a hierarchical order drove social change before the Age of Limits. As we shall see, economic inequality is growing for the main cases examined here, but the major characteristic of the Age of Limits is the separation between economic stratification and political rights.

Finally, what about scientific elites? A moment's reflection suffices to recognize that the authority of science is independent of its personnel: the validity of knowledge is impersonal. Scientists have no separate power base of their own (apart from autonomous institutions of knowledge) to further their interests, which lie primarily in expanding the influence of scientific knowledge in society, including the resources to pursue science, and they need allies among elites or the public ('people') or social movements. And even if experts can shape social agendas, this shaping capacity rests on their expertise or on maintaining or expanding the boundaries around their caste-like exclusive hold on knowledge, rather than on their force as a movement effecting social change.

But while a common denominator among elites and 'people' is economic growth, the autonomy of social orders is reflected in how the interests of elites are pursued within each order: political elites pursue re-election, economic elites pursue profit, and the technoscientific elite pursues truth and enhanced capacity for transforming nature. Clearly – again – these are orthogonal to each other, though the absence of strain or conflict between them also means that there is no struggle for primacy of one over the other. The exception would be if, as Mann argues (2013), economic elites, especially in the US, pursue primacy over political elites, outflanking them transnationally. Yet there is also a contradiction here (which Mann points to, but does not make explicit): if the aim of economic elites to concentrate wealth and income is achieved, then a healthy base of mass of consumption will be lacking. Yet concentrated – as opposed to broadly based – prosperity threatens long-term economic growth. On the argument made earlier, free markets do not allow the economic elite (or as Mann calls it, the capitalist class) to shape the economy towards a sufficient dispersal of wealth and income for broad-based mass consumption – as opposed to the political elite, which could try to shape markets towards this end. Thus economic elites are undermining their own interests in the long run: this class (to use the terminology often used) is working against its own future greater benefit, though of course in the short run and for individual capitalists, it is rational to maximize these benefits. Here it is worth recalling – in anticipation of the counter-argument that capitalists or economic elites might nevertheless benefit from more globally dispersed growth – that 80 per cent of economic activity takes place within states.

This detour has been necessary to anticipate the argument to be fleshed out in the coming chapters, that different political regimes (fragmented pluralism, state-centric corporatism, and the like) have shaped stratification, but in the Age of Limits conflict between elites and 'people' is no longer a central dynamic, so that fundamental economic redistribution or a major deepening of social rights, although they cannot be ruled out, are also unlikely, both because pressure from 'below' has become exhausted, and because the limits within each order reinforce the lack of strong interaction between them, including the separateness of free markets being shaped to a large extent on a supra-national scale, and the constraints they impose, including by the lack of power or authority to shape them. Instead, in the Age of Limits, the dynamic of social change can thus be located in how various limits strain against each other, though with different spatial and temporal horizons.

Hence for each of the cases (countries) to be examined, we will compare the shape of stratification, both economic – in terms of wealth/income inequalities – and political – in terms of penetrability 'from below' – but also how concentrated or evenly democratic control is distributed and how the state yields social rights. But again, this greater or lesser economic and political stratification or distribution of power is different among developed countries in the North but no longer drives social change – and in that sense it may be a single force field (and not multidimensional, as Weberians would have it) in which the forces are now too distributed to yield friction in stably institutionalized democracies: this, too, is a limit, though this limit does not apply to countries outside the North, as we shall see with India and China – but then, these are also an incoherent democracy and lacking in democracy respectively.

Global powers?

Before we turn to a fuller account of the dynamics of the three orders and their differentiation after the birth of the modern world, it is necessary to tackle one further question: apart from nation-states as units, is there a systemic level which encompasses the three orders at a more macro-level? This level, as mentioned earlier, is often discussed in terms of modernization or globalization, both of which implicitly posit the convergence between societies (or at least economic convergence in the case of the champions of globalization). Put differently, if we examine only a variety of developed (nation-state-bounded) societies, and markets and science operating at a transnational and planetary level respectively, how should we theorize the (international) relations between nation-states and other macro-social units? The idea that cultural diffusion towards a global society is taking place, as Meyer and his neo-functionalist colleagues have urged, only applies, as we shall see, to certain institutions like science (Drori et al. 2003) and not, for example, to a 'world society' (Meyer et al. 1997).[12]

One option would be to add, as Mann does, militarism as a fourth source of power. Yet militarism will only be treated here as a separate force for the first half of the 20th century and for the Cold War contestants into the second half, but not as a separate source of power during the Age of Limits and within the North. This is because militarism after the Cold War, and among developed societies, arguably only matters for the US: the hegemony of the US (some would even say 'empire'), even if it is supported by world-historically unparalleled military strength, is also undergoing decline and the international order is moving towards a multipolar or tripolar North. So while American and Northern militarism affects the globe outside of the North, there is no other effect on social change within the North (except in the event of a nuclear war, an eventuality which will not be addressed here, even if it potentially outweighs all else). Similarly with the American empire: this empire is in decline, and even if the imperial American 'external' role affected social change 'internally' in the past (for example, racism externally reinforcing racism within), this link no longer obtains straightforwardly.

Apart from militarism, geopolitics is difficult to theorize because it takes different shapes in different periods. For societies in the North, it is possible to distinguish the period of the world wars, of the Cold War and the period after the break-up of the Soviet Union. During these periods, the analysis must be 'open' to influences from the international system outside of nation-states – we can think, for example, of how the growth of state capacity was ratcheted up during the two world wars. Thereafter, however, in the Age of Limits, this external geopolitical line of causation is no longer of central importance (again, the US is a partial exception) to social change in the zone of peace in the North.

The reason that the first half of the 20th century and the Cold War will be treated differently is that the world wars, when mass mobilization impacted social change, were an exceptional period: these wars affected social change within, but in the period since then the geopolitical link between external and internal social change can be bracketed for the purpose of this analysis. As Malesevic argues (2010: 128), modern wars are directed outwards. And during the Cold War era, as Van Creveld (2008: 187) has pointed out, nuclear war has made wars between major powers impossible thus far: 'since 1945 no first-, or even second-rate powers ever engaged in more than border skirmishes with each other'. So while insurgencies and civil wars continue to take place in parts of global South – some have labelled it the Zone of Conflict in contrast with the Zone of Peace – militarism within the global North can be left to one side (as long as the consequences of the Cold War and the break-up of the Soviet empire in that part of the North are incorporated into the analysis in the period before the Age of Limits).

It should be noted that the argument is *not* that the international or global level apart from militarism is too complex to theorize. There is no reason in principle why this level should be more complex than other 'levels'. Outside of sociology, the supra-national realm is mainly theorized by international relations (IR), but the realist and liberal theories that are dominant in IR are not well-suited to coping with fundamental shifts or discontinuities from one set of asymmetries in power (or constellations among the macro-social orders) to another: for example, from the period dominated by world wars to a period dominated by the Cold War, and on to a period dominated by the North/South gap in economic power.

As Mann has argued (2013), there are in fact only two areas where power is truly global: nuclear weapons and climate change (I would add science, though in that case, as mentioned, it is best not to speak of power in the traditional sense since science by itself does not introduce asymmetries between peoples, even if it enhances power over nature by transforming it). Otherwise, the global level consists of nation-states and it is a 'system' only in terms of the diffuse powers of markets. These 'powers' are better described in terms of how markets and technoscience operate. Perhaps we could also include what has been labelled the 'soft power' of networks of institutions of international governance (Slaughter 2004). Yet one way to recognize the limits of this type of global power, or others, is to ask: How much coercion is there?

The North's economies currently dominate over those of the South, but this domination consists of imposing the rules of the game, with some implications that will be noted in the conclusion. Even within the North/South divide, however, states pursue relatively independent economic paths or strategies (Mann 2011). One faultline or cleavage of non-interaction between nations or regions at the supra-national level thus currently runs between the North and the South, with limited economic activity and diffuse power asymmetries between the two.

Yet even if free markets and technoscience are largely borderless, the nation-state can still be taken as a unit for comparison in what follows: measures of economic growth – and of economic stratification – are confined to nation-states or regions of similar nation-states (with important normative implications, as we shall see in the concluding chapter). Technoscience too is partly organized in terms of national systems of innovation or large technological systems whose reach is often defined by national borders, and we can compare how similar national units are in the role that technoscience plays in everyday life (Chapters 5 to 7), even if scientific knowledge, as argued earlier, is not just global but universal. Yet the main reason for focusing on the nation-state as a unit is not ease of comparison but political.[13] The international system thus consists of a system of states with asymmetric powers between Northern (American military, Northern economic) power, plus a set of diffuse economic (market) and cultural (consumerism, science) relations. Nevertheless, for the purpose of analysis, we shall often compare nation-states.

From the Age of Extremes to the Age of Limits

Against the background of the transition to a modern world of three dominant institutions within their respective social orders, plus how they relate to a system of nation-states and supra-national powers, it is now possible to return to charting the relations between them to the present day in a preliminary way. It has already been argued that such an account must be episodic; it must impose patterns on history. As Hall puts it: 'it is possible to occasionally distinguish moments in which one or other power source is the leading one, and when it sets the pace for the others' (1986: 22). Mann and Gellner agree, though it is difficult to find other social thinkers who address this issue apart from those that argue for the primacy of one particular type of power (economic reductionism, political economy, cultural construction) over the others. It is also possible, however, apart from the differentiation of three orders in the modern world, to consider de-differentiation: the main modern instance is the de-differentiation of state and economy during the world wars, or the trumping of both by militarism.

As we shall see, apart from these instances, it is useful to think about de-differentiation when it comes to the Age of Limits, if only to think negatively about why this is unlikely – and indeed how this constitutes one set of limits in contemporary social development. This unlikeliness has already been hinted at, but it can now be recast as a set of questions: how can it be, for example, that economic globalization does not constrain all political options in contemporary societies (as advocates of globalization or those on the political right claim), yet at the same time that political options are narrowed by a period of curbed growth in market economies (which those on the left deny, claiming that states should spend their way out of diminished growth, unless they see a looming economic cataclysm)? If social forces 'from below' have shaped paths of social development in the past, why is it that markets and states have nevertheless become separated in ways that the schools of 'political economy' or 'the varieties of capitalism' overlook (thus also overlooking that there are constraints which override these varieties)? Or, to take a different example, why is it that the state cannot easily impose constraints on potentially unsustainable consumption or on the technoscientific transformation of nature? The answers will have to wait until the different dynamics of the three orders have been elaborated.

The main pattern of social change in the modern period can thus for our purposes be broken down into a few main episodes: the long 19th century, dominated by the British empire (says Osterhammel [2009]; Mann [1993] agrees with British dominance, but focuses on the rise of nation-states and classes); the world wars as a period of extremes; a Golden Age of the North which overlapped with a global Cold War – between two further 'extremes' – which outlasted it until 1989–91; and after these an Age of Limits from the 1970s–80s onwards affecting the transformation of nature, economic growth and political options. As we shall see, the label 'globalization' does not fit since in the Age of Limits, economic strength remains highly uneven within the North and between the North and South, culture is homogenizing only in certain respects, and the drive towards extending social rights is stalled (and in some cases civil and political rights are incomplete or barely exist), while geopolitics is a 'thin' influence emanating from the global North. But to understand these limits and how they interrelate, we must first chart how each of the orders and their dominant institutions have developed separately, and how they have shaped and been shaped by their environments.

Before we move on, however, one question with which this chapter began must be resolved: which factor determined the transition to modernity – as there were three institutions which made a break with pre-modern society? As we have seen, there were decisive breaks within each of the three social orders (Table 1.2). Hence, whether we leave it as a laundry list of causes (Gellner 1988), the primacy of one or other source of power (Mann 1986; 1993), an economic-cum-scientific/technological determining force (for example, Mokyr 1990; Schroeder 2007), or the superiority of military technologies in securing the dominance of the West over the rest (Headrick 2010): disagreement can remain here, as long as we recognize that the break took place both from a global and a Western-centric perspective, especially since all of these views are compatible with the idea that three new, separate and dominant institutions were born.

* * *

An overview of the book will be useful: In this chapter, I have set the stage by leading up to the focus of this book; the current period which I describe as an Age of Limits: what sets this period apart within modernity, and what concepts should be used to understand the trajectories of economies, states and of culture within it? How does the analysis of social change in countries in the global North need to be located among modernizing or globalizing processes?

In Chapter 2, I go on to examine two cases, Sweden and the United States, in order to establish when and why their courses of social development diverged. The flipside is to ask what they have in common, given that these two countries are often seen as extremes among the range of options in advanced societies of the North. The first part of the chapter deals with the state. The second asks whether different cultures can explain what sets the two countries apart, specifically in relation to different conceptions of the individual in society.

Chapter 3 presents a broader account of political development in the global North. This chapter contrasts the (already mentioned) radical interpretation, which focuses on the struggle of working and other classes for incorporation into the state, with a liberal interpretation which places greater emphasis on a middle class and its alliances and on elite strategies. The chapter argues that there is nevertheless much common ground between these two views, but also that both come up against the fact that recently markets have become more autonomous vis-à-vis other social forces shaping states.

Chapter 4 argues against the notion that economies are embedded in other social structures. Instead, it proposes that markets have an autonomous logic based on the divisible and atomized nature of economic exchanges. It also discusses the pyramiding of these exchanges in financial markets. There are limits to the autonomy of markets, which are spelled out, and the chapter also discusses how the very openness of markets itself imposes constraints on social development.

Chapters 5 and 6 turn to how science and technology transform the natural world. Chapter 5 tackles the paradox that science is universally valid, and at the same time has a limited reach in terms of how its concrete instantiations, often in technological infrastructures, extend into everyday life. Nevertheless, it can be shown that the uses of technologies, such as for information and communication, are converging across the global North.

Chapter 6 moves on to the consequences of transforming the natural environment. Although much has been written about the looming crisis of resource use, the chapter argues that the continued momentum of economic growth, combined with an absence of countervailing forces to reduce the human impacts on the environment, entail that dramatic technological and/or state interventions are the most likely course when environmental constraints inevitably rebound on society.

The role of culture in social change has recently come to be regarded as central. Yet, as I argue in Chapter 7, there is ambiguity about whether science should be seen as part of culture or outside of it. In fact, science is autonomous of social contexts and indeed, as Chapter 5 will have shown, universal. Only two other components of culture, religion and consumption, play a major role, but religion is becoming residual while consumption is becoming at once more pervasive and at the same time yoked ever more exclusively to a need for continued economic growth.

Chapter 8 examines two cases from outside the global North, India and China, to see if the patterns examined so far shed light on the trajectories of these two countries and on various developmental models or options. China and India have both increasingly become market economies, but while China remains a single-party state, India's democracy has become increasingly captured by populist pressures. Their paths can be traced primarily via distinctive changes in developmental objectives of the state, rather than in longer-term cultural traditions. The same applies to the challenges they face, some of which they share with countries in the global North insofar as the capacities of their states are circumscribed by markets on the one hand and lock-ins to pressures from civil society – for further growth in China's case and the demands for social rights in India – on the other.

The concluding chapter draws out the implications of the increasing autonomy of states, markets and technoscience. The de-coupling between these orders and institutions, with limitations on resource transfers and steering between them, entails that there is limited scope for the emergence of forces to counteract the weakening capacities of states to support social rights, stabilize growth and financial markets, and promote a more sustainable transformation of the natural world. The chapter moves on to the terrain of political philosophy to argue for the continuing relevance of notions of the universality of equal capabilities and rights. While this universality is circumscribed in practice by the fact that social justice is primarily confined to nation-states, and politics is in turn affected by the other two social orders, the ideal of enhancing capacities can continue to be informed by social theory, including the identification of constraints – or limits – to its realization.

2
Convergence and Divergence

Chapter 1 has laid the groundwork and begun to map out a theoretical approach to the main processes of social change in the modern period. One question that has implicitly or explicitly been raised again and again here is: are advanced societies converging or diverging? Different answers could have important implications. If they are converging, taken to its logical extreme this might imply that there are no (or only restricted) options for social development. If they are diverging, this might entail that different paths of social development are not really comparable, and so they do not hold any lessons for each other. Put in terms of social theory, convergence often goes hand in hand with 'one best way' functionalism or 'survival of the fittest' evolutionism, whereas divergence supports (among others) the postmodern and social constructivist notions that there are irreducible differences between societies, and that generalizations across them are futile.

In this chapter, I will analyse the politics, economies and cultures of two countries that have often been compared, Sweden and the United States. The justification for choosing these two – and China and India, the other two main cases in Chapter 8 – will be provided shortly. Suffice it to say at this point that comparing concrete cases is preferable to treating questions like convergence or divergence in the abstract (the alternative is that the argument applies to all developed or advanced societies, and this kind of argument which puts countries into groups and compares them will also be used, especially in Chapter 3). In any event, against the background of a comparison of political and economic trajectories, I will then raise the question of whether this comparison is enough, or if it is necessary to add a comparison between the two different cultures. Finally, I discuss what can be learned from convergence and divergence and from comparing these two cases, as well as implications for the broader theory of advanced societies and a globalizing modernity.

Apart from the 'extremes' of convergence and divergence, there are two positions which implicitly and explicitly inform the debate: one is the idea that states are constrained by economic globalization and do not have a choice but to converge on a particular form of capitalist – here, 'market' – economy. This idea, if true, could have important implications for the argument that has already been made in Chapter 1 about the separation between the economic and political orders, and how the differentiation between their respective institutions has now become frozen. The other position can be found in the 'varieties of capitalism' literature which argues that the differences between 'political economies' will persist. In this case, states (the political realm) and the economic realm are deliberately fused, an idea that runs counter to the argument made here about the (now) frozen separation of the two realms. The main aim of this chapter is to see if it is possible to advance beyond these various positions, and to specify how advanced societies are converging or diverging.

Sweden versus America

To pursue this aim, the concrete examples of the Sweden and the US lend themselves to comparison because, as Blyth (2002: 12–13) puts it, they provide a useful set of 'most different' cases:

> Sweden is often seen as the social democracy *par excellence*, characterized by universal welfare provision, high labor density, and until recently, highly regulated capital movements. In contrast, the United States tends to be seen as the exemplar of liberal political economy with residualist welfare provisions, low union density and free capital movements . . . the United States can be seen as the case where the influence of business and the power of market-conforming ideas would be most likely to be apparent. In contrast, Sweden's social democratic institutions and strong encompassing labor organizations would constitute the least likely environment where such dynamics would be apparent.

Put differently, these two countries are typically placed at the extreme ends of a continuum.[1] Hence they also have different labels within the spectrum for developed societies, whether Sweden is labelled as 'social-democratic' as against the US with its 'liberal' welfare state regime, or if we place Sweden among the 'Nordics' as against the 'Anglophones' (Mann 2012, 2013), or if we contrast the US among the 'liberal market economies' with the Nordic 'social market economies' (Pontusson 2005).

These labels indicate divergence, as would a political scientist's classification of the two political systems. A political scientist would contrast a parliamentary system with a presidential one, a centralized state versus decentralized power in a federal system with three branches, and the long-term dominance by one party (the Social Democrats) versus a two-party system. We shall come back to these. At the same time, *both* countries are pluralist democracies, and so beyond political differences we also want to know how politics has shaped or is shaped more broadly by society, which is hinted at in the various labels that have just been mentioned. The main differences thus include:

- the role and capacity of the state; greater in Sweden with its cradle to the grave welfare state, as against the American minimal welfare state;
- a different type of engagement by the state with the workforce, which is highly unionized in Sweden and where the state plays an active role in wage bargaining and training. In the US, in contrast, the unions are weak and there is little by way of an active labour market policy;
- a more activist role of the Swedish state in economic policy, as against a hands-off approach to markets in the US.

As we shall see, these differences can be exaggerated. But in any event we will need to establish how they arose and how deep they are. And for differences that have persisted, we will need to ask (in the concluding chapter), how are they are shaping life chances, or liberty and equality, in the two countries?

A number of explanations have been offered for the different paths taken by the US and Sweden: these include the strength of the labour movement in Sweden as against the weakness of the labour movement in the US (Esping-Andersen 1990) which was, moreover, cross-cut by allegiances of ethnicity. This latter feature of labour in the US is often invoked in accounts of American 'exceptionalism' (Lipset 1996) or 'why is there no labor party in the United States?' (see Archer 2007 for a critical review of this debate). But the 'labour power difference' explanation has been challenged by Swenson (2002), among others, who compared the relations between 'capital' and 'labour' in both countries. Swenson argues that capitalists in the two countries, as represented especially by employers' organizations, were interested in finding an accommodation with labour which suited the needs of both sets of interests. In this respect, the period of the Great Depression was a critical turning point: Swenson says that in the US during the 1930s, employers needed to find a way to contain wages and ensure that labour remained weak by making sure that it was fragmented or segmented. In Sweden, in contrast, the main turning point was later, during the 1940s and 1950s, when employers managed to impose a nation-wide coherence on the labour unions, which resulted in workers accepting 'solidaristic' wages for the overall benefit of the economy. This resulted in two quite different systems, and Swenson traces these in detail up to more recent times.

Instead of a 'power' explanation (strength or weakness of labour), Swenson offers one based on 'interests', and especially the interests of employers in providing low wages and benefits, which applies to both countries, though with different outcomes. Without going into the details of his explanation, one implication is that it is not the strength of labour alone that is decisive, but that workers' interests must also seek accommodation with other groups – such as employers or parties apart from those representing workers' interests, and the agrarian party in Sweden (we shall come back to this shortly) – in order successfully to shape politics. The broader implication is a more pluralist and meliorist picture of how politics works, in contrast to the power and conflict picture.

Three other arguments about American–Swedish divergence can be mentioned. Blyth (2002) also takes the Depression era as his point of departure, but focuses on the role of economic ideas: he argues that in the 1930s, Keynesian ideas, in different ways in the two countries, put in place a welfare state that guarded against the failures and excesses of markets. This consensus lasted until the 1980s, when the Reagan era reversed Keynesianism in favour of ideas promoting the liberalization of markets. These free-market ideas also came to pervade the thinking of Swedish economists and policymakers, though they never took root among a wider public, which remained in favour of the state's role in the economy. Again, there are many details in Blyth's account that can be omitted for our purposes. The implication of his argument, however, is that rather than global markets imposing change on states from outside, it is the politics of economic ideas within countries that matter. Moreover, although similar economic ideas impacted the two countries roughly synchronously, they had different effects. A further implication of Blyth's account is therefore that these contingent ideas can be overturned or challenged, and that neither country needs to continue to be dominated nowadays by market-liberalizing policies.

A second set of arguments is presented by Steinmo (1993, 2010),[2] who bases his comparison on evolutionary ideas about the adaptation of political institutions to their environments. Thus he invokes 'contingent' factors, such as the homogeneity of the population in Sweden and its rich endowment with natural resources. But, like others, he focuses on the politics of the 1930s and the deal between labour and agricultural interests. The farmers were represented by the liberals and a compromise was made (which features in all accounts of Swedish politics at this time, of which more in a moment) with the farmers' interests which allowed for a certain amount of protectionism for agricultural products – in return for a labour and welfare policy desired by the Social Democrats. This compromise paved the ground for a strong coherent state and a long period of consensual politics.

In the US, in contrast, the weakness of the state was shaped by the fact that the Constitution was designed to prevent the concentration of state power before the arrival of mass democracy, combined with the legacy of slavery which delayed democracy coming into full force until the Civil Rights Act of 1964 (although Steinmo also notes how the 'contingent' resource richness of the American West shaped politics in the 19th century). Further, American ethnic cleavages and diversity have militated against consensual politics and the ability to forge an inclusive welfare state (see also Alesina and Glaeser 2004). Steinmo's explanation combines evolutionism, institutionalism and ideas about complex adaptive systems. The implications of his account lead him to list some of the challenges that this adaptation currently faces in both countries, and how the respective states in particular might address these challenges.

Finally, the contrast between the Nordics and the Anglophones also plays a role in Mann's larger comparative-historical account of power. Mann's account (2012: 241–312) is set apart by its acknowledgment that militarism also impacts on domestic social change. For example, during the Second World War, the American state put the economy on a war footing and the virtual absence of unemployment during the war (among other factors) – unlike the high unemployment during the 1930s – set back the welfare reform gains of the labour movement that had been achieved during the Depression. And although Sweden was neutral during the war, rationing and the state's economic planning played a role here too, in this case leading to a lasting strengthening of the role of the state.

We will come back to these arguments in a moment, but before we do so, we can ask more generally: how do these explanations compare? The first point to make is that the factors that explain the two different paths of development in the two countries are surely 'overdetermined'. That is, there are several factors which could explain the differences between them and they are not mutually exclusive. It is conceivable that the labour movement and its alliances, capitalist employers, economic ideas, ethnic homogeneity versus diversity, experiences in war, and other 'contingent' historical differences (endowment with natural resources which were crucial at different times in the course of agricultural and industrial development) all played a role. In fact, further explanations can be added: for example, political institutionalists have argued that the US has not been able to forge a coherent social policy because, with its pluralism, there are too many interest groups supporting different parties or parts of the policymaking or legislative apparatus so that they cancel each other out or can block (or 'veto') change. In Sweden, by contrast, a more centralized state and a dominant party have been able successfully to push for and implement welfare reform.

Another way to think about these differences is to ask: *when* did the consequences of the state's social and economic policies make themselves felt? And here a somewhat different pattern emerges: the US became increasingly egalitarian up until the 1960s and 1970s, and in fact was not very different in this regard from Sweden and other European countries, though it has since suffered a reversal (or again, the US has been a leader in education, ahead of European countries; see Garfinkel et al. 2010). Similarly, state spending in the US did not differ dramatically from that in Sweden (or other Western countries) up until the 1960s (Steinmo 2010: 203). On the other hand, Sweden, like other Nordics, was just as unequal as the US until the 1950s, then became more equal, and has since then maintained its position among the most egalitarian societies (Mann and Riley 2007). This timing of the rise and fall of equality in the US and the rise and stall of equality in Sweden suggests a further explanation; namely that the upswing in the post-war economy spread economic benefits more widely in both countries, but that either differing economic fortunes (American relative economic decline) or the distribution of political power (more even and centralized in the Swedish case, more divided in the American case) account for diverging paths in recent decades. These factors will be especially important if, as Steinmo has also argued, the contrast between a system of highly progressive taxation in Sweden as against a system of minimal taxes which favours the rich against the poor is oversimplified (we will come back to this shortly).

These ways of thinking about the two paths are different from, but not incompatible with, the analyses that aim to locate the most important break in economic and welfare policies in the 1930s.[3] This is the time when a combination of factors led to the creation of the welfare state and to new ways of governing labour markets in both countries. Yet in Sweden, as mentioned, there was an alliance between a recently industrialized labour force represented by the Social Democrat party and the still sizeable agricultural interests of small farmers represented by the Liberal party.[4] These two groups made a famous compromise – the so-called 'cow trade' of the Saltsjobaden agreement in 1936–8 (see Steinmo 2010: 50–2) – whereby the state, employers, workers and small farmers coordinated their interests for the sake of a national economic strategy of wage restraint in return for wage bargaining rights and welfare benefits.

The new social policy has come to be known as 'folkhem' ('people's home') and has set the terms of policy and political discourse ever since.[5] The consensus formed in the late 1930s has allowed the Social Democrat party to dominate politics up to the present day. And even if the Conservative party have occasionally led the government (as it does now), they nevertheless remain supportive of the 'folkhem' idea (the very name of the party, 'Moderaterna', or the 'moderates', is indicative). Thus Lindbom (2008) argues that the Moderaterna have adapted to embracing Sweden's welfare state tradition, rather than conforming to the Anglo-American conservative agenda of scaling back the welfare state. Indeed, the policies of the Moderaterna could be regarded as leftist in comparison to those of Anglophone liberals, and the shift of the party towards accepting the Swedish 'model' is arguably nowadays preventing the Social Democratic party from coming back into power since the latter party does not represent a strong alternative. And, as Steinmo (2010) notes, there has been no significant decline in public support for the state's role.

In the US, in contrast, the New Deal was contested from the start. In order to push through his welfare reforms, foremost the Social Security system, President Roosevelt had to compromise with conservative Democrats from the Southern states, thus weakening his agenda. Swenson (2002) describes the labour market policies that emerged at this time as 'segmentalist', setting a course whereby individual employers or employers in particular sectors could dictate the terms of wages and benefits – instead of having national bargaining between the government, employers and unions. Whether there was a comparative weakness of labour in this case, or if employer associations were able to pursue a more coherent strategy than labour, or if Southern Democrats could veto or weaken reform, the New Deal succeeded in creating the American welfare state, even if this achievement has remained conflict-laden. The lasting contestedness here is partly a product of employers continuing to have powerful organizational capabilities, partly because reforms have had to be to a large extent fought for and against via the courts (a source of power that has no equivalent elsewhere as a separate branch of government), and partly because there has been a weakening of the labour and union movement.[6] In the pluralist American political system, labour and welfare policy have thus been contested to this day.

How far back do we need to go in order to identify these divergent paths? If we look back even further than the 1930s, it is possible to start with how *modern* politics became democratized: in the US, as mentioned, democratic political institutions were established before citizen-classes struggled for a share of power within the state. A pluralist and stable democracy was entrenched among affluent white males with the right to vote early on, but without the struggles to incorporate a broader population that character-ized European paths of social development. And although labour conflicts were intense and violent in the US, especially in the late 19th century and up to the Depression (Archer 2007), these conflicts were not nationwide and they were marked by cross-cutting ethnic and other cleavages within a highly decentralized political system. Thus many different groups have continued to be represented within a fragmented state.

In Sweden, in contrast, most of the labour force nowadays is union-ized and the state, including coalition governments, has continually sought to integrate the interests of various organized social groups via compromises. This strong state can be traced back to pre-industrial abso-lutist Sweden, where the monarchy did not, as elsewhere in Europe, have to contend with a powerful nobility or urban bourgeoisie, and which at the same time faced a strong class of independent small farmers whose interests could be incorporated into a liberal representative parliamen-tary system (Anderson 1974: 173–91; Mann 1993: 716–18). A strong centralized state administration has remained its legacy ever since.

An account of the main difference between the state and politics in Sweden and in America can therefore be based on more long-term com-parisons of the state–society relationship (see also Chapter 3) – *and* at the same time take into account specific forces operating in particular periods. The relatively strong inclusion of forces from below (farmers and workers) and weaker elites 'above' explain why Sweden has been dominated by a social democratic party for most of the era in which civil society or class-citizens have become more powerful, resulting in a state that has been able to incorporate these forces via reformism. The result, a universalist welfare state and lower levels of inequality, did not crystallize until well into the post-war period, but this may to be do with the fact that Swedish industrialization and economic growth also occurred later and within a shorter period than in, say, Britain and the US.

In America, in contrast, the pluralist state has been fragmented, penetrated by different party interests (Southern conservative Democrats are perhaps the prime example) and by many interest groups pulling the state in different directions. Put differently, powerful elites and interest organizations have had greater control in this case than elsewhere, whereas weaker groups have been more marginalized – all within a highly decentralized political system. As Steinmo puts it: 'The increasing fragmentation of political power in America has not built walls between public and private power as might have been hoped' (2010: 232). Or, as Hall and Lindholm (1999: 112) write:

> The institutional weakness of the central state, the separation of powers, and the internal divisions of the political parties allow American politicians to be less tied to national programs and more responsive to their constituents, but the same factors also make them more reliant on partisan pressure groups and lobbies for financial and political backing.

Equally, in the language of Chapter 1, we could describe the contrast between how the two democratic states respond to or control their respective environments (the rise of 'the people') as a difference between a centralized and coherent as against a more pluralized fragmented ordering, with consequences that will be discussed shortly.

In any event, these long-term trajectories of the state have, in turn, shaped social development, but it is difficult to say that economic and political power are more intertwined in the US: it may be that economic interests are able to penetrate the American state more powerfully and thus to shape it, but it is also the case that the state is less shaped by and shaping of economic forces in view of the 'hands off' nature of the state. And perhaps the two reinforce each other such that the business interests 'in' the state shape it towards a more laissez-faire attitude towards the private sector. Yet it is difficult to make these factors responsible on their own for American distinctiveness: until the 1970s, welfare states expanded in both countries and throughout the West, and the decline in rates of economic growth have since then also affected all advanced economies, including that of Sweden, even if American economic power is singularly affected by the overextension of its military reach and the unique extent of the 'financialization' of the American economy (see Chapter 4). Swedish politics, however, is also hemmed in by economic interests, in this case due to a reliance on export markets.

This brings us to recent times and how the role of the state has changed in an Age of Limits. The responsiveness of the American state to many diverse interests has had a cost – literally: Steinmo says that the US is 'unique in the extent to which it attempts to regulate, reward, subsidize and manipulate decision making through its tax system' (2010: 153). In fact, he argues that if public and private social expenditures are combined, the US spends more per person than Sweden (2010: 152–3; see also Garfinkel et al. 2010: 51 for a similar argument). To this we can add, following Pontusson (2005), that taxes, which are high in the Scandinavian countries, do not explain social inequality in a straightforward way: in Sweden (and Denmark) taxes have a regressive effect on redistribution, and redistribution is in fact achieved via benefits, whereas it is only in the US that taxes have a greater redistributive effect than benefits. So in addition to the quantitative divergence in levels of equality, it is necessary to add how these distributive effects are achieved: via benefits for all combined with universal taxes in the Swedish case, and taxes targeting groups differently combined with benefits which are highly unevenly distributed in the American case.

Thus it is necessary to pinpoint the consequences of the role of the state. As indicated in Chapter 1, there are at least two ways to interpret how states have diverged: one is that the stronger civil society actors have been able to balance against or penetrate the state, and the second is that a relatively weak state allows itself to respond to these actors or to be penetrated by them. In both cases, the account is not solely based on the state; rather, it is the interaction between the state on the one hand and civil society or forces from below on the other. From a comparative perspective, the Swedish state provides a mirror image to the American one: strongly centralized, it can coordinate policy and give direction to the interests of a few well-organized groups. But the reason for this greater coordinating capacity lies not just on the side of the state, but also in that the state confronts more aggregated and homogeneous interests – such as the almost entirely unionized workforce, a strong national employers' organization, and parties that regularly engage with both. The American state is more penetrable, but it also faces more diverse and conflicting interests, as we have seen with labour, but we can also think of the 26,000 lobbyists that are represented in Washington (according to Steinmo 2010: 151).[7] Or we can note that the Swedish employers' organization (SAF) is also strong and coordinated: Blyth notes that it is stronger than comparable bodies anywhere else in terms of funding (2002: 210). In the US, even the names of the equivalent organizations indicate their non-coordinated nature: business roundtables, chambers of commerce and political action committees (see also Pontusson 2005: 20).

These are all differences, but we can ask whether they have been exaggerated – or to put it differently, whether there has recently been more convergence. Take, for example, state spending and taxes: a common perception is that the US state has minimal spending and low taxes as against Sweden's high spending and high tax state. And indeed, if we compare, for example, government expenditure as percentage of GDP in the mid-1990s, then the figures are 32.9 per cent for the US (1995) and 68.3 per cent for Sweden (1994) (Tanzi and Schuhknecht 2000: 141). However, this does not include 'fiscal churn', which 'measures the extent to which the same households both receive government payments and pay taxes' (ibid.). If we include this fiscal churn, the figures are 23.9 per cent for the US and 34.1 per cent for Sweden (for the same years).[8] This difference is not as large as the contrast between a 'socialist' Sweden and a 'pro-market' US might initially suggest.

It is also important to understand that taxes and spending can mean different things: in the US, the government taxes people and businesses, but then gives them tax rebates of various types. As Steinmo points out (2010: 154), such rebates could be seen as spending since they are revenues lost. In Sweden, the government taxes people and businesses more, and also taxes the benefits they receive (pensions and social security). The Swedish state thus spends a lot, but that is because it taxes universally, whereas the American state is able to spend little because it gives so much money back to taxpayers. One implication that Steinmo draws out is that Americans therefore (rightly) perceive welfare as handouts (they are means-tested), even though they perceive the handouts to themselves (rebates) as not something that their state provides for them: 'Americans have grown increasingly skeptical of government at the same time that they try to use government to solve their private ills' (Steinmo 2010: 150). In Sweden, in contrast, where all pay a high price for social spending, people perceive this as equal and fair treatment and they have not become more ill-disposed towards taxes.[9]

Perhaps an even more important contrast than levels of equality can therefore be made between a universalist Swedish state and one that is more responsive in different ways to particular social groups in the case of the American state. To anticipate, this mirrors nicely a contrast that can be made between a neo-Hegelian civil society that is articulated in an engagement with the state in Sweden (Tragardh 2010) and a Toquevillian civil society balanced against the state in the US.

To be sure, there are also differences between the economic systems of the two countries. The main one may be that, like other 'small states in world markets', Sweden has had to maintain an economy that is more open to the world since it is more dependent on exports.[10] The way that small states compensate for the exposure of the labour force to global change is by providing re-skilling or training for workers. The main openness of the US, on the other hand, is the increasing 'financialization' (Krippner 2011; see also Chapter 4 below) of the American economy. Those who argue that states are constrained by economic globalization are therefore partly right, but not for the functionalist/evolutionist reason that there is a single – one best – free market solution: 'capitalism' (or markets, in my view) imposes certain conditions, but for rather specific reasons in each case (export openness versus financial openness) that enable and constrain countries in different ways as economic actors. Thus economic and political institutions or orders are separable in both cases.[11] Further, there is no reason why the US and Sweden should not pursue autonomous politics – except where they are constrained: in terms of trade openness in the Swedish case, and supporting a globalized financial sector in the US.

True, post-war growth lifted the American and Swedish economies both, and spread the American model of an advanced economy with large multinational and multidivisional corporations (Van der Wee 1987). American managerial techniques and consumerism spread to Europe and beyond, just as Fordism and Taylorism had diffused in the manufacturing industry in the 1920s and 1930s (Hughes 1989: 249–294). Markets also diffused, including systems of innovation (Schroeder 2007: 38–40) and means of meeting consumer demand such as supermarkets and marketing techniques (de Grazia 2005). But politics, unlike markets and technology, is not equally subject to diffusion, and is subject to different pressures from below (to which we will return in Chapter 3), so that different types of state have persisted.

Americanization or globalization?

If the dominant institutions in Sweden and the US can be analysed under the same umbrella, even if they also diverge, what about culture?

As with economic globalization, arguments about cultural globalization often revolve around Americanization. Two issues can be treated separately in what follows: how and whether Swedish culture has become Americanized, and how and whether American culture has become globalized. To begin with, it can be noted that both cultures, and indeed all advanced societies, became more national over the course of the 19th and 20th centuries in the sense that their sub-national cultures were diminished: 'National education systems, mass media, and consumer markets are still subverting localism and homogenizing social and cultural life into units which are, at their smallest extent, national' (Mann 1996: 298). Thus American influence on Sweden is on national culture, whereas the globalization of American culture is something broader.[12]

For Swedish Americanization, it is relatively easy to trace pro- and anti-American attitudes over the course of time: the most pro-American decade was the 1960s, the most anti- the 1920s and late 1960s (according to Alm 2009: 196). At the same time, the influence of American popular culture more broadly, especially via the media, has persisted throughout the whole of the post-war period, whereas German cultural influence was stronger into the early part of the 20th century. To be sure, during the Vietnam war, Sweden was also one of the countries at the forefront of protest against American politics, but that war also caused political upheaval in America. Perhaps the peak of American cultural influence thus generally coincided with the peak of its post-war geopolitical dominance. Whether this means that American cultural influence is now in decline can be left to one side: if consumer culture and science are dominant, then consumer culture is no longer peculiarly American and science has always been universal in principle, whatever its geographic origins.

Individualism in Sweden and America

Nevertheless, it is interesting to ask: does culture converge, or does it diverge such that it matters for social change? To tackle this question, we can examine a component of culture that must be as fundamental as any to understanding social change: beliefs about the individual in society. In America, as Hall and Lindholm argue, the ideal of continual self-improvement needs to be displayed by the evidence of self-transformation, for example in status goods. In Hall and Lindholm's words, 'the pervasive pragmatic modular approach to life permits Americans to . . . [visualize] the world around them as a machine that can be retooled, or taken apart and rebuilt, in order to achieve maximum efficiency . . . even the self is considered to be a kind of modular entity, capable of being reconfigured to fit into preferred life styles' (1999: 86). They continue: 'each striving individual seeks to become "all you can be" through ceaseless labor, accumulation, consumption, and display' (1990: 90). Hall and Lindholm base this understanding of American selfhood both on comparative-historical sociology and on anthropological studies of households.

Swedish individualism, in contrast, is oriented more, on the one hand, towards nature, and the peace and isolation that can be found there, and, on the other, towards living up to the expectations of a communitarian society in which norms are highly transparent (Frykman and Löfgren 1987). The characterization by Orfali sums this up: 'The dream of every Swede is essentially an individualistic one, expressed through the appreciation of the primitive solitude of the vast reaches of unspoilt nature' (1991: 443). She says that 'in Sweden, perhaps more than anywhere else, the private is exposed to public scrutiny. The communitarian, social democratic ethos involves an obsession with achieving total transparency in all social relations and aspects of social life' (1991: 418). Again, this understanding is grounded in social history and (in Frykman and Löfgren's case) anthropology.

From the point of view of social history, individualism could also be equated with the increasing role of consumer choices. Thus Fischer argues that the key cultural difference between early America and today is 'more': 'The fundamental contrast between early Americans and today's Americans in their circumstances of life' is that 'modern Americans have so many more choices . . . generally, more Americans gained access to more things material, social and personal' (2010: 2). But it is hard to see what is peculiarly American about this, since Swedes have undergone a similar change. And in Sweden, consumerism is of course nowadays no less powerful than it is in America (Löfgren 1995). O'Dell describes how Swedes think of Americanization in terms of consumption: 'Ask what is American, and Swedes will draw up a list of consumer items which are commonly found throughout the country and which are used daily' (1997: 114). Perhaps this reflects American influence, but surely these attitudes are no longer perceived as particularly American since consumerism has spread throughout the developed world.

A different way of characterizing American exceptionalism, according to Fischer, is to say that Americans are the 'most accepting of economic inequality, the most religious, the most patriotic, and the most voluntarist of Westerners' (2010: 13). By 'voluntarism', Fischer means a 'sovereign individual' in the sense of 'self-reliant', but also 'believing and behaving *as if* individuals succeed through fellowship – not in ego-istic isolation but in sustaining voluntary communities' (2010: 10); in other words, through the associationalism that Tocqueville discerned in American society. Hall and Lindholm put this distinctiveness more strongly: 'In most other cultures, the community precedes the individ-ual, who finds a place in it. In contrast, for Americans, "individualism" is natural, community problematical. *Society has to be built*' (1999: 102, citing Varenne 1977). Kent describes the Nordic countries quite differ-ently: the 'wellbeing of the collective identity,' he says, 'is perceived to take precedence over individual rights' (2000: 371). Perhaps it is neces-sary then to discuss not just individualism, but also its opposite.

Yet the temptation to equate Sweden with greater collectivism and the US with greater individualism should be resisted. As Berggren and Tragardh have argued, the Swedish welfare state, or the 'people's home', has not produced a more collectivist mentality in Sweden than else-where. Instead, they trace a distinctive type of individualism, a 'state individualism' (2006: 10), to its roots in 18th-century Swedish liberal-ism. As we have seen earlier, this freedom in relation to the state has its origins in the comparative strength of free small farmers in Sweden (perhaps there are echoes of America's farming and frontier roots here). This kind of individualism, Berggren and Tragardh argue further, has only been further entrenched by the Swedish post-war welfare state. They note that the Swedish welfare state is aimed at individuals, rather than favouring households or worker collectivities or other civil soci-ety institutions – which chimes with the universalism of the Swedish state discussed earlier. Thus it is important not to extrapolate from a strong welfare state a zero-sum opposition between collectivism and individualism.

Similarly, we might be tempted to counterpose the greater religiosity of Americans – they are the most religious Westerners – to individual-ism. But this would also be misleading since, as Fischer and Hout have documented, Americans have also become more tolerant of other faiths over the course of the 20th century (2006: 245). It would be equally misleading to contrast American individualism with Tocquevillian associationalism in a zero-sum manner since, as we have seen, Fischer also sees connections between voluntarism and individualism. In any case, according to the figures compiled by Baldwin, Americans belong to more civic associations, but the Nordics (including Sweden) are close behind the Americans and ahead of other European countries in this regard (2009: 152; only Iceland is ahead of the US); whereas if the meas-ure is volunteer work, Swedes and Americans are ahead of other Western

OECD countries, with roughly half the adult population engaged in this activity (ibid.: 154).

The difference thus relates not to individualism as such, but to individualism in relation to the state: belonging to a group is not as problematic in Sweden as it is in the US. Swedes, with a more positive attitude to the state, do not regard state-related associationalism as being opposed the individual. Tragardh (2010) therefore thinks that what makes Swedish civil society unique is that it is state-centred. Americans, on the other hand, are ambivalent about the state (Hall and Lindholm 1999: 109–28), even if they then engage in much self-organized collective activity. This difference in relation to individualism might seem to be an exception to the argument that culture plays no structural role – as it could underpin different political attitudes. But how necessary is it to invoke culture here, as political divergence has already been accounted for by a number of factors? Furthermore, invoking culture faces a problem with timing: if the two types of individualism and associationalism in relation to the state would be critical, then this would be difficult to reconcile with what I referred to earlier as the rise and fall of the American welfare system and the Swedish rise and stall (which are both relatively recent) – to speak nothing of the fact that the cultural patterns in both countries are rooted in longer-term histories, whereas in both countries, the state grew enormously over the course of the 20th century.

To conclude: culture *qua* culture can be separated from political ideas, but its role in fostering divergence needs to put into context. American 'anti-statism' and Swedish 'collectivism' have persisted, even while global waves of political ideas and social movements, like the counterculture of the 1960s, have come and gone and affected both countries. Second, distinctive cultures are increasingly nationally bounded, at the same time that a global consumer culture has emerged, and the mass media have spread popular culture (but again, the two – national and global – do not need to be seen as zero sum; Norris and Inglehart 2009). Put another way, if what defines the distinctiveness of high and popular cultures (or the culture of everyday life) of the nation is taken to constitute modern cultures, these distinctive cultures are nevertheless increasingly mediated by the same technologies (see Schroeder 2007: 74–120). Finally, since political differences are over-determined by factors other than culture, it is difficult to assign a macro-sociological function to culture, except perhaps to reinforce the boundary around the national unit.

Is it possible to say that there are wider lessons that can be drawn from all these differences and convergences? For example, it could be argued that the US would need greater universalism and solidarism to shift towards a Swedish welfare system generating greater equal capacities, or that Sweden's universal welfare state will face the challenge of including a more diverse immigrant population coupled with a population that is ageing more quickly or replenished less quickly (which, in turn, means that a greater influx of immigrant workers is needed). But resolving these tensions would require cultural shifts that are difficult to conceive, and perhaps we are at the limits of social science inasmuch as engineering cultural change – even if social science can provide insights into how that can be done – surely moves beyond science and into norms.

Politics, as we saw in the first part of this chapter, has diverged in the sense that the two countries have yielded different capacities of the state and levels of social rights – as well as levels of economic inequality.[13] Yet in both cases, after the push from below for the expansion of social rights, particularly from the Depression until the 1970s, the state's room for manoeuvre has narrowed. In what sense these are more general limits is the subject of the chapters that follow. But as we have seen (and will pursue in greater depth), the opposition between convergence and divergence can be reconciled if it can be understood how the three orders within and beyond both countries, despite their differences, to some extent share a pattern of differentiation that has become increasingly frozen.

3
Paths towards Pluralist Democracy: Liberal versus Radical Interpretations

A crucial gap in sociology in recent decades has been the lack of a general theory of the state and power or of the state and social development.[1] There are several reasons for this: one is the demise of Marxist political sociology, with its unifying idea that the state is the instrument of class power. Marxist theory has been replaced, if at all, by Foucauldian or constructivist ideas on the one hand, or institutionalist theories on the other – neither of which have produced comparative-historical and systematic accounts of the variety among contemporary states. A second reason for this gap is the popular idea that the state's powers have diminished in recent decades because of globalization and neoliberalism. On this view, the state's powers are undermined by a globalizing economy, and if the state is eroding at the expense of larger economic forces, it becomes difficult to see the state as the locus of power.

A further problem with contemporary theories of the state is the legacy of Max Weber: although he put forward a definition of the state that is still widely used – the state as the monopoly of legitimate violence – he had no fully fledged conception of democracy (Breuer 1998; Schroeder 1998). To satisfy sociologists, such a conception of democracy would require an analysis of how different interests are represented in the state; in other words, an understanding of plural powers. Yet while concepts of pluralism (or polyarchy) and democracy abound in political science (Dahl 1998), there are no such concepts in sociology (we will encounter the exceptions below). As we shall see, the problem of democratic pluralism which eluded Weber is still not resolved in sociology. At the same time, unless the state is regarded as the instrument of a (unified) ruling economic class or elite, some notion of pluralism is required inasmuch as the state represents various different interests or powers.

I will not spend much time on countering the argument that the state has been in retreat due to the pressure of globalization. As we shall see later in this chapter (indeed, in relation to Sweden and the US, the previous chapter dealt with this argument), this idea is misleading. However, I shall argue that apart from an account of the plural interests represented in democratic states, it is also necessary to take into account the autonomy of the economic order and how it counterbalances the state. This autonomy goes against another influential school of thought about the nature of the state which has already been discussed in the first two chapters – 'political economy' or the 'varieties of capitalism'. Although this school is not directly concerned with democratic plural-ism, it nevertheless aims to account for the differences between how states relate to their societies. The problem here, as implied by the label 'political economy', is that the political and economic orders and their institutions are elided. Against this, this chapter will argue that even if economic forces can contribute to explaining the differences between states 'from below' and from a long-term perspective, there is no reason not to keep the economic realm separate. Secondly, and in keeping with the idea of limits, I will argue that the main forces from below have recently become eclipsed.

The argument will proceed by outlining two major alternatives in sociological accounts of the modern state and democracy: one has reframed ideas about classes in terms of citizenship rights (Mann) and the other focuses on the balance of power between the state and civil society (Gellner and Hall). Both are sociological – after all, they are about power and about comparisons between societies – but they also have quite different political implications. I will label Mann's account 'radical' since the core of his account is to uncover asymmetries of power. The accounts by Gellner and by Hall (who have somewhat dif-ferent positions) I will label 'liberal' because their focus is on how civil society counterweighs the state's power.[2]

Before setting out on this comparison, it should be noted that both the 'radical' and 'liberal' accounts are not, in the first instance, 'political' in terms of espousing the values of particular regimes or parties: in both cases, the imperative in the first instance is to be true to the facts. Yet there are obviously political implications in the two approaches to social theory: in the radical case, the theory aims to uncover structural imbalances of power in order to criticize them (in societies represent-ing a variety of political stripes), whereas in the liberal case, the idea is to see how elites and other groups can respond to the challenges that are presented to states in the environment that shapes them (ditto).

To be sure, the two positions are being stylized here for the sake of contrast. Yet the point of presenting them side by side is to compare their strengths and shortcomings – and go beyond them where possible.

The chapter will begin with what is to be explained; the endpoint of a range of states in advanced societies in terms of their plural powers, and how this differs as between the liberal and radical accounts (in this respect, it will be possible to build on the argument about convergence and divergence in Chapter 2). Once these endpoints are surveyed, there follows an account of the role of the state in economic development, including the development of welfare states and their limits vis-à-vis markets. At this point, the chapter will sketch the trajectories of states and the forces that shaped them in both the radical and liberal accounts. It will then compare the two and end with implications.

Some limitations can be mentioned because the chapter tackles an enormous topic: the chapter will not deal with the relations between states, even though these have been shown to be a key to state capacity in the past (Tilly 1990; Collins 1999a: 19–36).[3] Second, the state plays an important role as an economic actor apart from its provision of citizenship rights or transfer payments – as a consumer of products and services. This role will be excluded in this chapter because it bears mainly on economic rather than political development. Third, the chapter confines itself to Western or advanced societies (Chapter 8 deals with China and India), though implications for developing societies will be mentioned in the conclusion. And finally, the chapter adopts a comparative-historical approach and neglects engagement with constructivist and rational-choice or institutionalist perspectives: all that can be done in this respect is to note (again) that these have so far failed to provide a coherent comparative account of the trajectories of modern states and social development.

Liberal and radical endpoints

Ultimately, the radical and the liberal accounts wind up at different endpoints of state development and of the range of states, so it will be useful to preview them. There are two dimensions to this range in both accounts: one is the extent to which the state is penetrable by different social groups. This is an endpoint because the extent to which states are responsive to or controlled by their citizens – democracy – is a crucial distinguishing feature of states. The explanation here in political science would be in terms of elections and parties, but a sociological account must go beyond this to show how various groups or forces shape the state – focused on the relation between ruling elites and less powerful groups. Further, it can be anticipated that a highly penetrable state is not necessarily the most democratic – if the interests that permeate the state may, for example, skew its power disproportionately towards one or other grouping. Or again, the penetration of the state may result in a stalemating of all these groupings, and may thus be suboptimally democratic.

A second dimension comprises rights vis-à-vis the state. As we shall see, one point of departure here is Marshall's conception of civil, political and social citizenship rights (see Turner 1986). In this respect, since civil and political rights have become well-entrenched in all advanced societies, we can focus on what sets states apart from each other nowadays; their social citizenship rights, which determine the well-being of citizens.[4] How generous and extensive is the state's provision for the well-being of citizens of different states, and how stable is this provision? Rights can also be interpreted differently, with the emphasis on rights *against* the state, and in this case rights can be seen in terms of the scope for the untrammelled expression and coordination of interests among individuals. To what extent the state ensures a minimal degree of social well-being, or if the state's role is to enable a market economy to flourish and otherwise empower individuals: the scope and depth of these rights constitutes the second dimension that shapes the trajectories of the states, with different radical and liberal interpretations of these.

There are no doubt other dimensions in which states vary. Still, the core of a sociological account of the state is arguably the relation between the state and society – a combination of the first dimension, penetrability by interests, and the second, extent and depth of citizenship. At one extreme of these dimensions are what Mann calls the Anglophone states, with the US the best example, permeable by a diffuse set of interests and with restricted social rights. At the other extreme are corporatist or social democratic states, where societal interests are articulated more coherently and coordinated by more statist governments, with extensive – but in some cases bounded or selective and in others universalistic – social citizenship. Again, these two dimensions – the way interests are articulated in the state, and the way individuals are accorded social rights – account largely for the variety among states. We have already encountered these in Chapter 2, in relation to 'convergence' and 'divergence'; now we must see if there are broader patterns.

At this stage it is worth reiterating a point made earlier: it might be expected that the liberal interpretation would lean toward supporting the Anglophone end of the spectrum of states whereas the radical interpretation would lean towards the social democratic end of the spectrum. But it is important to stress again that both interpretations are, in the first instance, politically neutral. If there are political implications to different approaches in social theory, it should be possible to separate these from predilections for different political regimes. A value-free account can nevertheless be related to normative implications, albeit in an indirect way, and we will return to these implications in the concluding chapter.[5]

The state and economic development

The role of the state vis-à-vis economic development has shaped how 'pluralist' or otherwise states are.[6] To see how, we can review the contrasting liberal and radical interpretations of the state's role in economic development. In the liberal view, capitalism developed before industrialization. In this case, a middle class emerged whose economic interests and property rights provided a counterweight against the state. Other states, where industrialization occurred later, required stronger states, and the capitalist or radical elites in these states were forced, reluctantly, to yield rights to working classes via authoritarian regimes with ideologies legitimating collective goals rather than individual liberties. Further, these regimes also took a much more active part in economic development, as opposed to regimes where capitalism emerged and industrialization took place earlier and which allowed more autonomy to markets.

The radical theory, in contrast, argues that the trajectories of the state depended on conflict between classes, which we can simplify for the moment to the conflict between 'capital' and 'labour', with various paths to be described later. The important point in terms of economic development is that a variation at the endpoint of contemporary states is that in some (Anglo) states, there is a zero-sum power stand-off between capital and labour, whereas other states – the Nordics and Christian Socials, as Mann labels them – have yielded more cooperative relations between capital and labour which promote a more cohesive social order. This way of interpreting the range of contemporary states is obviously quite different from the liberal interpretation.

These vast simplifications will do for now, but one additional element needs to be mentioned: with industrialization, the state needed to provide a more extensive infrastructure for rapidly growing markets and larger skilled workforces. These infrastructural powers (education, health and public services) that were created from the late 19th century onwards also expanded the scale and scope of the state's functions (Mann 1993), and these, as we shall see later, were a precondition for social citizenship.[7] But in addition to the infrastructural aspect of state capacity, state capacity also relates to how infrastructures are used by states in promoting economic development. Thus Weiss and Hobson (1995) have argued that stronger states have a greater capacity to achieve developmental goals. They point to South Korea and Japan as examples of states that played a powerful role during the early phases of industrialization; a role which, they say, continues today. They call this 'governed interdependence', or the 'state's capacity to mobilize elite collaboration in pursuit of developmental goals' (1995: 162). This kind of state capacity is characteristic not just of East Asian developmental states, but also of Germany and France, and contrasts with a weak state in Britain and in the US.

Here we can leave to one side precisely *how* these states promoted economic growth, but hold on to the idea that in some states there are strong linkages between political and economic elites that can be aligned towards common goals, and others where the goals of economic and other elites diverge. The important point to keep in mind is that this way of thinking overcomes seeing the opposition between a strong organizing state and a weak one as zero-sum: instead, strong states can coexist with strong societies *and* promote economic development (and thus deeper social citizenship rights) to a greater degree. Governed interdependence thus entails that the state is somehow more 'embedded' within the economy, and so requires 'power *through* society' rather than 'power *over* society' (Weiss and Hobson 1995: 168; they draw on Mann's conception of infrastructural power for this formulation).

Put differently, cohesive elites within the state are able to harness forces in society towards common goals – although, as Hobson and Weiss say, the state also needs autonomy from society in order to promote economic development. To return to the theme of pluralism then, the options are: a neutral, minimal (Anglo) state whose main purpose is to ensure that strong interests from civil society are able to guide society and which does not coordinate these interests; strong and coherent (social democratic) states that have this coordinating capacity; and finally, late developing states where cohesive elites play a strong role in steering society towards desired ends. We will see later (in Chapter 8 with India and China as 'late' developmental states) that the last of these complicates the spectrum from Anglos to social democratic states.

The state's fiscal growth and economic transfers

Before we turn to politics as such, it is necessary to consider one further aspect of the economy that intersects with the state: state spending and how it relates to markets. This issue is often framed in terms of how much spending the state can 'afford' insofar as the economic growth of markets permits it. This way of thinking pervades contemporary political discussions, but it is important to put these in a larger context of how state spending has grown historically and if there is anything new about the constraints that exist today.

Tanzi and Schuhknecht provide the figures for this long-term historical development: government expenditure in advanced societies as a percentage of GDP has gone from 10.8 per cent on average in 1870 to 45 per cent in 1996 (2000: 6–7, Table 1.1). The range in 1996 is from the US, which is lowest (32.4 per cent), to the highest in Sweden (64.2 per cent). We have already seen in Chapter 2 that this difference is not what it seems. But in addition, the figures can be broken down into the difference between real expenditure ('the sum of government wages and salaries and materials and supplies purchased by government') which goes from an average of 4.6 per cent in 1870 to 18.2 per cent in 1995, as against spending on subsidies and transfers, which goes from an average of 1.1 per cent in 1870 to 23.2 per cent of GDP in 1995 (ibid.: 25, Table 2.1 and 31, Table 2.4). What this means is that health and pensions have become the largest share of social spending.[8] The main point is simply that: howsoever this expansion occurred, the constraints that may operate now did not prevent it happening in the first place. And whatever else we may say about these constraints, Tanzi and Schuhknecht and others indicate a plateauing in recent years, not a 'rolling back' of state spending.

At this point, it is useful to distinguish between state spending as a proportion of GDP (zero-sum simply by virtue of being a proportion), state spending overall (larger as long as the size of the 'pie' is growing, but also limited by the growth of the pie), and state spending as it is constrained by 'markets' and citizens (limited by what markets 'tolerate' and citizens are inclined towards; that is, what businesspeople and citizens think about state spending). The two are linked, but the link is 'fuzzy' since it rests on perceptions and on the diffuse power of markets.

The 'toleration' by markets allows us to jump to recent times, when the focus has been on arguments to the effect that taxation regimes are under pressure from globalization and this leads to a 'race to the bottom' whereby states try to outdo each other to slash taxes and spending to avoid 'crowding out' capital for investment. The idea of a 'race' implies that countries that tax too much will lose out to others that don't. Hobson has examined this argument and suggests that instead there has been a 'race to the middle', or the negotiation of an equilibrium between state revenues and the needs of capital (Hobson 2003: 38–9). He shows that while there are still differences among OECD tax regimes, there are also indications that aggregate tax burden differentials have declined (ibid.: 48). If this is correct, then states may have reached a high plateau where they are moving to a balance that is converging across states and markets.

Against this background, we can come back to more theoretical points: states centralize and concentrate power, whereas in markets, power is dispersed and diffuse (see Chapters 1 and 4). The implication is that whereas states determine the distribution of resources, markets can only bolster or limit them in a diffuse way. Thus the bounds of the state vis-à-vis markets – nowadays – are where the limits of growth and the vagaries of markets constitute a barrier to the extension of social citizenship. As we shall see, and as has already been mentioned in Chapter 1, this is also a problem of 'translation' between the two orders: even if social citizenship consists of rights that are bounded by economies and their growth rates (whether in a zero-sum manner or not), unlike markets, these rights are not 'disembedded' – they are not transferable – but rather embedded by virtue of being subject to the state and how the interests within it determine their distribution. Put differently, rights are not goods that are subject to the same type of adjustments that are characteristic of markets or to contractual exchange; they are 'package deals' (to use an expression of Ernest Gellner's), and even if they can be adjusted, these adjustments are within the bounds of political power.

Like other citizenship rights, social citizenship rights can be seen as either universal or restricted to some groups (as we have already seen in Chapter 2). Yet such a binary opposition can be too simple: these rights can also be stratified by the way that the state provides 'lumps' of economic resources, or if it requires self-provisioning or regulates benefits. There are thus various ways to draw the boundary between states and markets in terms of social citizenship rights. One way that has been used to describe this boundary (Esping-Andersen 1990) is whether labour or other services are 'commodified' (subject to purchase in a market) or de-commodified (subject to non-market implementation by the state). In all advanced societies, there is a mix, and the state varies in terms of providing different levels of 'protection' from 'commodification'. The limits to commodification can thus be added to the universality or restrictedness of social rights: are rights restricted to certain categories of nationals, to those who contribute voluntarily to social insurance, to those seeking work, and the like? It can be noted, however, that even if market 'commodification' represents a diffuse boundary of resources around these rights, these rights as they are secured in the state (outside of commodification) are a matter of kind and not degree.

Social citizenship rights are thus indivisibly provided by the state but at the same time enabled or constrained markets, where growth has been in relative decline in recent decades. Before pursuing this point further, it can be mentioned that so far we have only considered states and how they have expanded their powers and been constrained vis-à-vis markets. The consequences of this expansion, and especially the effect on economic stratification, have so far been left to one side (though they were touched on in Chapter 2). In this connection, the main recent expansion of the state, as we have seen, has been in progressive taxation and welfare or social security (transfer payments). Tanzi and Schuhknecht argue that the effect of this spending on reducing inequality is small and the main purpose of this – again, large share of total spending – is to benefit that part of the public that provides the largest share of votes: 'Relatively little improvement in income distribution is actually caused by taxation and by transfer payments, even though the latter expenditure category accounts for about 50% of total public spending and tax revenues are a large share of GDP' (2000: 96). Their 'findings suggest that public transfers do not aim mainly at improving the lot of the poor but probably at gaining political support from the middle classes or certain socially important groups' (2000: 114). This argument is highly controversial, and does not fit with the contrast between Sweden and the US made in Chapter 2 (or with others who have examined this relationship, for example Garfinkel et al. 2010).

We can leave the debate about inequality to one side for now, except to note that prima facie, the lowest levels of inequality can be found in the countries with the highest social spending (Mann and Riley 2007). However, in terms of the contrast between the liberal and radical accounts presented here, Tanzi and Schuhknecht's liberal pro-market position points to an endpoint of this liberalism: either the middle classes need to be 'bought off' ('bribed') with state-sponsored economic benefits to ensure continued political and social stability, or these benefits can be cut to favour private choices which, it is argued, favour economic growth. This is a liberal viewpoint, but more emphasis could also be placed here on sociological ('stability') as opposed to economic ('choice') liberalism. And this 'buying off' depends in any event on the bribe's continued availability.

A radical account of the varieties of capitalism

At this point, it will be useful to give a brief account of Mann's position, again focusing on the relation between states and capitalism or the relation between political and economic power (leaving out other forces such as war and the economic relations between states). Again, Mann's position is much more complex than this brief sketch allows and involves all four sources of social power, but for the purpose of comparing rival positions, it is useful to concentrate on economic and political power.

Three types

Mann argues that several types of political economy have persisted into the 21st century. Again, he calls them Anglos (or Anglophones), Nordics and Euros. These correspond roughly to Esping-Andersen's three welfare regimes – liberal, social democratic and corporatist (here we will likewise restrict ourselves to these Western ones).

Anglos (here always the US and UK, to simplify matters) institutionalized their liberal (or in the UK, reformist labour, not socialist) class compromises early, before the Second World War, but these compromises were only 'lightly entrenched in their states', partly because these countries had weak or reformist working class movements (Mann 1988: 192–4; Mann and Riley 2007: 104). Hence 'only interest groups and individuals, but not classes' (Mann 1988: 192) were represented in the state. The Anglos could thus be described as weak and pluralistic states facing strong markets. As we have seen in the case of Sweden, the Nordics had settled their class compromises by the end of the Great Depression, with the state directing the agreement between labour and capital, which led to generous and universal welfare provision after the Second World War. This also led to social democratic regimes with workers and capital both represented in the state. In the Nordic states, strong social citizenship rights have provided a counterweight against market forces. Finally, Euros converged after the Second World War with the state as the locus of power-sharing between capital and labour – not via universal social citizenship rights as for the Nordics, but via more segmented benefits, with different benefits for different occupations and familial status. In this case, the corporatist compromise between different groups was entrenched in how parties shared power. For the Euros, power sharing among parties thus shapes how the cushions against the pure workings of economic power are distributed.

When did these political regimes first emerge, and what factors shape them today? Their origins lie in the late 19th century, whence growth in the infrastructural capacity of states led to the 20th century mobilization of classes, nations and other social movements (such as women's political representation) 'from below'. Here we will not go into these 'movements', or discuss how the authoritarian regimes of the right and left, which were defeated in 1945 and 1989–91, derailed the process. In any event, the first part of the 20th century was when working classes were collective actors in Europe (Mann 1995; Hicks [1999] labels them a 'supermovement') but when there were also conservative reactions against the rise of working classes (religious, nationalist and technocratic). The key point is that this era was the height of working class mobilization. Crouch has called this the 'parabola of working class politics' (2004) with the ascent in the first half of the 20th century when there was the strongest need to accommodate working classes within the state's representative democracy followed by a decline in the post-war period.

The 'Golden Age' of the post-war period until the 1970s nevertheless continued to extend social citizenship, funded by a period of world-historically unprecedented economic growth. Subsequently, since the 1970s, there has been an increasing 'financialization' of economies (Krippner 2005), but this is much more characteristic of the Anglo economies of the US and the UK than in other regions. This financialization emerged 'interstitially'; new financial instruments could develop in the unregulated arenas of capitalism outside individual national economies and subsequently grew unimpeded until the recession of 2008, since when there have been feeble attempts regulate financial markets. Since the 1980s, according to Mann, there has also been a dominance of neoliberal ideas according to which the role of states should be minimized and the role of markets maximized. But even if these ideas have become (until the recession of 2008) widespread among policymakers, this has not led to convergence towards neoliberal institutions. Instead, the three regimes persist.

Among the Anglos, citizens' economic positions (their housing or property, investments and pensions) increasingly depend on the financial sector. At the same time, increasing inequality among the Anglos means that there is not enough breadth (widely distributed assets) among a 'property owning democracy' to anchor the financial sector. Uniquely among the Anglos, the conflict between capital and labour has been exacerbated because class compromise was less institutionalized in the state. Thus, finally, the recession has hit the Anglos, with their large financial sectors, hardest.

In other parts of the North, among Nordics and Euros, welfare states have stalled, but only among Anglos have social citizenship benefits been cut back significantly. Among the Nordics and Euros, they have been defended. The same goes for the power of workers' rights; this has been significantly curtailed only among Anglos. Still, this is a major change, since Anglos were the most egalitarian into the 1950s and 1960s, and they have now become the least egalitarian countries in the North, whereas the Euros and Nordics started from a low level of equality in the 1950s and they have become the most egalitarian parts of the North (Mann and Riley 2007). This divergence took shape in the 1970s.

These differences mean that some countries are shaped more by markets, others by states – or that power lies more with dominant economic elites in the one case and political elites in the other. This has consequences not only for governance, but also for citizens' welfare and their economic position. Among the Anglos, the balance has shifted to economic imperatives trumping political power, with the result of growing inequality. Mann nevertheless departs from a widely held view whereby the size of the state has become unsustainable during the period of relative economic decline. There is no clear relationship, he argues, between economic efficiency and the size of welfare state spending (see also Lindert 2004 for Sweden). This goes against the arguments of Tanzi and Schuhknecht (2000), encountered earlier, who claim that less state spending has been better for economic growth. In any case, states still redistribute 30 to 50 per cent of GDP, despite neoliberal ideas about rolling back the state. In short, globalization has at best stalled, but not undermined, the power of the nation-state. Mann's arguments are compatible with the idea of a 'parabola of working class politics', or that pressure from below decisively shaped the nature of politics into the post-war period.

To begin to contrast his ideas with rival views (presented more fully below), we can note, first, that in the post-war era the picture has become more complex (and here we can go beyond the limited focus on states and their capitalisms in these three regions) and there are additional factors that play a role in these trajectories of the three types of state: 1) the long-term costs and decline of the US empire (perhaps also a long-term hangover of the place of finance from the former British empire); 2) financialization, which may have impacts on growth that are separate from those related to the (non-financial) varieties of capitalism; 3) the decentralized nature of political power of Anglophone states (the US is perhaps the main example again), leading to gridlock and a veto on national (universal) programmes; 4) the long-term cycles of economic growth and slowdown since the Golden Age, which have affected all three regions; 5) classes have become ever more diffuse as collective actors while other social movements have partly – though in a less concentrated way – taken their place as influences on states; and 6) states have reacted to changing economic realities even without alleged lack of control over outside-in (global) economic forces. All these are compatible with – though they also go beyond – the thrust of Mann's arguments about how the state was shaped from below, whereby class-citizens push and entrench their interests to a greater and lesser extent within the state, which is more penetrable by diffuse and incoherent market interests in one case, or by a more cohesive ordering of the interests of social groups in others (cohesive, or if they diverge – say, over the universality of social citizenship rights – incorporating them differently). In any event, the key argument is that different paths persist within capitalism.

Before we compare this radical with the liberal account, a contrast can be made between Mann's ideas and Marxist world-systems theorists. Mann's view does not, like that of world-systems theorists, depend on the idea that capitalist economic growth is continually in crisis. This (ultimately functionalist and economistic idea) leads to the notion that capitalism must look ever further afield and 'push' class conflict from the centre (which has been discussed here) into the periphery of the developing countries. Put differently, class unrest in one part of the world is being displaced to another (a global 'spatial fix' of capitalist reordering), which means that the 'parabola' of working class politics is far from exhausted and can be found nowadays in the countries where the new engines of capitalist growth can be found, such as China (Silver 2003). Instead, Mann's pattern is politics-centred; classes gained citizenship rights via the state (Mann 1988: 188–209), not primarily because of capitalist crises (though these also played a role at certain points, and especially during the Great Depression [Mann 2012]). Nor, in Mann's view, do crises in the periphery – in the long run – boomerang back to impact the economies of states in the centre.

However, there is an affinity between Mann's radicalism and Marxists (and where I depart from both, at least for the Age of Limits), which is that capitalism remains a core concept, with its entwining of political and economic power (which the concepts of 'political economy' and 'varieties of capitalism' share). All these approaches ignore the separation of economic and political power, or of markets and how their form of social organization has become orthogonal to that of states. This separation has hardened in the Age of Limits, which is recognized – at least partly – by liberals.

Liberalism and the varieties of capitalism

At this point we can turn to the main contrast with Mann's argument, which is the liberal approach whereby state and civil society (sometimes including markets, sometimes not – we shall see that this makes a big difference) are everywhere in tension with each other. In the liberal view, civil society should provide a counterweight to states, in two senses: first, there should be a plurality of interest groups providing strong inputs into the state. Second, there should be sufficiently extensive scope for markets to allow for their efficiency which, in turn, provides the growth that is a prerequisite for legitimacy. Note again that the liberal view (and Mann's view) should, in the first instance, simply provide an accurate account of how the politics and markets of advanced societies work. Still, the normative or philosophical ideals on which they are based or which they lead to – a drive for universal (equal) social rights as against providing the conditions for the individual's (free) flourishing – can already be flagged in passing (we shall return to them).

The liberal account of how classes shape modern democracy has a similar continuum from Anglos to different versions of social democracy, but with a subtle and key difference from the radical view: in this account, the bourgeoisie or middle class has a larger part to play as its growing prosperity gradually comes to promote softer rule. In this case, the explanation allows for the contingent effect of wars on the internal dynamics of democratizing states, but more generally rests on how elites adapt to a changing external capitalist economic environment. This account emphasizes better and worse responses by elites to the economic pressures from middle and working classes from below and vice versa, with the responses of both sides having room for manoeuvre. In the end, however, the endpoint of this account is that the economic interests of a sufficiently large middle class steered by a prudent elite can together successfully adapt and maximize the state's flexibility within the larger capitalist world.

To see how liberalism arrives at this endpoint, it is necessary to begin with how, in early modern Europe, capitalism was already a larger unit within which states had to accommodate themselves from the start. In the subsequent struggle for democracy from below, it was the economic interests of a growing middle class which slowly asserted themselves against states. In the United States, this struggle was relatively mild because the middle and then working classes had sufficient power within the state so that the various political interests could slowly be accommodated within it. Contingency plays a greater role here than in Mann's account: the economic pressures for liberalization do not necessarily lead to pluralism because adjustment to changing external economic and geopolitical conditions is also needed (Hall 1988).

A further disagreement with Mann's account is that the combination of capitalism and authoritarianism could not in any event have survived the two world wars (Hall 1987: 118) – with the implication that ultimately, the economic prosperity resulting from industrialization would have led to political softening (the affinity with the functionalist 'industrial society' theory of modernization, mentioned in Chapter 1, can be noted here in passing). Nevertheless, the liberal account admits of different political economies within capitalism, so that in the case of social democratic or corporatist states, the state engages in more bargaining with classes. However, even in the (to change to Mann's labels) Nordics or Euros, it is important that state elites have sufficient flexibility to respond to larger economic external forces when they engage in this way. Hall's favourite example is Denmark, which has managed this successfully, even if there are continuing challenges.

A closely related but somewhat different delineation of the relation between pluralist democracy and the social forces that shape it is to focus on civil society. This aspect of the liberal account derives, among others, from Tocqueville, but the concept of civil society has also undergone fundamental changes. Hall and Trentmann note a shift from the 16th and 17th centuries when the concept originally meant 'civil society *as* political society', to the 18th and 19th centuries, when civil society became an 'independent universe, *distinct from* state and market' (2005: 3). In the late 20th century, they say, there is an 'ongoing ambivalence about the pairing of commerce and civil society' (2005: 10). In other words, civil society has meant both politics and what is outside of the state – and it has both included and excluded markets. Hall and Trentmann conclude that there can be no closure to the different interpretations of civil society (2005: 21–2). But this is worrisome: if – for the sake of a thought experiment – civil society does not include markets, *and* an analysis is preferred which does not include classes, *and* we also exclude social movements as being distinct from the kinds of voluntary civic associations outside the state and counterbalancing it that Tocqueville had in mind, then we are left with no political forces vis-à-vis the state at all (except parties, but these become part of the state when they rule).

Clearly this will not do, and nor will another remaining option, which is to shift the main emphasis of civil society on to a public sphere of media, a tradition commonly associated with Habermas: the public sphere of media can be seen either as a transmission belt or mode of input into politics (Luhmann's functionalist view), or as a separate arena which provides a check on politics.[9] Even in the latter view, however, unless we think of the public sphere of media as merely expressing the aggregate of atomized public opinion, the public sphere would need to represent or be shaped by precisely the powers (classes or social movements) that have just been ruled out, or the media could represent political parties and interests without the autonomy of a public sphere (or the media would themselves be an autonomous actor). A further option would be to focus, instead of classes, on business interests and organizations versus those of labour – though in this case the analysis is closer to the radical view than to liberalism.

This dilemma, of potentially ruling out all political forces apart from markets in a liberal sociology centred on civil society, is also evident in Gellner's writing. Gellner's definition of civil society is 'that set of diverse non-governmental institutions which is strong enough to counterbalance the state and, while not preventing the state from fulfilling its role of keeper of the peace and arbitrator between major interests, can nevertheless prevent it from dominating and atomizing the rest of society' (1994: 5). But Gellner himself notices that this definition is not satisfactory; it is negative (preventing authoritarianism) and while 'it may, indeed, be pluralistic and centralization-resistant . . . it does not confer on its members the kind of freedom *we* require and expect from Civil Society' (1994: 8), where the 'we' refers to members of liberal democracies.

Here lies the rub for liberals like Hall and Gellner: liberals can often only offer negative definitions of civil society (as with liberty), and not substantive ones. Hall and Trentmann say, for example, that 'civil society must be at once an agreement, a consensus, and a recognition of difference' (2005: 21). Perhaps this position is tenable normatively, but social science also needs a structural account of the social and political forces that are at play in this plural arena. For such a full-bodied concept of civil society, it can therefore be proposed that this consists at a minimum of: first, non-state economic (market) forces, plus how the economic interests arising from it are embodied in middle and other classes; and that these, secondly, provide a counterweight to the state. In this way, a vibrant civil society therefore allows some flexible responses in how elites, themselves composed of plural interests, respond to other social forces in maintaining a balance between state and civil society that maximizes the scope for individual and organized interests.

This is a tangled definition, and it leaves to one side the issue of what other forces may be included in civil society in addition to this minimum (such as social movements, a public sphere of media, and other politically relevant associations) as they do not bear on the argument here. On the plus side, however, this conception of civil society aligns perfectly with the argument about middle classes above (adding markets as a counterweight to the state), and it is a structural account, therefore also making the liberal account in both Hall's and Gellner's versions comparable to the radical account above.

Before we proceed with this comparison, one point remains: such a counterweight has been achieved among Anglo, corporatist and social democratic states, and one issue for the liberals is to gauge how successful these variations are in coping with social change – and especially with changes in the capitalist economy. A further question that is thus left open is the nature of the economy itself: Hall and Gellner are clear that any complex economy requires a state-managed infrastructure to function properly (Hall 2010: 266). However, the economy also needs to be autonomous from the state, especially as it is part of the minimal definition that civil society should counterbalance the state (Hall 2010: 155, 358; Hall 2013). Perhaps this is not clear-cut, as in the notion of a 'mixed economy' (Hall 2010: 363), and we can leave this issue unresolved for now – except to note the possible overlap with Mann's notion of 'infrastructural power' discussed earlier.

Finally, my criticism of liberalism can be briefly anticipated: if the concept of 'capitalism' were avoided by liberals (Gellner says the concept is overrated), and we also leave aside the contingent responsiveness of elites and other classes to their environment, then little would be left except for markets counterbalancing the state: little, except that liberals do not regard the hardened separation between the economic and political realms as a structural problem under conditions of relatively diminished and constrained economic growth – as I do. A second criticism is that the liberal argument also implicitly rests on the possibility that growth will be able to buy off the discontent of middle and other classes (Perhaps. But this functionalist idea should not, in my view, override that states can engender greater and lesser degrees of inequality and rights.)

Comparing the radical and liberal accounts

The liberal view, as we have seen, emphasizes the contribution of bourgeois or middle classes in generating a sufficiently large group of property owners to balance the state's power. This view conceives of civil society as the sphere of contracts and self-organized civil associations that counter but also influence the state. The growth of a bourgeois middle class can be regarded as an 'organic growth' (from below) within liberal democracies, in contrast with the mass mobilizations of right and left authoritarianisms or with mass mobilizations in times of war. Thus the liberal view interprets the process of gaining rights as a product of democratic revolutions, or of 'party' mobilizations – party in Weber's sense of political groupings outside of the state that seize state power – whereby parties gain the power to have their interests represented in a pluralist state. This contrasts with mobilizations 'from above'; that is, from revolutionary or state elites, typically mobilizations which occur later when the state is stronger, and which lead to various types of illiberal states. Finally, this view sees history in terms of the victory march of the bourgeoisie stalled by fascism and communism, a victory march that resumes after the fall of both. Note that this view does not exclude the idea of working class struggles from below, but the emphasis is different: the working class obtains property ownership and welfare rights in a compromise with capital, in contrast to the radical (or Gramscian) interpretation of civil society whereby the struggle of labour vis-à-vis capital continues.

Thus the liberal and radical interpretations can both be seen a struggles for rights: in the liberal view, if we regard civil society as consisting of political groupings, or if 'the market' and contractual property relations are included in civil society, then the representation of the interests of citizens 'in' the state can be seen as a kind of feedback mechanism between the state and its direction-giving (civil) society. In the radical view, on the other hand, the state (in relation to all paths or varieties) is the locus of an ongoing struggle. This radical idea can be taken one step further, because this struggle could also be a reformist struggle to extend and deepen social citizenship. In Nordic social democratic or Euro corporatist states, workers are 'inside' the state and pursuing this struggle 'reformistically', whereas in other states such as America there is a more direct or conflictual confrontation between capital and labour.

Mann could agree with the liberal account that the tension between state and market (or the flexible autonomy between the two) exists in liberal (Anglo) regimes, but not elsewhere. In Anglo societies, as we have seen, workers did not have to take on the state since citizen rights had been achieved early on and conflict was confined to the economic realm of the workplace, a reformist path. Mann and Hall agree on this point, but the consequences are different: for Mann, this resulted in a state of incoherent plural interests facing an all-too-powerful market; this contrasts with Hall's liberal view which sees here a plurality of interests that need to adapt flexibly to a dynamic market. The alternative paths involved the state and its elites 'taking on' workers, repressing them and inflaming struggles for rights. To this was added, in some cases, the upheavals of war. The result of these struggles, in any event, were rights for workers and other groups in terms of a share of state power, gains that have since become embedded in the state via parties representing their interests.

The liberal sociologist, in turn, might say that all three types of regimes, with different levels of social citizenship in place after the 'parabola', simply have different power balances and can be gauged by the extent to which they provide the greatest level of market-based prosperity and the most dynamically diverse forms of political participation. At this point the debate might need to go beyond the bounds of the nation-state because it would include external factors (war and openness to markets) that influence this market-based prosperity. Still, both accounts can recognize that capitalism is now globally practically unchallenged as an economic system. Both accounts also agree that there is no single dominant political system, even in the West or North, which entails that the scope and limits for manoeuvre in this system continue to be open – even if there would be disagreements about the constraints. A key point that is left open in the two accounts is one of the continuing tension between states and markets: in the end, the two positions perhaps differ most on how to interpret the link between economic growth and the scope of the state's role in markets (this might be expected, given the labels – but it is important to pinpoint the difference sociologically).

In Mann's view, labour is more nationally caged and economic ruling classes much less so. This is a major cause of regional differences in inequality and therefore of the asymmetries of power in contemporary societies. Mann's view is thus close, for example, to that of Walby (2009), who regards the continued deepening of economic equalities and of democratic forces pushing for social rights as an ongoing project of modernization. Hall's and Gellner's view, on the other hand, concentrates more on the continuing benefits and challenges of open economies and how elites cope with these challenges and simultaneously expand the room for a (hopefully thriving) plurality of interests. Their ideas have a greater affinity with non-systemic or non-structural ideas in social science disciplines apart from sociology, such as political science, economics and international relations.

The difference between the two positions can be linked to the critical – though as yet unresolved – debate (see Walby 2009: 326–30) about whether capitalism increases or decreases economic inequality on a global level. If there is global convergence towards equality, this would lend support to the idea that a global middle class – represented in this case perhaps most of all by China – is growing and that markets therefore ultimately have a trickle-down effect. If, on the other hand, inequality is growing globally, the implication is that there is a persistent gap between global 'classes' and that markets favour some at the expense of others. Unfortunately, this debate does not admit of a straightforward resolution since a closing and increasing inequality gap varies by regions of the world (Mann and Riley 2007).[10] Further, as we shall see in Chapter 8, there are open-ended questions about how inequality in China – and in India – relates to the recent decades of market liberalization in both countries.

In any event, there are two main sociological interpretations of democracy along these lines: the liberal interpretation proposes that there are many interests that are constantly adjusting to each other, whereas the radical interpretation is that there are a small number of contending forces which tend to be skewed towards the most powerful ones. Note that both are pluralist (unlike the ideas of Weber and Marx and their followers), but in the one case, there is room for continual open-ended contestation, whereas the other emphasizes the structural imbalances in this contestation. This returns us to where we started, with the bourgeoisie as the carrier of liberal individualism and the working class as the carrier of socialist egalitarianism – but we are now in a position to see how the different trajectories of these class-citizen movements have resulted in the variety of pluralist democracies, with the fragmented American pluralist democracy at one extreme and the corporatist or social democracies at the other. Both the liberal and the radical account thus provide a sociological understanding of the plural forces that shape a more and less penetrable democratic state – even if they differ in how they do so.

One shortcoming of both accounts is that even if class-citizen-based trajectories have shaped the balance of interests and forces within the state in the past, it has been argued that they no longer do so in any discernible or systematic way (Crouch 2004).

To be sure, there are still groups that are excluded systematically from power, something which the liberal and radical positions could agree should not be tolerated. Hall and Lindholm (1999: 129–44) point, for example, to the illiberal exclusion of African Americans in the United States; and Mann (2012) argues that this exclusion, rather than the absence of socialism or of a labor party, is the main reason for American 'exceptionalism'. The radical interpretation adds that there are inevitably various power imbalances. Finally, in relation to the absence of any discernible pattern of class-citizen dynamics today, we can see that democracy – pluralism in the cases of both open-ended liberal contestation and of radical structural imbalances – seems to be more subject to electoral drift and a technocratic concern with economic growth rather than political ideology. If this is the case, perhaps it is important to focus on the forces that have emerged following the 'end of the parabola'.

The implications of this comparison are as follows: the liberal account, however conflictually the emergence of pluralism is charted, is open-ended in seeing politics as subject to ongoing perfectibility. Even if there are distortions in the balance between plural powers or systematic exclusions from the powers of the state, these can, with growing skill, be overcome. The radical account, on the other hand, points to the conflicts or contradictions within contemporary democracies: the predominance of powerful economic elites, systematic exclusions of disadvantaged groups, and imbalances that are bound to lead to further conflicts.

At this point we can move on to where my argument departs from the liberal and radical accounts: first, I have suggested that the various conceptions of civil society – as a counterweight to the state which includes or does not include market relations, or as the sum of classes-citizens and social movements that struggle to obtain a share of the state's power – cannot provide a complete picture. In my view (elaborated in the next chapter), it is necessary to recognize that markets have their own, disembedded logic which, especially after the Golden Age, imposes its own constraints, particularly on the extension of social citizenship, but also on curtailing the open interplay of plural interests inasmuch as economic interests force their own priorities upon democracies. Second, an additional interpretation of state power that places limits on pluralism (though this has not been developed so far, but see Dandeker [1990], and we will return to it in Chapter 9) is that the state has its own, non-pluralist, logic inasmuch as technocratic elites have become more powerful over time within an expanded bureaucratic apparatus. These 'experts' control a machine-like state that is able to contain or outweigh contending plural forces, and their technocratic power also militates against the idea of increasing democratization by means of tighter or denser relations between, or a greater interpenetration of, state and civil society. And finally, although the liberal and radical accounts provide important insights and capture different aspects of the formation of modern states and democracies, the ideologies (of freedom and equality) with which they are associated no longer have as much purchase within contemporary democracies as they once did. This is because the social bases which 'carried' them have eroded and other forces, including the two just mentioned, but also a long suppressed divide between cosmopolitan elites and locals, increasingly undercuts them (see Collins 1975: 64–5).[11]

A sociological account of modern democratic states, as we have seen, focuses on how forces 'from below' have shaped different kinds of states. Whether the varieties of contemporary democracies (not, as should have become clear, political economies or varieties of capitalism) are regarded from a liberal or radical perspective, in both cases it is possible to identify tensions which continue to affect this variety. To go further, it will be necessary to take extra-political factors – levels of economic growth – into account in shaping this variety. Moreover, it will be necessary to add the increasing primacy of economic power or of relatively diminishing growth, or the hardened separation between the political and economic orders, beyond the end of the 'parabola', as well as environmental limits to economic growth – all of which increasingly constrain political options.

Still, it can now be seen how state spending and the state's role in economic development relate to the shaping of the state 'from below': as for state spending, we have seen that this has plateaued at a high level, but with differing consequences. How the state is balanced by other forces in the liberal account, and how a certain level of social citizenship has been reached in the radical account – both accounts are more realistic than a-sociological theories which regard the state as a matter of 'choice', but are also more realistic than theories which regard the state as primarily a tool of oppression. As for the state and economic development, similarly, this is a matter of when and how much, rather than of whether at all or that it is an indispensable tool at all times (though this constraint has taken on a new shape in the Age of Limits, as will be seen). There is thus also a shortcoming that the liberal and radical accounts share: since state spending and the role of states in economic development have reached a more or less steady state, does this mean that the balancing function of the liberal account and the function of extending social citizenship on the radical account should now be replaced with a different function – such as the state's coming to terms with its limits?[12]

Put differently, where the radical account focuses on how persisting inequalities shape the state and vice versa, and the liberal account focuses on how the state and its elites learn to adapt in and to a larger environment, a third account – elaborated below – focuses on the persisting divide between an autonomous economic system and a constrained state, with both 'cages' confronting each other and social change being driven by the tension, but also a lack of tension, between the two.

There are two sets of implications:

1) Among developed societies, there are a variety of options in the relations between state and economy – but one sees flexible adjustment to external open markets and elites maintaining this openness as key, while the other sees continuing political conflict by partly caged (largely working) classes within states and a deepening democracy as key. The liberal account stresses the agency of elites and a possible evolution towards improvement, whereas in the radical account the future of the state and social rights is decided (except for the American empire, where external factors play a role) by the structural confrontation between capital and labour;

2) For late developers, different options of imitative development or departures from these models of development follow from these two ways of understanding the state and pluralist democracy.

These options will be revisited in Chapter 8, which focuses on China and India, and Chapter 9, which will assess the centrality and limits of the political order.

4
Free and Unfree Markets

The easiest way to highlight the argument about economic change that will be made in this chapter is to point out what the argument is *against*: the dominant orthodoxy in economic sociology is that the economy, and markets in particular, are always embedded in social contexts, or in culture and politics. The argument here is that the *modern* economic order is in fact characterized by disembeddedness and untrammelled markets. This deepening of disembeddedness can be traced back to the 19th century and to the processes whereby market relations were lifted out, on a large scale, of particular geographic and social contexts, and increasingly came to consist of individual 'atomic' transactions. These transactions could henceforth be seen as part of a single interconnected market including, at its apex, financial markets. This disembedded market operates internally in a relatively unconstrained way, even if a number of structures can be identified which impose constraints on disembeddedness.

The orthodoxy that the economy is 'embedded' in political, cultural and other institutions applies throughout the social sciences – except in the discipline of economics, where rational actors pursue the maximization of welfare and happiness in free untrammelled markets. At first sight, it may appear that economics and economic sociology are interested in different phenomena: economics is concerned with the vast numbers of transactions or interactions – and the fine-grained mutual adjustments that add up to equilibria – within markets, which are the dominant institution in the economic order; economic sociologists are more interested in the role of the state and of macro-actors such as classes (or capitalists and labour). In economics, the vast sea of non-embedded self-interested individual transactions connect the micro and macro realms, whereas in economic sociology macro-institutions (again, the state, or culture) and micro-contexts of exchange are rarely connected. And, finally, economics approaches phenomena in terms of quantification and modelling relations mathematically (hence, too, there is a seamless web from micro to macro), whereas sociology deals with 'lumpy' structures, unless it is argued that these are de-composable into rational choices or the cultural role of 'agency'.

This chapter begins by expanding on comments made in the introduction (Chapter 1), where it was argued that despite such fundamental disagreements about starting points and approaches, there is in fact considerable agreement among economic historians and others that a shift to market economies took place in the 19th century. This story can be extended into the 20th century: Polanyi, among others, argued that in the post-war period, the capitalist economy became re-embedded after a period of dysfunctional disembedding. I argue against Polanyi that disembedding has in fact been much more linear, even if the world wars represented setbacks, and that further disembedding has taken place with growing mass production and mass consumption. The mechanisms of these markets, I argue, are close to how economists conceive of them, though without any of the baggage of the assumptions that economists make about the efficiency of free markets or about free individual actors. This also includes financial markets, which are often regarded as the most disembedded of all markets. Financial markets, however, also provide a good example of how disembeddedness is both enabling and constraining (as are non-financial markets, again, a point where I depart from economics). Finally, a distinction can be made between where free or disembedded markets operate and where they don't. It is a shortcoming of contemporary economics that this limitation has never been – indeed cannot be, given the premises of economics – spelled out systematically. The lack of a boundary around disembedded markets in economics, and conversely the lack of a recognition of disembedded markets in sociology, constitute an impasse for both disciplines in contemporary social science. This impasse can only be partly resolved in this chapter, but its implications for the overall argument will also be pursued in the chapters to come.

The emergence of disembedding

There is widespread agreement that a fundamental transformation of the economy took place during the 'long' 19th century. But since, as noted in the introduction, this book wants to avoid making capitalism into the prime mover of this transformation, it can be recalled briefly why 'markets' are more important than 'capitalism'. Three terms have conventionally been used to explain the 19th-century transformation towards a modern economy: capitalism, industrialism and markets. The main dichotomy is between those who favour the term industrial society as against those who favour capitalism, the former implying open-ended growth on the basis of technological innovation, the latter (in the Marxist version of 'capitalism') entailing endless conflict between the owners of the means of production and those who are exploited by them. But the dichotomy between these two concepts has always been misleading: it is widely agreed that the industrial revolution (or two of them) caused qualitative changes towards higher rates of growth. One problem with the concept of industrial society, however, is that the dominance of the industrial sector did not last very long since it was eclipsed in the 20th century by a services or information sector. Similarly, the problem with 'capitalism' is that classes, which, even if they crystallized during the 19th century, have not been a uniform motor throughout history and have never again regained the organizational capacity that they achieved during their heyday and into the first half of the 20th century (as discussed in the previous chapter) – although it can be acknowledged that stratification exists at all times.

But whereas markets and capitalism pre-dated modernity in *non-modern* economic forms, the industrial revolution(s) obviously did not. For markets and capitalism, it is therefore necessary to spell out how they *became* modern.[1] Fortunately, again, this is a point on which there is much agreement: markets in the sense of *mass* markets which encompassed all or most of production and consumption only came about in the course of the industrial revolution (Swedberg 2003: 146–9). Moreover, it is only since the late 19th century in advanced economies that the vast bulk of goods became produced as commodities and exchanged in markets (Swedberg 2005: 11; Turner 1995: 59). And according to O'Rourke and Williamson (1999: 41–55), both national and international markets become strongly integrated in the late 19th century and up to the First World War (before this integration was temporarily thrown off course by the wars): an important indicator of this integration was the convergence in prices of basic commodities. The idea of markets as a 'natural' mechanism for redistribution of wealth was new in the 19th century (Osterhammel 2009: 1182), but took hold ever more firmly.

What then, apart from markets, are the unique features of modern capitalism? Swedberg says that 'what is unique about capitalism, as compared to economic systems based on redistribution and reciprocity, is that it alone is primarily driven by the profit motive. The two most important social mechanisms of capitalism are consequently *exchange* and *the feedback of profit into production'* (2005: 7). But for the profit motive to be institutionalized in production, there were two prerequisites, property and money:

> For much of human history, property was not a way of defining the world . . . but once a certain threshold is reached in the proportion of objects that can be *possessed* by actors, property becomes a self-escalating force . . . eventually, as in the case of modern capitalist systems, property rights penetrate all relations and virtually all objects are defined in terms of property considerations. (Turner 1995: 40)

At this point, property can be used in exchange relations to pursue profit, via money – as long as money is separated from non-economic relations – a further feature of *modern* capitalism: 'It is only with the separation of the economic order from the rest of society in the modern era that money takes on its historically exceptional role in representing private property and private contracts,' says Ingham (2004: 90). Here again (as with the state), we can see an argument about a turning point towards a new type of economy, and a condition for a subsequent intensification in scale and scope.

With this, we have arrived at a *modern* economy in which economic relations have been separated and lifted out of (or became disembedded from) other, political and cultural, relations, and we can jettison the term 'modern' if we restrict the use of 'markets' to its incarnation in industrial and post-industrial societies. Thus we can also hold on to the view that science and technology played a necessary (if not sufficient) role in the industrial revolution (Schroeder 2007: 60–6), even if it is not necessary to see science, technology or industrialization as mysterious prime movers. Instead, the focus can be on what industrialization *does*: the growth rates produced by the industrial revolution(s) now allow economic exchange that goes beyond the constraints of local subsistence economies on a large – society-wide – scale.[2] After industrialization, economic exchange also took place on a mass basis beyond the constraints of the given natural world.

Part of this disembedding from nature is also a disembedding from locale: 'In modern societies most of the social structure does not vary with natural conditions, because all sorts of deficits for all sorts of activities can be filled by fast, efficient transportation systems'

(Stinchcombe 1983: 80). Finally, trade, too, played a related role in disembedding:

> It is worth remembering that the expansion of world trade and the process of commodification rests on an anthropocentric view of the world. As goods became commodities, humans increasingly came to believe that the world existed to satisfy human needs and wants. All efforts were bent toward turning nature into 'natural resources' or 'factors of production' and making these useful or profitable for people. (Pomeranz and Topik 1999: 183)

Put differently, the transformation of the natural and social environment – their commodification – for growth beyond subsistence became taken for granted.

In terms of institutions, how did the separation of the economy from other – political and cultural – institutions (or orders, as I have called them, following Weber) come about? Weber, too, argued that the decisive feature of modern capitalism is accumulation for profit rather than for meeting needs, and this is also the defining feature of the capitalist firm (Swedberg 2003: 56–7, 90) or the corporation, which has become an autonomous (legal) entity (Perrow 2002) interacting in a market of other such entities. Exchange relations generally, at the level of interactions of firms and other actors, at this point became divorced from traditional economic needs and insulated within capitalist markets as a goal in themselves:

> With the moderns, a revolution occurred in this respect: the link between immoveable wealth and power over men was broken, and moveable wealth became fully autonomous in itself, as the superior aspect of wealth in general, while immoveable wealth became an inferior, less perfect, aspect; in short, there emerged an autonomous and relatively unified category of wealth. It should be noted that it is only at this point that a clear distinction can be drawn between what we call the 'political' and what we call 'the economic'. This is a distinction that traditional societies do not admit. (Dumont 1977: 6)

From this comparative-historical or anthropological perspective, the economic order has become divorced from the political and cultural order. And if we want a sociological approach that focuses on economic *power* rather than institutions – in this case the power to overcome nature in order to satisfy human needs (for example, Mann

1986: 24) – it is possible to shift the emphasis to a form of economic power which moves beyond locales constrained by nature and via a disembedding mechanism (money) towards economic production oriented to profit-making.

What defines this order, in terms of individual activity and the aims of economic activity as a whole? Here we must reach for a further characteristic of disembeddedness, its open-endedness. As Gellner explains:

> The fact that, in the very nature of things, there *cannot* be a single well-defined overall aim for production, that there is no inherently neutral entity that constitutes 'wealth', means that, in the long run, instrumental rationality cannot govern us in this sphere. Men seek life styles, roles, positions. These are many-stranded and culturally defined. They involve the use of material objects as tokens, but they are not made up of such objects. Power helps men to attain them, but power assumes a complex variety of forms. (1988: 265)

In other words, economic power, including wealth in whatever form this takes or can be translated into, has become an end in itself (or a means towards open-ended consumption, as we shall see in a moment). Yet in the meantime, production (the other side of the economic order, apart from consumption), even if it no longer simply has the aim of meeting needs, must now proceed in an instrumental and single-stranded way to enhance wealth and consumption, or as a separate means to political or cultural power (even if it may not be *directly* translatable into these).

Thus disembedded markets have become the dominant institution within *modern* markets (or of capitalism, if the term is preferred *and* restricted to the economic realm). But this also means that the very conception of markets has shifted from being concretely concerned with production for meeting needs towards being abstractly concerned with prices, a shift which also entails that the whole of the economy can be conceived of in terms of markets (Swedberg 2003: 104–30). To be sure, this commoditization which translates goods and services into prices – the most concrete sense of disembedding – took many forms during a very long-term transition. For our purposes, it will suffice to summarize how economic practices were transformed into relations of monetary exchange in the main institutions of *mass* market relations.

If we break markets down into four types – for production, labour, consumption and financial markets – then for three of these, the rise of mass markets is well-established: The 'American system' of mass production (Hounshell 1984), the extension of contractual labour

(Osterhammel 2009: 996) and the extension of consumption to mass publics (Stearns 2001: esp. 44–52). An additional element is scale, which developed alongside the means of mass distribution (Beniger 1986) which tie together production and consumption via innovations in bureaucratic organizations, and also include the innovations in office technology that provide informational and communicational transmission mechanisms (Yates 1989). Labour similarly turned into 'mass' labour markets as these became increasingly national (or supranational). (We will come to the fourth, financial markets, shortly). All of these transformations took hold initially sometime in the late 19th or early 20th century, and even if this is a matter of degree, the shift to mass markets is ultimately also a shift in kind. Thus, with modern market relations, the relationship between economy and society changed: now, the economy transcended localism and nature, it has become separated from the other orders, subject to its own 'open-ended' logic, and consists of a 'mass' market at the same time.[3]

At this point we can come back to disembedding, which Giddens (1990: 21) defines as 'the "lifting out" of social relations from local contexts of interaction and their restructuring across indefinite spans of time-space'. Yet this is only *part* of the disembedding of modern economic relations, whereby social (here, economic) relations become national or supranational geographically and subject to an open-ended time horizon. But economic relations are also separate from political (or military) and ideological/cultural power and separate from the context of everyday subsistence needs, as well as from other social relations (for example, households) in which they were traditionally entangled. Hence they are also atomized and calculable in a 'lifted out' context – a market – of money and prices, and at the same time not subordinate to other orders or authorities which dictate the aims of these (wealth- and profit-seeking) economic markets.

Note that the argument runs counter to the often-cited essay by Granovetter (1985) which (along with Polanyi) created the 'embedding' agenda in economic sociology, but it does not go against its spirit: Granovetter, too, wanted to identify macro-structures, and to do so in a manner that regards Weber's notion of economic action as a special type of action (1985: 507). What Granovetter overlooks, however, is that Weber would have agreed with what I have argued here, that economic action above all 'atomizes' modern social actors: Weber thought that modern capitalism is subject to an inescapable process of rationalization and leads to the increasing dominance of instrumental rationality, which is at once corrosive of existing embedded social relations and at the same time cages actors in new, more impersonal ones. Granovetter has subsequently admitted that economic sociology has been misled by his concept of 'embeddness' inasmuch as he did not intend this to be a concept that applies universally; it is aimed at the meso-level and does not address macro-changes or link to micro-level processes (Krippner, Granovetter, Block et al. 2004: 114–15). Moreover, he thinks that the concept has become 'stretched to mean almost anything, so that it therefore means nothing', and that he 'rarely use[s] "embeddedness" any more' (2004: 113).

This brings us to the second main use of 'embeddedness', which follows Polanyi's well-known argument (see Block and Somers 1984) that disembeddedness applies to a period of capitalist upheaval which resulted in the chaos of two world wars in the 20th century, after which markets became re-embedded in the welfare states of the post-war period. True, the period of the world wars saw diminished global trade. Yet markets still operated, often even across enemy lines, and disembeddedness was not irreversibly set back by the political retrench-ment into the political authoritarianisms of the right or left. And even if, as Polanyi argued, the consolidation of welfare states in the post-war period has contributed to varieties of welfare states (discussed in Chapters 2 and 3), the post-war period has also seen a further disem-bedding of markets. If Granovetter's ideas are (by his own account) best deployed on the meso-level, Polanyi's apply mainly at the macro-level. But the former has only (and can only, unless a more general argument is made) led to individual case studies of meso-level embedding of one or other economic institution (this shortcoming has been recognized [Krippner, Granovetter, Block et al. 2004]). And Polanyi's macro-level ideas could only be validated by an (again, general) demonstration that an embedding has taken place across many countries and on a long-term basis. Yet this picture does not fit the 'liberalization' of economies in the post-1970s era. Moreover, the embedding agenda has not been able to link the various levels (macro- and micro-). At the same time, as we shall see, disembedding is widespread, takes place on several levels, and these levels can be linked.

Markets and their mechanism

Modern capitalist firms are oriented towards profit and growth, and disembedded markets are the institution that dominates the economic order, once mass markets and permanent growth have been enabled by industrialization. The onus has thus been placed on the distinctive workings of the central institution *within* the economic order – *modern* markets – rather than apostatizing one of the other labels for the whole of the social order (capitalist or industrialist society). But *how* do these markets work? One way to address this question is to say how they don't work: 'free markets', the preferred term of economists, have not in certain respects converged in the manner that neo-classical economic theory says they should, since there continue to be uneven distributions of growth around the globe without signs of a general decline in this unevenness (this has already been discussed, and we will return to it shortly). Nevertheless, there is an obvious affinity between 'free' and 'disembedded', and this can now be pursued further.

Swedberg (1994: 256–7), as noted earlier, argues that the four main types of markets, 'the financial market, the mass consumer market, the labor market and the industrial market', came into being in the 19th century in the US and parts of Europe and have since spread across the world – and 'free' can thus be taken to mean expanding without running up against barriers. What are the mechanisms of these markets? 'Labor markets have become the standard organization of employment for wages under industrial capitalism,' say Tilly and Tilly (1994: 287). They also argue that 'capitalism stands out from other economic systems for its stress not only on compensation relative to commitment and coercion but also on *fungible* forms of compensation: money and similar rewards that easily convert into other goods' (1998: 87). Industrial markets might better be termed 'production markets' (as White, to be discussed below, conceives of them), but a distinction could be made between how they work and who controls production. Yet 'the ownership of the means of production' only makes sense in tandem with a *political* analysis of class, and is otherwise problematic because the distinction between ownership and control has been blurred in 20th-century managerial capitalism. Mass consumption markets have already been discussed, and their mechanisms are well-known. All that needs to be added here is that they spread to Europe and beyond in the 20th century (de Grazia 2005; Stearns 2001). And finally, again, financial markets need to be treated separately (in a moment).

The key consequence of disembedding, however, is that *all* markets, both the four types of markets and the geographies and different sectors of markets, are interconnected. This, as Hamilton and Feenstra explain, is the central insight of Walrasian economics, whereby 'markets must continually adjust price and wage structures according to what is happening in other markets. A change in the price of commodities will change the price of final goods. A change in the wage of labor will change the demand for goods, which will also change their price', and so on (1998: 161). Walras also developed the theory of equilibria, giving economists a tool to understand the workings of these interconnected markets: 'Equilibria are generated from a price system that is internal to the model of economic activity . . . the organization of economies represents an emergent process that is generated reflexively from the interaction of knowing participants' (Hamilton and Feenstra 1998: 175). Here then lies the nexus of micro- and macro-economics, which is that the actions of many economic actors add up to a single whole which operates on the macro-level. This is also where the difference between what is of concern to sociologists and economists lies: sociologists would like to know what type of aggregate effects the 'interaction of knowing participants' has resulted in on a large scale, and they focus on the enduring structures which give shape to this micro-aggregation, whereas economists both at the micro and macro levels aim at calculating how the sum of these interactions affects wages and prices under the condition of – or on the assumption of – equilibrium.

Yet, as Hamilton and Feenstra argue, and I agree, this is also where sociology and economics could overlap: the sociology of an order of disembedded economic relations might recognize that the multitude of micro-economic interactions simply add up to a mass of market interactions which are somehow adjusted in an 'equilibrium' and nothing more. Sociologists do not need to take the further step to follow economists and presuppose that this interconnectedness results in one or more *stable* equilibria of wages and prices – instead, they could recognize that disembedded economic actions simply constitute a larger sea of mutually and constantly adjusting exchanges – and thus result in one or more equilibria in everyday life and institutions rather than in the technical sense of the word. This is why there is much convergence or interconnectedness that stretches across the micro, meso (organizations) and macro-levels:

> While enterprises attempt to increase their power in relation to each other, organizations that attempt to regulate the economy in some respect attempt, on a formal basis, to spread their system logically and consistently throughout their prescribed domains. The reflexive actions of both sets of economic actors increasingly channel and standardize the actions of all economically active participants. (Hamilton and Feenstra 1998: 173)

And while Hamilton and Feenstra also recognize that there are structures apart from these equilibria, the point is that one or more equilibria – or, put in non-economic terms, large-scale aggregations of market interactions which somehow adjust to each other and stabilize themselves – are a key mechanism of markets.

Again, whether the market tends towards a single or multiple equilibria, and how this relates to the contiguousness of different markets (sectorally or geographically), or if there are hierarchies within markets, are secondary questions. And these questions are dealt with in particular ways by economists: for example, they will use the idea of one or more equilibria as a means to quantify, model and predict economic change, based on 'universal' ideas about how economic actors behave, and invoke institutions to segment or layer them. What is important from the sociological perspective is that the idea of one or more equilibria is obviously correct if we take it to mean that at some level, the aggregate of disembedded market exchanges adjusts to the overall level of what is possible in the struggle to extract our needs and requirements for consumption from nature, based on a certain level or levels of the extent to which such power over nature has been achieved: in short, that there is a relation between supply and demand.[4]

The economic approach to thinking about markets – aggregating actors quantitatively and on a large scale – thus allows us to see why the structure of the economy has been such a problem for sociology: the question of how many routine everyday micro-interactions can translate into macro-changes is not unique to the economic order, and applies to political and cultural sociology as well. But there is a difference: many routine micro-interactions in the political and cultural order do not need to be aggregated – as do economic exchanges in terms of potentially contributing to an overall level of economic activity – and there are widely accepted concepts for macro-level political and cultural change which make do without them (we can think of states and revolutions, or religion and secularization).[5] Economists have solved this problem by turning the aggregation of the vast sea of micro-interactions into a calculable whole. Sociologists would rightly regard this sea as less interesting than the islands, the macro-structural changes that rise out of the water and determine the long-term horizons of economic change. But economists are correct that the vast sea of economic interactions also has an interconnected structure of its own; namely, again, in constituting a calculable whole (or a number of wholes) where all the interactions affect one another. Sociologists – and economists – might like to add, again, that this whole is not completely open-ended at any given stage since it faces the constraints of the existing level of economic production, a constraint which is constantly being overcome (we shall come back to this).

Thus sociologists don't have to make assumptions, as economists do, about the efficiency of markets or about particular versions of rational or self-interested actors. They could agree with rational-actor models simply in the sense that atomized individuals and 'aggregated atomized' actors, such as profit-seeking firms, aim at enhancing – economists would say maximizing – their economic advantage. They could also agree with economic approaches to markets inasmuch as there is a fluidity and open-ended nature to economic needs and wants, combined with the fact that different types of markets are fluidly connected to each other. A different way to say all this is that power is diffuse in markets, and even if markets do not automatically tend towards an equilibrium that can be captured in equations, markets are infinitely adjustable and in this sense tend towards stability – unlike other social structures which are subject to breakdown or upheaval (the Great Depression and other milder economic crises could be seen as counterexamples, but how states intervened in this and other economic crises was also severely constrained by financial markets, and thus these crises do not disconfirm disembeddedness. This will be discussed further below).

Again, it is worth spelling out what the argument does not say: there is no implication that there are no monopolies within markets; Schumpeter and others have argued that a key feature of capitalist markets is the temporary monopolization of opportunities. And there is no implication that markets work according to an optimal balance between supply and demand (although there must be some relationship between them – since otherwise the interconnectedness of markets would break down). And it is misleading to focus solely on markets – markets are only the nexus of exchange which connects the more important reality (for social actors) of production (or work) and consumption. Still, the view put forward here shares with economic theory the idea that market relations consist of impersonal change; that is, other social relations are bracketed out and the exchange can be seen as based on the interest of atomized units and as being (formally, though not necessarily substantively, to use Weber's distinction) voluntary (Swedberg 2003: 132–3).

The argument also emphasizes the importance of micro-interactions, though not necessarily in the way economists do. As Mann puts it,

> economic power is the most deeply entrenched in everyday life. Its routines involve half of our waking lives and energies; it yields

subsistence without which we would not survive. It combines diffuse markets with authoritative production units. Its rhythms are characteristically slow. The metaphor of economic 'revolutions' misleads . . . Britain's industrial revolution took over a century . . . Depression and inflation can impact more suddenly, but they do not, unaided, generate major social change. (2006: 386)

This way of characterizing economic action alerts us to structures outside the disembedded market to which we must turn (in a moment) in order to identify change and persistence: long-term inequalities in wealth and income, sectoral changes in production, shifts in the economic power of nations and regions, and financial markets, which are more volatile than other markets. But disembedded markets mainly drift, rather than changing suddenly *or* congealing into permanent structures. Put differently, there is no centre of power in the economic order, nor is there a 'cockpit' of capitalism, unlike in the other orders of society (the leaders of parties or states, for example). While some economists and political thinkers would celebrate this decentralizedness and freedom from concentrations of power, in fact it can equally be regarded as a major constraint and source of social dysfunction. In any event, the main mechanism of markets is interconnected exchange.

This focus on disembedded markets must finally be contrasted with the notion that markets are 'free' in another sense: If 'free' entails extensive and *formally* free markets on a large scale – in wage labour, goods and services, property and capital – then 'free' overlaps with disembedded. This does not exclude, for example, many forms of exchange whereby labour is coerced or firms operate in monopolistic ways as long as 'formal' contractual relations (or 'formally rational' relations, again – as Weber called them) are maintained. In short, free markets have no necessary connection with free*dom* (since such formally free relations exist in politically and culturally 'unfree' societies). And there are many structures which curb and shape formally free markets. But before we turn to these, we need to examine one market which has so far been left out.

Financial markets

We have so far put aside financial markets – with good reason: they are distinct from the other markets, even if they nevertheless tie all the other markets together. At the same time, financial markets, as mentioned, seemingly go against the idea that markets that are disembedded are separate from politics and culture: even if they are disembedded from local relations and contexts, isn't this where capitalism is ultimately tied to the state and embedded in politics? As we shall see in a moment, the answer is: only partly. Before we turn to this question, let's tackle the questions of their distinctness and how they tie other markets together.

We have already seen that money is one of the disembedding mechanisms of markets. But when did money itself become part of a system of disembedded markets? Not fully during the 19th century, since, as Heilbron (2005; see also Osterhammel 2009: 1291) has pointed out, among private investors, government bonds, at least in Britain, constituted the largest portion of the stock market in terms of value. Heilbron nevertheless also charts how, in the late 20th century, despite continuing differences between the types of financial regimes, stock markets have become penetrated by global investors everywhere.

In any event, financial markets are not just about stock markets, but also about the range of mechanisms for dealing in credit and debt, whether of firms or governments or financial institutions themselves. As Ingham says, 'the capitalist monetary system's distinctiveness is that it contains a *social mechanism* by which privately contracted debtor-creditor relations – for example, bank loans, credit card contracts – are routinely monetized' (2004: 134). So 'the question of the production of money may be considered in terms of demand and supply for credit' (ibid.: 136). Hence there is a point at which money becomes part of financial markets with their own logic. Ingham further argues that the money supply and demand has to go outside of orthodox framework of 'money's fundamental value, which, it is held, resides in the long-run equilibrium between quantities of money and goods' (ibid.: 82). Ingham's argument is that there is a sociology of power which is superimposed on this orthodoxy of an equilibrium – or, to put it differently, money (the demand and supply for credit) is embedded in power.

On the crucial nexus between financial markets and political power, however, Ingham's account goes against the argument made here, so his analysis is worth following in detail in order to challenge it: Ingham says: 'The money market is the "headquarters" of capitalism' (ibid.: 202). Who is in charge in these headquarters? Ingham argues that there is the conflict between the state, its ruling elites and the rest of society for control over money (or credit). A struggle thus takes place between the state and the market to produce capitalist credit and there is a balance of power between them (ibid.: 144). In the end, however, Ingham is inconsistent: he says that even if the state, via central banks, has some control over money, this control is also limited (ibid.: 137), particularly since, 'by its very nature, the creation of the money in the capitalist system is indeterminate' (ibid.: 142). In other words, to some extent at least, no one is in charge or in control in the 'headquarters', and there is an open-endedness (or, in my argument, disembeddedness) to the creation and circulation of money.

Ingham's argument that links money to embedded power becomes even more inconsistent when it comes to changes in recent decades. These changes, he says, concern how money is conceived (he says 'socially constructed'): there is a 'discoverable, *naturally* optimally efficient state in the "real economy" . . . in this, there can be no "real" basis for opposed interest . . . the struggle for economic existence can only be the struggle for rationality' (ibid.: 149). So on the one hand, he wants to introduce power relations into this struggle, but on the other says there can be no 'real' basis for this struggle and shifts can take place at the cultural level (the 'struggle for rationality') which are exempt from power and which entail that the very attempt to define the nature of money – and thus the financial system – is subject to open-ended interpretation (or, again, a degree of disembeddedness).

But there is also a simple reason why financial markets are – ultimately – not socially constructed, and that is that neither governments nor financial institutions can create more money or credit than what workers and firms earn and can translate into the purchasing power for the goods and services they buy. Financial instruments that pyramid on themselves can emerge and escalate (as we shall see in a moment), but they are – again, ultimately – tethered to the purchase they have on the world of goods and services.

Along the same lines, Ingham suggests that 'modern independent central banks continue to attempt ideologically to *universalize* social and political relations' (ibid.: 149). To be sure, insofar as central banks try to define a system of credit and debt, this is also an attempt to shape society, and this attempt is obviously disembedded insofar as it tries 'to *universalize* social and political relations'. However, independent central banks only partly represent political interests (otherwise, they would not be independent), and partly represent the economic interests of those who want to shape the financial order. Are these elite interests, as Ingham argues, embedded? If so, one would expect the 'headquarters' to shape the financial order in accordance with the interests of a geopolitically or geoeconomically dominant elite, in this case perhaps the combination of Wall Street and Washington. Yet in fact, as Abdelal (2007) has shown, it was a technocratic elite, with a European political but also a 'universalizing' economic agenda, which has in recent decades done most to reshape the financial order in the direction of a more open one. Further, the project of this elite is, as ever, incomplete and always outside the full grasp of any set of interests. Incomplete, however, does not mean that there is a systematic opposition to disembedding financial markets: the response to the financial crisis of 2008 (the largest since the Wall Street Crash of 1929 which led to the Great Depression) has not put in place mechanisms to embed financial markets; it has only – feebly, many would argue – regulated them so that they can continue to run smoothly.[6]

A final point that Ingham does not address and which could be seen as operating outside of the equilibrium of orthodox economics is the workings of financial instruments that revolve around credit. By means of these instruments, as Collins has argued, financial markets have pyramided upon themselves by developing ever more complex markets. Collins calls these 'superordinate markets', new markets that serve to perpetuate capitalism: 'Capitalism is an omnimarket society . . . omnicapitalism stays dynamic by creating new markets for superordinate goods, including both financial instruments and consumer goods impregnated with social status' (1999: 206). The open-endedness of consumer markets has been dealt with earlier (and here Collins notes the interconnectedness of consumption and financial markets, whereby financial products are themselves objects of consumption), and financial instruments can thus also be seen as creating superordinate goods which make credit itself into an ever more manipulable commodity. These superordinate markets, separate from but also tied to 'subordinate markets', then need to be placed in the context of the extent to which a 'financialization' of economies has taken place, whereby profits are derived from the financial sector rather than through trade or commodity production. Krippner (2005) has argued that such financialization has taken place much more in the United States since the 1970s than elsewhere.

At this stage we can come back to the other point made at the outset in this section, Schumpeter's insight that it is (in Collins' words) 'the competition for capital (credit) that ties together all economic sectors' (1986: 125). We have seen that a disembedded market for credit and debt sits on top of but separate from other markets, tying them together but consisting of goods and instruments that are divorced from them (though they are also interconnected). Few would disagree with this separateness, even if they might disagree about the extent to which the rise and fall of economic and geopolitical power (in the sense of 'clout') and the control of financial markets are de-coupled from financial power. Thus, howsoever financial markets are politicized within nation-states, again, they partly transcend the nation-state.

If not an elite, what about the control of (superordinate) financial markets that is embedded in the everyday dealings by ordinary people? Shouldn't even financial markets ultimately be embedded in everyday economic life? Indeed, it has recently been argued that there is 'agency' on this level, since individuals have become part of and partly driven the rise of 'shareholder capitalism' (for 'agency', see Hobson and Seabrooke 2007; for 'shareholder capitalism', see Fligstein 2001). But such an argument returns us to the very reason for turning away from the aggregation of micro-interactions and towards macro-interactions and structures in the first place: namely, that these every-day interactions – within the economic order – do not add up to more macro-changes, except in an aggregate and impersonal sea of relations over which, as a structure, they have little control – even if they can engage in formally free transactions *within* this sea. Perhaps for a large part of society in certain, especially Anglo-American, capitalist societies, financial markets have become part of people's everyday lives, but people exercise little individual power or control in the 'casino capitalism' (Strange 1986) of financial markets that has spread across the globe. To be sure, one embedding constraint on financial or superordinate markets could be that individuals and institutions curb or scale down their investments in these markets. However, even after the financial crisis of 2008, it is difficult to foresee a systemic constraint on these pyramiding markets (and if a diminution has been seen, again it is in the manner of attempting greater stability, and not of curbing the activity of financial markets beyond this aim).

The economic order: embeddedness versus disembeddedness

Before drawing out the implications of the argument, it is necessary to consider the other side, the way that structures are imposed upon, against and within the overall disembeddedness of markets: put differently, how embedded structures work against or side-by-side with disembedded structures, or with how the economic order is structured from the outside. Before we do so, it is worth mentioning that in each case, it will be necessary to identify specifically how these structures do – and do not – detract from the disembeddedness of markets, or how they impose boundaries on disembeddedness. Obviously this topic deserves to be treated in much more detail, but it can be limited for the purpose of the present discussion to simply counterposing embedded versus disembedded markets. These structures or forms of embeddedness can be put into five categories which push disembeddedness into place, impose variety upon it, and shape it from within:

1. Stratification, including the 'superstratification' of the rise and fall of economic powers, which imposes shape on disembeddedness;
2. The varieties of capitalism or of political economies, which impose themselves upon disembeddedness mainly via states;
3. Monopolies and other congealed markets, or different business systems or geographically based sectors, which shape markets within the fluid sea of disembeddedness;
4. Constraints on growth, which impose limits 'from below', or from the limits to the extraction from nature;
5. State and cultural power or institutions (the non-economic powers and institutions), which shape markets from above (in addition to the varieties of capitalism) and push against them.

1. Stratification is obviously a way in which fissures emerge from – and are introduced into – markets. But where do these make a difference? If the economic interests of nations or sets of nations are stratified geopolitically or geoeconomically, then this can be termed 'nationalist' superstratification (Mann 1993: 32). This nationalist superstratification pushes against 'disembedded' markets insofar as, for example, power relations impede free exchange, as when tariffs are imposed with the aim of gaining advantage in nationalistic economic competition. Disembedded markets outflank these restrictions, but the economic order is often shaped by this form of stratification. The problem is that patterns of, for example, a core exploiting a periphery have mainly been identified in networks of commodity chains (Gereffi 1994), which are 'free-standing' rather than forming a single or general superordinate structure that shapes exchanges between, say, the global North and the global South.

To be sure, there is another type of stratification in the continuing divergence between regions during the post-war period in terms of income inequalities, as Mann and Riley (2007) have shown (for Latin America, East Asia, South Asia, Anglo, Nordic and European Continental; see also Milanovic 2011). This divergence goes counter to the expectation of convergence within neo-classical economics. Most importantly for the argument here, it goes counter to the notion of disembedded markets insofar as economic growth and power should spread evenly. But we can note, first, that the differences are regional and porous as opposed to between stratified and bounded blocks such as the global North and the global South, or between hegemonic and subordinate economic powers. The second is that is that these regional income inequalities must be placed among other structures of inequality; first, among inequalities in wealth as opposed to income, and second in relation to the political varieties of capitalism (to be addressed shortly) which are among the prime determinants of these inequalities. Finally, there is no unilinear historical pattern to these inequalities: during the Golden Age, as Mann and Riley (2007) show, they were attenuated, but they have since re-emerged. Nor is there a unilinear pattern in the rise and decline of the most powerful economies – the historical pattern of this rise and (relative) decline is clear, but it does not betoken systematic market inequalities.

Another form of stratification, classes, as pointed out earlier, has waxed and waned in significance, as has the importance of status groups. The economic competition between these groups shapes markets, but in modern society, this shaping must, again, be explained side-by-side with stratification via different social citizenship rights within nation-states, which are political struggles vis-à-vis the state, and put into the context of the waning of economic class struggles during the second half of the 20th century (Chapter 3). These patterns of political struggle, not market mechanisms, have recently shaped, for example, the share of GDP that is redistributed in different countries. Further, even if 'varieties' in respect to redistribution remain (see point 2 below), there has also been, as mentioned in Chapter 3, a 'race to the middle' (Hobson 2003) among the OECD countries in terms of taxes for redistribution.

On the micro-level, individual market exchanges are 'voluntary' and formally 'free', but here too there is stratification and inequality in the exchanges people make. Even the lubricant of money and credit, as Ingham points out, is something people make use of in a stratified way (2004: 138). But for the reasons mentioned earlier, it would be difficult to aggregate this stratification on the micro-level of everyday life into larger patterns (even if these micro-interactions, again, ultimately constitute the main reality which shapes the economic lives of individuals or households). Hence exchange is also not easily captured by 'power' and 'control' (discussed in Chapter 1), and the question of whether states or markets contribute more to economic equality and inequality is also rather vexed (as we saw in Chapters 2 and 3, though again, it is clear that the welfare state has contributed to equality for a time;

Garfinkel et al. 2010). And yet, economic inequality, and stratification in this sense, has been growing in the four cases discussed here in recent decades (as we shall see for China and India). Thus markets may be shaped by economic interests, but this formally 'free' exchange also results in constraints.

In short, a series of forms of stratification – or inequalities – runs from the micro- all the way up to the macro- of economic orders, intersecting disembedded markets at each level. How systematically these forms of stratification go *against* disembedded markets has been partly addressed in the analysis of the political order (Chapter 3), and how stratification of social rights in the political order can translate – or not – into stratification of resources in the economic order is a point to which we will return in the concluding chapter. The point here is that stratification on all levels does not supersede disembedded markets *within* this order.

2. The varieties of capitalism, or the varieties of political economies of capitalism (discussed in previous chapters), in contrast, shape disembedded markets not in penetrating them sideways, as stratification does, but from above. These varieties are in tension with the uniform nature of markets, but they also fail to penetrate them deeply. A key point to recognize here is that variety and uniformity in this case are not a zero-sum game. Even if capitalism is practically universal nowadays, its varieties have also in certain respects remained or grown. There is a large literature on the 'varieties of capitalism' (see, for example, Hall and Soskice 2001) that has already been discussed in previous chapters and which catalogues and explains the differences in key institutions of capitalist (here 'market') societies, from macro-economic policies and business systems to labour policies and welfare regimes. Yet if the varieties of capitalism literature should not just be a set of descriptive histories, then, as Swedberg (2005: 30) argues, it needs to be theorized. And the main differences within capitalism are those that have been discussed in Chapters 2 and 3, where the idea of the intrinsic connection between the two orders in 'political economy' was rejected. Here we can simply note that disembedded markets are shaped – from above – by this continuing divergence, but that this divergence must be offset by the convergence towards disembedded markets across the globe.

3. A different type of embeddedness is that *within* markets. This includes monopolies which dominate and prevent the free entry and exit of actors. As Collins notes, 'monopolies ... are part of the dynamism of the economy' (1986: 125), as when innovations are temporarily monopolized.

But they are also limited: 'monopolies are temporary over the long haul' (Collins 1986: 125). This includes infrastructures or large technological systems, which produce lock-ins or monopolies by virtue of technical standards congealed within political structures. These infrastructures or systems can have a long-term momentum which can shape markets as well as being shaped by them. An equally important embeddedness within markets, finally, are those markets which operate outside of ordinary interconnected markets and are 'political', such as illegal drugs, healthcare and defence, the three largest sectors in the US economy. All these fall outside of disembedded markets, but also interact with them.[7]

A related type of embeddness *within* markets are the structures resulting from the persistence of different business systems. The post-war period, as Whitley points out, has not seen a '"global" business system with its own actors and rules of the game, it would be more accurate to regard it as the internationalization of the American business system' (Whitley 1999: 132). This internationalization received a major impetus in the post-war period, as developed economies adopted American practices, for example, in management (van der Wee 1987) and business services (Dicken 1994). Even more fundamental here are sectoral differences, differences in the distribution of types of economic activity. Again, these will continue to push against the disembeddedness of markets, in this case mainly against their geographic disembeddedness.

4. A fourth limit on the disembeddedness of markets is external – the physical limits of what can be extracted from nature at any given time in view of the available technologies for manipulating the physical world. This limit will be discussed further in Chapter 6, but, to anticipate, it places an upper ceiling on open-ended growth. Yet even in this respect, as we shall see, disembedded economic relations do not have a firm or clear boundedness. While the role of innovation in economic change has slowed overall since the Golden Age (Maddison 2001), innovation will continue to push against this limit. Still, scarcity of exploitable physical resources and the extent to which this scarcity can be overcome in relation to mastery of nature provide some structure – in this case limiting the level of needs and wants that disembedded markets are able to support. In so far as these 'limits to growth' threaten the future of disembedded market economies, they can be regarded as a reembedding force, though, as we shall see in Chapter 6, it is difficult to foresee the urgency of this constraint.

5. Finally, the separateness and unconstrainedness of markets does not entail that globalization 'trumps' the differences in the political

or cultural orders. As critics of the view that 'globalization' constrains domestic politics have pointed out, 'around 90% of production is still carried out for the domestic market and about 90% of consumption is locally produced. Moreover, domestic investment by domestic capital is financed mostly by domestic savings and far exceeds the size of FDI [foreign direct investment] flows in all major markets' (Weiss 2003: 14, see also Mann 1999). As Weiss also argues (along with others), openness to global markets can enable rather than constrain domestic politics. Yet even if the evidence points against the strong 'globalization' thesis that the global economy undermines states, it is important not to go to the other extreme to say that states determine the shaping of the economy. As Dandeker puts it, 'modern capitalism is ... bigger than the nation-state. No single political authority can surbordinate the global operations of the world system to overall administrative control' (1990: 134). Disembedded markets outflank states, even if they are also 'contained' in them.

The argument that markets were initially fostered by the state (Swedberg 2003: 142) or that economic development was enabled and initially shaped by the state (Weiss and Hobson 1995) are important, but they do not alter the fact that, once established, markets operate in a disembedded way.[8] In Weberian terms, 'the rational market can be described as a market wherever renewed profit is at the center and substantive regulation is kept at a minimum' (Swedberg 2003: 145) – or, it could be added, where there is more than minimum regulation, this regulation is aimed at optimizing the disembedded workings of markets.[9] This type of rationality does not mean that it is necessary to subscribe to the model of a rational or utility-maximizing actor, but entails that this 'rationality' (though 'rationality' could be equally be replaced by the adjectives used earlier: open-ended, atomistic and divisible) should be seen as the central characteristic of an economic order that is on various levels promoted by bureaucrat policymakers and politicians everywhere.[10]

Similar arguments apply to the cultural order. There are different cultural forms of economic order (see di Maggio 1994; Hamilton 1994; Swedberg 2003: 218–40), but these, too, are overridden by 'rationality' and by how disembedded markets become diffused throughout global capitalist markets. In sum, disembeddedness is limited, but not outweighed by, non-economic orders and powers. Within the economy and in the forces that shape it, power is diffuse and relatively dispersed: we can contrast the 'open-endedness' of disembedded markets with the political and cultural orders, both of which have an apex of legitimate authority (the state, or religion and science, respectively) and hence often sharp boundaries. But there is no ultimate or centralized authority in the economic order – unless we want to assign this authority to the sacrosanctness of property rights or to money as the universal exchange mechanism. Yet, as we have seen, these are not authoritative in the sense that they can be identified with a single controlling institution, but rather constitute the very mechanisms whereby the economy is becoming disembedded.

Beyond disciplinary turf wars

Swedberg points out that in the analysis of the markets, which are '*the* central institution of capitalism' (2005: 12), economists mainly focus on price and sociologists mainly focus on social relations and institutions, and 'each hold half of the truth' (2005: 11; see also Swedberg 1990 for the relations between the two). The view presented here is somewhat different. As it relates to disciplinary perspectives, it has been argued that sociology has not addressed the economists' half of the story, with Hamilton and Feenstra (1998) a notable exception. Even though recently a veritable 'embeddedness' industry has grown up in economic sociology (or perhaps even more recently a 'performativity' industry, where it is claimed that the economy is socially constructed, and in this sense embedded), none has directly addressed the disembeddedness of markets. Neo-classical economics, on the other hand, has taken little notice of the embeddedness literature, even though economics as a discipline is becoming more heterodox, and its boundaries with other disciplines are becoming fuzzier (see Coyle 2007).

Yet the argument here also sidesteps the question of the scope of economics (I cannot say, for I am not an economist). The order that *envelops* the disembedded market structures sketched in the previous section embeds (or structures, if you prefer) but does not determine it, since, as we have seen, markets are also insulated from determination by these structures in different ways. (Using a different image, we could say that markets, even if they are partly embedded, nevertheless constitute an insuperable disembedded apex; or a separate order. This links to the question of 'primacy' which will be discussed in the concluding chapter.) At the same time, the abstract models that are prevalent in economics will not satisfy sociologists who are interested in substantive structural changes. *Within* disembedded markets, neo-classical economics might take one approach, whereas the main purpose of sociology is to identify causes, mechanisms and consequences of disembeddedness from within its disciplinary purview.

The complex interactions between structures as sociologists see them, even those which occur *within* disembedded markets, may not be of interest to economists – with their need for quantification and the models based on this. This kind of quantification and modelling, on the other hand, is not possible in sociological accounts of disembedded markets because even though interest-oriented and 'atomized' behaviour operates at all levels, it is unclear when the sociological characterization could fit the kind of maximizing or rational choice behaviour demanded in economic (quantifiable and modellable) analysis. Perhaps, instead, sociologists could describe economic action as (rational) restlessness in Weber's sense, or as a constant struggle to overcome an uncertain future. In any event, sociologists could agree that this type of behaviour is unlike that found in the other, political or cultural, orders. Yet this kind of behaviour does not represent 'choice' since, sociologically speaking, there is no reason why behaviour in disembedded markets should be any less enabled or constrained than elsewhere, even if it consists of atomized actions that are often self-interested.

This viewpoint can be contrasted with that of Beckert (2009), who asks about the motives or causes of economic action from the standpoint of an economic sociologist. Among the causes he points to, for example, are status competition, profit maximization, and the like. He sees these motives as more embedded than those in the neo-classical view, whereby individuals maximize in the face of scarce resources. But neither Beckert (nor the neo-classical view) ask: why engage in economic action in the first place? The obvious answer is: to meet the basic need to subsist, and over and above this to accumulate and consume. Taking these two motives further, it can be recalled that Marx distinguished between meeting basic needs and everything beyond this (surplus production). But this distinction points to a key feature of *modern* – and only modern, on a society-wide scale – economies or markets; namely, that *modern* markets make it impossible to distinguish between the two in terms of their mechanisms (though it *is* possible to distinguish between them analytically, from an extra-market perspective). In this sense, too, markets have become disembedded.

There are two implications that follow from this analysis about how to analyse economic change sociologically: one is that embeddedness – or rather the economic orders and powers which push against and penetrate disembedded markets – must be conceptualized more precisely so as to capture how these external forces shape markets. The way these forms of embeddedness are conceptualized here departs from other ways to do this: There are currently two versions of 'embeddedness' explanations, the first whereby economic change is embedded in non-economic institutions and powers (which might be called the sociological imperialist or social constructivist solution), or the second whereby economic change is embedded in rationality ascribed to and constrained within institutions (as in the 'new institutionalism' of principal agent theory or rational choice imperialism that strays outside of economic relations and into other non-economic institutions). Both ignore the disembeddedness that has been described here, and thus the vast sea of non-embedded interactions that take place.

The institutional view, following Bowles (1986, cited in Hamilton and Feenstra 1998: 160), describes '"the capitalist economy as a multiplicity of mini-command economies operating in a sea of market exchanges"'. But this, as Hamilton and Feenstra point out, means ignoring the larger economy and focusing, in my words, on islands in the sea. On the view presented here, there are also constraints on the sea of exchanges (such as the environmental limits to overall growth as per point 4 above). Furthermore, it will be necessary, to continue with the analogy, to map the boundedness of all land masses and the way they are constraining in various ways. But this picture should not overlook the fluidity of the sea or the mechanisms of flows or perhaps turbulences within it, or the fact that bodies of water themselves constitute a macro-structure in modern economies – and are not only micro-mechanisms.

How, then, to conceive of this 'sea' of disembedded market exchanges? I have argued that it cannot be conceptualized as embedded or as a structure operating via authoritative power – if we think of the dispersed nature of economic activity and the diffusion of practices, at all levels from the micro to the macro, whereby market exchanges take place. This diffuseness is also evident in DiMaggio's and Powell's notion of 'institutional isomorphism' (1983) at the meso-level, whereby organizations copy each other's organizational forms. Or again, if we think simply of shifts in this 'sea', such as shifts in the international division of labour or within nation-states in terms of sectors of the economy. Or, again, what of shifts, for example, within manufacturing whereby organizational changes take place to subdivide labour processes? Or when there are adjustments to new forms of competition and conflict within the economy? Adjustment, shifts (geographical, sectoral, demographic and the like), isomorphism (which could be seen as diffusion applied to organizations), and the diffusion of other practices – none of these are structural in the sociological sense of structural functionalism or authoritative institutions or analytical mechanisms (though they might be an analytical mechanism if the mechanism could be seen as an atomistic response within a set of disembedded relations).

At the same time, many phenomena within disembedded markets can be explained without the rational actor model of neo-classical economics (though also without ruling it out) but which use the idea of maxiziming self-interest to explain a variety of market phenomena. So, for example, Collins' idea (2004: 141–82) that people pursue an enhanced status in encounters by maximizing emotional energy in interaction rituals, or White's (1981) notion of how firms monitor each other in production markets in order to compete effectively, or Gereffi's (1994) buyer- or producer-driven commodity chains in which various actors seek to maximize profit at different points along networks.

Whichever term we use – diffusion, adjustment, maximizing behaviour and the like – these all express the idea that atomized actors (again, actors should not be taken to mean individuals; they could be meso-organizations) make fine-grained calculations about how to enhance their economic benefit, and this fits well with the idea of a sea of disembedded exchanges. But although this type of behaviour has not been well-theorized (apart from in economics, where it is postulated as an abstract universal), it is how most practices are spread most of the time in disembedded markets, and these practices or interactions are the most common mechanisms whereby they are spread. How to aggregate these micro-interactions into a macro-account, again, is similar to the question of how to turn micro- or everyday interactions or encounters into aggregated social changes – with the exception that within the 'interconnectedness' of all markets, there are effects of aggregation which add up to – if they are converted into, say, prices – overall changes. And this is quite unlike, say, in the political or cultural orders, or in the study of local micro-interaction in everyday life outside of the economic order, where such aggregation does not result in overall changes in the same way.

The implication of the analysis is that the disembedded part of the economy needs separate analysis – identifying its scale, scope and mechanisms. And while a detailed account of economic relations is beyond our scope here, this separation nevertheless provides us with the needed answers to questions such as: what type of effect do the workings of disembedded markets have – given their scope – on the rest of society (here, the other two orders)? Such a sociological account of economic life of disembedded markets must in some respects be quantitative, specifying the size of these markets and the volume of goods and services that can be converted into monetized units and that are exchangeable – and this provides one clue to the failure of translations between the orders (to be discussed in the concluding chapter). Perhaps patterns of growth are the closest we can come in this brief account. Further, it should also specify the mechanisms whereby such exchanges can take place in the manner of 'atomized' market exchanges. The discipline of economics takes a particular approach to these mechanisms by quantification and modelling ('laws' of the market), but again, it is not suggested here that sociology should follow or copy economics in this respect. After all, the 'laws' which model the relations between quantities in economics in equations inevitably need to be put into words, and sociologists could equally spell out these relations between quantifiable transactions in different formulae of words.

Finally, a point about what is *not* being argued: the idea of disembedded markets is not intended to endorse the 'liberal' view that goes along with neo-classical economics. This liberal view suggests, for example, that the removal of trade barriers in the 19th century or the absence of state power were the key to the success of capitalism. Yet as Chang (2002) has shown, states were crucial to economic development of the major and smaller industrializing powers during key phases of take-off. At the same time, Chang's arguments do not rule out the view of disembedded markets put forward here: the state helped to create some of the conditions for market activity, but this does not explain the dynamic of market activity once markets are in place. Similarly, while the analysis does not endorse any particular political viewpoint on disembedded markets, it can be acknowledged they *do* enjoy widespread political legitimacy. This is because markets are held (rightly or wrongly) to be responsible for producing economic growth (Gellner 1979). There may be preferences for particular versions of capitalism, but disembedded markets are stably institutionalized if only because their power is so diffuse and malleable, including (though not resting on) the widespread belief that they work. This makes it difficult to identify social forces which push for particular types of embedding – and hence for simplicity's sake, in what follows these markets can be called 'free' rather than disembedded, if only because 'disembedded' is rather unwieldy.

5
The Paradoxes of Science, Technology and Social Change

Science and technology commonly do not play a separate role in macro-accounts of social change.[1] Nor do they constitute a separate social order, as here. At the same time, they are frequently and popularly invoked as agents of radical social change – as when, for example, it is asserted that information and communication technologies are drivers of globalization. New scientific discoveries and technological advances are regularly heralded as bringing about momentous transformations, yet little thought is given to the workings of routine technologies and older scientific discoveries that shape our lives (as Edgerton 2006 has pointed out). In social theory, in the meantime, the most prominent current perspective on science, technology and social change is the idea of 'social shaping' or 'social constructivism', whereby science and technology never do any autonomous shaping, but they are always already shaped by social or cultural contexts. These different approaches are clearly at odds. One reason for this can be previewed, which is that in addition to enthusiasm about scientific discovery and new technologies, there is also often a fear of 'technological determinism', of runaway social change, and a hostility to the idea that scientific advance leaves no scope for human volition, as for example in the case of genetic determinants of behaviour.

A further tension is that any account of the social implications of science and technology must, in keeping with the overall approach taken here, be grounded in everyday practices. In other words, it must show how technoscience affects social change concretely in everyday life – as opposed to postulating these at an abstract level. Yet the institutions of science and technology are rather remote from everyday life – if we think of the abstract nature of the scientific worldview on the one hand, or of how the effects of routine technologies have become practically invisible in everyday life on the other. This too is an odd – paradoxical – characteristic that we shall come back to.

Furthermore, the everyday effects of science and technology are at the end of a chain, which begins, in the first instance, with laboratories or research and development, which, again, is remote from everyday life. Thus any account must also cover the social institutions that produce scientific knowledge and new technologies, and we can proceed roughly along a path from origins to end uses: first, describing the institutions whereby scientific knowledge is generated, often in the autonomous research university, moving on to research and development, big science and large technological systems, and innovation systems. At that point, some examples can be provided of how consumer technologies – here we can focus on information and communication technologies – affect and have become an integral part of everyday life. With these implications for everyday life, we will have come to the end of the chain whereby scientific knowledge and artefacts are created, and ultimately end up transforming social life. One further step will be necessary, however, and this will be tackled in the next chapter: how technoscience has transformed the natural world at its furthest extent, in societies characterized by permanent economic growth and open-ended consumption, and how the spread of this transformation across the globe is reaching physical limits.

The 'linear path' leading from science to technology to everyday life that has just been sketched immediately highlights a somewhat misleading idea about the relationship between the two: it implies a simple 'linear model' whereby scientific ideas are discovered and then, via a process of research and development, followed by diffusion, and ultimately translate into the artefacts that we use in everyday life (see Edgerton 2006 for criticisms). As we shall see, this model is partly incorrect, since, for example, research technologies often lead to new scientific discoveries. Still, we shall see why it is nevertheless useful to have a comprehensive, end-to-end view of science and technology and their effects in everyday life.

Another issue that can be mentioned at the outset is globalization, since science and technology are commonly regarded as a key factor that accelerates this process – at least by those outside of the specialism of the sociology of science and technology. So, for example, Guillen (2001), in his review of the social science literature on globalization, describes how (as already mentioned) information and communication technologies are regarded as being responsible for a world-wide 'information', 'knowledge' or 'network' society. Similarly, historians see science (Bayly 2004: 312–20) and technology (Osterhammel and Petersson 2003: 107) – again, especially information and communication technologies – as drivers of globalization. On the other hand, within the subdiscipline of science and technology studies (STS), the dominant view could be labelled 'globalization denial': within STS, science and technology are regarded as inescapably less than global since they are always shaped by local social or cultural circumstances.

The truth, as we shall see, is more complex: the argument that will be made here (put forward in greater detail in my 2007 book), is that while sociologists of science and technology are right to question abstract generalizations about the impact of science and technology, they are wrong to reject the idea that such generalizations are possible at all. The reason STS scholars reject such generalizations is because they also reject the idea that scientific truth is universal: science, it is argued, is shaped by social context, a notion that is dominant in the sociology of science and hence leads to the charge (justifiable, in my view) of relativism. Similarly, STS scholars reject technological determinism and any idea that technology goes beyond local social shaping, which has meant that sociological accounts of technology typically consist of case studies and avoid larger historical processes. This tradition within the sociology of science and technology goes back to the fact that it was dominated first, by 'materialist' (neo-Marxist) ideas about science and technology being shaped by economic and political power, and more recently by the idea that they are shaped by cultural forces – in line with social and cultural constructivist theory (see Hess 1997 for an overview) – and again, oriented to the idea of critiquing cultural power. Against this, I shall defend the notions of scientific truth and technological determinism, which also entails, as we shall see, that science and technology are important globalizing forces. In agreement with sociologists of science and technology, however, I shall argue that the social implications of technoscience must always be concretely instantiated (in keeping with the structural and 'from below' overall account of social change here).

Before proceeding, the discussion can be related by looking back to Chapters 1 and 2 and convergence and globalization: however defined, 'globalization' should entail that social phenomena are becoming world-wide in scope. How does this apply to science and technology? The brief answer is that scientific knowledge is universal and its institutions are becoming global, but high levels of technological development are confined to the global North or developed societies. In other words, when we speak about 'globalization', we really mean the developed societies in the North (which includes Australia and New Zealand), with the implication that the processes will spread to – or converge – in the developing world or the global South. Thus globalization, modernization and convergence are interrelated. Here we encounter a further apparent paradox: science is universal, its legitimacy is transcendent, and it is independent from political and economic shaping. At the same time, the effects of science and technology are also geographically constrained in practice. Whatever else needs to be shown or arrived at, this tension between the universality of science and technology and its local instantiations will need to be resolved.

The production of scientific knowledge and technological innovation

There are two sides to the relation between science and technology and social change: one side is how the natural or physical world are transformed by science and technology, and the other how different parts of social life – social institutions and everyday practices – shape and are transformed by science and technology. To understand why, we must define our terms: modern science can be defined, following Hacking, as 'the adventure of the interlocking of representing and intervening' (1983: 146), and technology in the same vein as the 'adventure of the interlocking of refining and manipulating' (Schroeder 2007: 9). What these definitions entail is a realist and pragmatist view of science and technology: by means of the advance of scientific knowledge, we have been able to intervene more powerfully in the natural or physical world, and by means of technological artefacts we have been able to manipulate the human-made world more powerfully.

It can be anticipated that these definitions, which will be elaborated in a moment, address some of the paradoxes that have been mentioned, especially about the geographic scope of technoscience: insofar as intervention in – and manipulation of – the natural world takes place, this takes place universally; scientific knowledge and technological artefacts operate the same way everywhere in relation to the natural or physical environment. Indeed, they do so not just world-wide but throughout the universe (insofar as we know it). This greater exercise of power by means of refining and manipulating also has a social side, however, which is that the world around us has become increasingly 'rationalized', as Weber argued. The mastery of the world entails an increasing rationalization or instrumentalization of the social world. Rationalization led, in Weber's words, to disenchantment and to an 'iron cage'; or rather, it has provided us with a more powerful 'exoskeleton' with which we dominate the natural world. Environmental historians thus speak of the expansion of the human footprint in the environment, which has accelerated at an unprecedented rate in the 20th century and now encompasses the globe (McNeill 2000: 4).

These features of science and technology are distinctively 'modern' (to take issue with Latour 1993). Only modern science, emerging since 1600 or so in Europe, is 'high-consensus rapid-discovery science' (as Collins 1998: 532–8 calls it). Collins argues that 'research technologies' played a crucial role in scientific advance whereby laboratory instruments, which could be endlessly modified, provided physical demonstrations of phenomena and could reliably repeat experiments (Collins 1994a: 163). Note the inversion here of the 'linear model' that was mentioned earlier: it is technology that drives science rather than the other way around. Note also, however, that when we move from how individual discoveries are made by means of more powerful research instruments to the growth of knowledge and technological innovation *generally*, it becomes difficult to say that one precedes the other.

These laboratory instruments can, in turn, be exported from the lab so that ultimately they turn into consumer goods:

> After modification at the hand of scientists, the equipment may become commercially viable when reintroduced into the lay world . . . Once this happens, the research process is legitimised to a high degree: not merely on the level of ideology (which may wax and wane), but in the taken-for-granted practices of everyday life. (Collins 1994a: 165)

This is why it is important to establish which technologies have this taken-for-granted character – and how far globally this taken-for-grantedness extends. Even if, therefore, we conceive of the spread of science and technology in terms of concrete networks of social relations, as many social thinkers, including for example social constructivists ('actor-network theories') that are popular in the sociology of science and technology, want to do, then science and technology can still be said to have a global reach:

> The world that once existed only in the immediate vicinity of certain European scientists has now expanded around the globe. That Western technoscience works, in Polynesia or Brazil, does not have to be treated as an abstract epistemological question; it is an empirical,

sensuously material, practical pattern of how far certain networks have expanded. (Collins 1999b: 28)

In other words, laboratory instruments ultimately translate into consumer goods in everyday life, and how far these networks of artefacts extend throughout the world can be demonstrated empirically, not just in theory.

So how did – and does – scientific knowledge come to be global? First, we can note that there are limitations to its global nature: scientific knowledge has the exclusive monopoly on legitimate knowledge about the natural or physical worlds. But this legitimacy extends in the first instance to the professionals whose role it is to produce truth (Fuchs 1992). These professionals have obtained the power and autonomy to police the boundaries around truth. It can be added that these professionals have a system of scientific communication that is universal (the norm of 'universalism' that Merton [1942] saw as one of the hallmarks of science) – or 'open' according to Fuchs (2002) – which again, is evidence of the global nature of science: it is formally open in the sense that communication cannot stop, for example, on epistemological grounds and simultaneously practical ones: if communication were to stop on the basis of the insistence on a particular epistemological standpoint, no further communication would be possible. Instead, scientific knowledge must be open to criticism and to further refinement. In practice, again, we can note that even here there are limits to the global nature of science communication: to take just the simplest one, scientific journals are not available everywhere, and not all researchers have access to computers or to the World Wide Web where they might find articles even if they were available online for free.

But there is another side to this global or universal nature of science; which is that scientists must orient themselves to a common object – an object of knowledge production, as Glaeser (2006) calls it – in order to advance beyond the state of knowledge regarding this object. There is therefore a social organization to the 'transcendence' or autonomy of science: the social organization consists of a constantly moving research front, which remains open and open-ended because of its system of communication. Researchers orient themselves to advancing beyond the current state of knowledge wherever this may be in relation to their particular common object of investigation. In this way, research is aimed at an ever more powerful transformation of the physical world. It is not shaped by economic forces, except when and insofar as the aim of advancing knowledge is economic reward ('innovation'), and similarly not shaped by political forces unless these dictate particular social goals. Even in these cases, however, it is only the selection of which area of knowledge to focus on, and not knowledge in relation to the physical world itself, that is shaped by these extra-scientific forces.

Here it can be noted in passing that social science and social theory – including this book – should illustrate this focus on a common object and advance it in relation to this object. Indeed, I hope that it does so, for example, in weighing the evidence for the two interpretations of state development in Chapter 3 and moving beyond them, or by overcoming an 'embedded' conception of the economy with a 'disembedded' one that fits more closely (as argued in Chapter 4) with the autonomy of markets. In my account of science in this chapter, I depart from social science orthodoxy and existing debates more radically, but that is because the 'social shaping' and 'constructivist' ideas of science and technology resonate more with the interpretivist stance of the humanities and cultural studies than the scientistic aims of the social sciences (Fuchs 1992; Schroeder 2007). Alas, the shortcoming of this argument can already be anticipated: social theory does not (or does only indirectly) provide an advance on mastering the natural world, but mainly advances how current knowledge about social change is organized – a limited but important advance in knowledge (we will return to this point in the conclusion).

In any event, bringing science and technology down to earth in this way, or translating them into social processes, allows us to pin down their global nature still further: although the vast bulk of science communication takes place within the global North (just as the vast bulk of trade and financial flows take place in the global North), there is no reason *in principle* why science communication is geographically restricted. The same applies to the vast bulk of scientific knowledge produced, the amount spent on R&D, and many aspects of technological development.

An array of institutions which have spread from their geographical origins nowadays ensures that the production of scientific knowledge and technological innovation continues to advance: first, there is the autonomous research university which emerged in late-19th-century Germany and has since become transplanted around the world. Second, there are the large-scale research and development laboratories which were pioneered early in the 20th century in the United States and which, again, have become widespread across the globe. Third, with policymakers increasingly taking the view that innovation is essential to economic growth, national bodies for research funding and for promoting 'national systems of innovation' have been created.

Drori et al. (2003) have charted how the institutions of science, including professional bodies and ministries dealing with science and technology policy, have spread across the world in the 20th century. This includes national policies investing in scientific research and promoting a scientific work force in the belief that innovation fuels economic growth. In a similar vein, Frank and Gabler (2006) have shown that higher education systems, which national governments believe to be essential to developing the skills for a 'knowledge society', have also become globalized, providing increasingly uniform curricula around the world.

During the 20th century, science and technology have also changed shape. Science has become 'big science', with research organized on a large scale (Galison and Hevly 1992). Physics is often seen as exemplary, with instances where more than a thousand researchers are organized in a single effort, as with the atomic bomb in 1930s and 1940s in the United States, or physicists world-wide nowadays who participate in the experiment of the large-hadron collider at CERN (the European Organization for Nuclear Research) based near Geneva. On an even larger scale, the development of 'large technological systems' (Hughes 1987) has to a large extent been driven by the need for social infrastructures (transportation, communication, energy) which support the increasing scale and scope of industrial production and of the service industries – as well as a consumer society. We have already encountered these (in Chapter 4) in the discussion of the increasing scale and scope of markets – national and beyond – and of the state's capacity internally and externally (Chapter 3).

It is true (as those in the 'social shaping' or 'social constructivist' schools argue) that these systems, which constitute the most large-scale extensions of technological mastery into the environment, are closely entwined with political and economic factors. Infrastructures such as energy provision, for example, typically extend at least to national borders and there are complex regulatory and economic issues, especially when they cross them. Note, too, however, that these systems also have a 'technological momentum' (Hughes 1994) of their own, or purely as physical artefacts, insofar as they become all-encompassing and more stable over time – although they can be technically refined and made more powerful – so that they are difficult to change in any fundamental way. This momentum can therefore be seen as a conservative (no fundamental change of direction is possible) as well as a progressive one (whereby the system continues to be improved and extended).

In the cases of other institutions of science and technology, too, it is possible to identify limits to 'globalization' and 'universalism'. The scientific research front, for example, is also limited in the sense that it is concentrated in a few areas and groups. The same goes for the objects of research: this research front has migrated in terms of which fields are at the leading edge of science. Roughly speaking, this leading edge migrated from chemistry in the late 19th century, to physics in the middle of the 20th, to electronics in the post-war period and now on to biotechnology or the life sciences. It therefore true, as mentioned earlier, that scientific and technological advance are shaped by economic and political forces in a general way: chemistry came to prominence when the dominant economic sector was agriculture, and the heyday of physics was in the middle of the 20th century when it was in the service of geopolitics. Today, the pharmaceutical industry dominates research, and with it the life sciences. In this sense science serves other social structures.[2]

It is a similar case with the concentration of research and development (R&D). As Edgerton points out, 'pharmaceutical firms now account for around one-third of all development and research expenditure. Pharmaceuticals plus the motor-car industry perform around half the world R&D total' (2006: 202). In this sense, too, science and technology are not 'global': R&D efforts are not spread equally across all areas of research (or scientific disciplines) but rather concentrated in a few areas. Furthermore, R&D for the pharmaceutical and motor-car industries is, of course, concentrated in a few geographical locations rather than being spread around the globe. To sum up: there is no need for abstraction, or for an 'idealist' account of why science and technology are global or universal. They are physically so – despite the limitations of where they are concentrated and of their scope – and the institutions which support them have proliferated. The same, as we shall see, applies to consumer technologies in the household.

Technology in everyday life: the example of information and communication technologies

It has already been mentioned that technologies can be exported from the laboratory and ultimately assume the form, among other things, of consumer devices. Yet it is important to base the argument about their widespread social implications not just on technology diffusion, but rather on the actual uses of technology. Here we can take, in the first instance, the uses of telephones and television, which are well-established and widespread throughout advanced societies and are becoming so around the world. Nowadays, the internet or mobile phones are complementing them and taking their place, yet it is more problematic to generalize about these newer technologies-in-the-making. Still, what we find is a global spread of these technologies: global in the sense that the telephone and television and their successors have become practically universal throughout the developed world, not just in terms of the diffusion of technologies, but also in the uses of these technologies for spending leisure time to socialize and to be entertained.

To make a concrete comparison, we can once again briefly focus on Sweden and the US, two countries that are, as mentioned in Chapter 2, in important ways at different ends of the spectrum among the developed countries of the global North. How different are these two countries in terms of information and communication technology (ICT) uses? If a widespread general effect on society is taking place (and bearing in mind that we are focusing on use and not just on the diffusion of devices), we would expect these uses to converge in these two countries, and perhaps around the world. Yet discussions of convergence – or the homogenization of cultures – are rare in comparison to studies which focus on differences (but see Rantanen 2005; Schroeder 2007), even if there are no a priori reasons why one should be more likely than the other.

To narrow the topic still further and to instantiate a set of specific uses, we can focus on leisure or consumption, as distinct from the political and economic orders – or also of work. This separation is often hard to make in practice, but it is warranted by the nature of uses of ICTs themselves: peoples' uses of ICTs for leisure are different from their (economic) work uses. If we think, for example, about connectedness for leisure and work (including unpaid work), there are quite different constraining and enabling factors: coordinating care for children or working with others in an organization means that much of the volume of one's communication is a requirement of the job that one cannot opt out of – unlike the comparatively untrammelled and optional nature of leisure communication. The same applies to the political uses of ICTs, where communication between those who govern and those who are governed faces different constraints and possibilities from those that hold the fabric of everyday relations together: think, for example about the spike in the importance of political communication during brief election periods, versus the steady stream and regular rhythms of everyday leisure communication. In confining ourselves to consumption or leisure, in contrast, we restrict ourselves to culture as separate from the economic and political orders.

If then we examine telephones and television in Sweden and America since their beginnings, then a long-term change that is common to both countries is 'more': more time is being spent on both, a greater number of contacts are maintained via phones (and via more multiplex channels, as we shall see in a moment), and more hours are spent on a greater variety of television programmes that are consumed in more diverse forms. Overall, there is a greater and more uniformly diversified mediation of interpersonal relations and consumption of mediated content for leisure – a generalization that applies to both countries. Differences remain, such as the availability of publicly funded television in Sweden (which plays a minor role in the US). Yet these differences were arguably stronger in the past before commercial television became added to the public broadcast monopoly in Sweden.

Nowadays, the internet and mobile phones add to the uses of land-line phones and of television, but also extend and complement them. The main factor that limits this extension and the additional use of devices is not so much technological innovation, but the total amount of time that can be spent. Total time available for leisure is constrained, and so a substitution effect takes place to some extent, as when time spent using the internet eats into the amount of time spent watching television rather than (or as well as) adding to it (for example, World Internet Project 2009: 319), or when mobile phone uses are to some extent being squeezed into 'dead time' such as travel (Haddon 2004). Similarly, the number and frequency of social contacts cannot be expanded indefinitely. So, for example, nowadays, one finding among researchers who study mobile phones is that although people like to be able to reach others, they don't like to be reachable all the time themselves (Katz 2008: 435).

One problem with gauging the uses of ICTs nowadays is that it is difficult to tell new ICTs apart from each other. Mobile phones, for example, can be used to access email and the Web and to play music, while personal computers (PCs) can be used for making telephone calls, as a photo album and to watch videos. Compare this situation with old media – television, radio, telephone – which were single-purpose devices. However, if we can delimit uses to the cultural order and consumption, then we can take all the uses of ICTs together: there is a widespread view nowadays that ICTs enable 'access to anyone, anywhere, anytime', which implies that the technology causes radical social changes such as disembedding people from their sense of place and altering the rhythms of time in their everyday lives. This view, however, as we have seen, overlooks a number of limits, including the number people that we typically maintain relationships with and the overall time spent in the consumption of ICTs for mediated entertainment. The point is not that there is a 'global village', but that within limits, ICT uses are converging.

To be sure, there are differences: so, for example, some countries such as Korea and Japan can be described as mobile-phone-centric in comparison to countries like Sweden and the US which are more PC and internet-centric: there is a high degree of use of mobiles and comparatively low use of internet with PCs in Japan and Korea (though email and the Web are commonly accessed on mobiles) versus the low uses of mobile phones for internet and high use of internet with computers in the US and Sweden. But it is difficult to see what difference this makes when the different devices all enable a kind of multimodal (voice, text and image) connectedness and access to various types of content. With digital devices, some have argued that an 'always on' connectedness (Baron 2008) or 'perpetual contact' (Rule 2002) are emerging.

But perhaps the question of geographical constraint – or the lack thereof with greater globalization – is about freedom. So we can ask: does the greater use of ICTs enhance freedom? Katz, for example, has argued that mobile phones enhance physical and social freedom: physical, because it allows people to go further and still stay in touch, and social, because 'it increases the choices in life' (2008: 444). Yet this position is doubly misleading: To be sure, mobiles increase choice, but they also constrain choice, since, as Katz himself points out, there is no choice about having a mobile. Not to have a mobile, at least for those under the age of sixty in parts of the developed world, is frowned upon or worse (ibid.: 443). This means, secondly, that there is no choice but to take on what Katz calls the 'added new complexity to the management of personal relationships' (ibid.: 444). Such complexity adds to freedom, but also imposes new constraints: those with mobiles are tethered in additional ways to maintain relationships, and the only 'choice' is about which devices and modalities to use in engaging with others (here it may be useful to recall the notion of an 'exoskeleton' with its technological determinist implications which guide this chapter).

At the other extreme, it is common to argue that social patterns of ICT uses are culturally specific. Yet, howsoever we regard concrete uses, the effects are to create more frequent, longer, more multimodal and more extensive ties. And mobile phone ownership, for example, has become a universal feature of belonging to a consumer culture, joining telephones, television, PCs, and, increasingly, internet access. And of course, consumer culture is not just Western but has become globalized throughout the developed world and beyond (de Grazia 2005; Stearns 2001). An immediate reply will be: aren't the uses of ICTs quite diverse when we think of the enormous differences between countries of the developed North and 'the bottom billion' (Collier 2007)? Indeed, when we think about new technologies and global social change, we tend to think of the vast and possibly growing gulf of inequalities that separate developed and developing countries, or more accurately between different regions of the world (Mann and Riley 2007). The next step that is often implicitly taken, however, is to assume that the divides in wealth and income will also be reflected in digital divides or divides in access to ICTs.

Yet it needs to be remembered that economic inequalities pertain to industrialization and living standards as a whole, and to expensive infrastructures, whereas digital or communication divides may apply far less to relatively cheap consumer goods and technologies that have diffused rapidly (and relatively cheap infrastructures) – such as with mobile phones (World Bank 2008: 72–5). The fact that the vast majority of the world's population does not have access to the internet (one of the 'digital divides') must be put into the context that there are billions of mobile phone users, and that 'mobile use in the developing world is more common than any other ICT, that is, personal computers or fixed-line telephones' (Shristava 2008: 22).

There are thus common patterns in developed societies produced by technologies of consumption and leisure towards an ever more uniformly diversified way of life (Schroeder 2007: 116–20). The main significance of this cultural change is not 'anywhere, anytime, and any-one', but rather the increasing and multimodally tethered relations to each other, and to an array of mediated cultural content. What can be added to this is an important emergent cultural pattern whereby there are limits on the mediated time spent and on the mediated engagement with others and with information and entertainment.

In Sweden, in America, and across the developed world, there will continue to be more dense, more extensive, more time-consuming, and more non-location-specific ties – since it can be assumed that the increasing popularity of mobile devices will continue, and they will continue to tether people more to each other (though less to place). Along the same lines, there will continue to be a proliferation of content in different formats on traditional broadcast television and its digital successors. Cultural homogenization in this sense may thus be as important as cultural differences.[3] Yet these similarities across cultures may ultimately be shaped above all by the possibilities for the extension and proliferation of multimodal tethered connectedness and of the consumption of mediated entertainment, which are beginning to face limits, even while they are still growing.

These consequences of ICTs may seem a long way from a discussion of the social implications of technoscience. Yet this detour has been necessary because the argument here – as throughout the book – has been that social change should be analysed from the ground up, and encompass the widest possible scope. The production of more powerful scientific knowledge and technological artefacts is one side of this process. The other side, how this increasing power, autonomously, affects everyday life, has been demonstrated here in relation to ICTs, which are often seen as emblematic of these effects. Even here these effects need to be instantiated. Once this is done, it is possible to see limits, but also widespread effects. It can be added that the argument has been made here in relation to leisure and ICTs. It could equally be made in relation to political communication, though in this case, the differences between Sweden and the US might stand out more, even if there are some similar effects here too (a more mediated and more 'managed' form of politics, see Schroeder 2007). Finally, it is important to be clear about limits: so far, limits have been identified to leisure uses in terms of time and connectedness. Arguably, these cultural changes in leisure or consumption and limits play a minor – purely cultural – role in social change without further repercussions. When it comes to the transformation of the natural environment, however, and in the case of other technologies requiring vast amounts of resources as in the case of transport, these limits will have wider ramifications.

Globalization, science and technology, and social theory

In the previous section, the argument was made that the culture of consumer uses of ICTs – though not society as a whole – has become globalized (at least for two countries, though with wider implications). This argument is closely linked to Chapter 4, which argued that the market economy has become driven by open-ended consumerism, though the arguments are also separate or free-standing: while it is impossible to envision a market society fulfilling consumerism on a large scale without the technological infrastructure which supports it, this consumerism does not necessarily entail homogeneously diversified uses of ICTs, or vice versa.

Still, apart from a consumer culture, the relation between science and technology on one side and culture on the other is a complex one: in some respects, science displaces formerly authoritative cultural belief systems like religion. In other respects, too, science and technology increasingly mediate culture (discussed in more detail in Chapter 7), just as they transform the political and economic orders (as mentioned in Chapters 2 to 4). Sticking with the examples here of the uses of ICTs for consumption or leisure, there is a link, since much technological innovation is aimed at – and harnessed for – providing an endless stream of novel artifacts in a culture of consumption. Hence, too, the intertwining of culture and technology in a 'technology–culture' spiral, whereby novel artifacts provide increasingly mediated experiences of cultural consumption, which in turn generate ever more needs for novel artifacts, and so on in a never-ending spiral (Braun 1994).

ICTs such as the telephone and television, but also the automobile and other forms of transport for leisure, provide among the most visible examples of the 'technology–culture spiral' in contemporary culture. They illustrate how technology impinges on the rest of culture insofar as it leads to an increasingly technologically mediated culture (but note again: technology also obviously has functions outside of its role in culture). Science is thus separate from culture (as cumulative knowledge) and mediates culture (in the form of technologies of consumption). This way of understanding the relation between technology and culture avoids a technology-centric view by focusing on everyday life. It also avoids what Edgerton calls an 'innovation-centric' view, which is focused on the promise of the newest technologies among early adopters. So for example, he says, the 'musings of information society gurus' recently have been about the internet and the Web, whereas in his view, 'today's globalisation is in part the result of extremely cheap sea and air transport, and radio and wire-based communication' (2006: 113, 115). In other words, technologies which have become an established part of everyday life are far more important than recent innovations. Here, such a skewed and innovation-centric view of globalization has been avoided by rather focusing on mundane technologies and 'technology-in-use' (ibid.: 2006: xi).

Nevertheless, there are many critics of the association between science and technology and globalization. Here we can take just two examples; Shapin on the side of science and Edgerton for technology. Shapin is a critic, not of globalization as such, but of the modernity of science. To his question: 'Do we live in a scientific world?', he answers 'assuming that we could answer what such a statement might mean, there is quite a lot of evidence that we do not now and never have' (2008: 436). He proceeds to criticize the key assumption whereby modernity and science are interrelated, 'that scientific beliefs have got much grip on the modern mind writ large' by arguing 'that just isn't true' (ibid.: 439). His main evidence is that many Americans believe in God and hold many beliefs that run counter to science. Further, American scientists believe no less in God than people generally do (ibid.: 436–8). But Shapin's argument is misleading: the point is surely that scientists' religious beliefs are not allowed to enter into their professional role or into scientific communication (I would be interested to see evidence to the contrary). Similarly, peoples' beliefs are not exhausted by their scientific worldview, but in the modern world, when serious matters related to nature (such as health) are at stake, science is the only legitimate worldview.

Edgerton similarly criticizes 'techno-globalism', pointing out that technology has often reinforced nationalism and served, for example, military purposes which have reinforced the boundedness of nation-states (Edgerton 2006: 113–17).[4] We have also seen that Edgerton criticizes an 'innovation-centric' technological determinism and the idea that the link between technology and globalization is new; in fact, he argues, earlier technologies may have played a greater role in this process than more recent ones. To be sure, globalization theorists have often underestimated the role of the nation-state (Mann 1999) and asserted that ICTs (often the prime example) promote globalization without demonstrating how this takes place in practice. Yet, as I hope to have shown, a specific kind of convergence can be shown for two countries, and by implication for others. Moreover, if the process can be demonstrated for specific technologies (telephone and television), it is still the case that these technologies must be put into a more holistic context of how they fit with the technologies that have come to complement and add to them (internet and mobile phones).

Both Shapin and Edgerton want to deny the idea that technoscience can be associated with globalization in the abstract, outside of practice or apart from its use. I agree. Where they then go wrong is in claiming that science and technology are not globalizing in practice, but they do so only negatively without putting any broad patterns about science, technology and social change in the place of what they criticize. Modernity and globalization are related: the expectation is that the kind of mastery over the natural world that was inaugurated with *modern* science and technology will diffuse across the globe. Critics of this view, including most sociologists of science and technology and 'constructivist' social theorists, deny that there is such a 'master trend' in society. They would argue that there are no translocal impacts of science and technology and no 'grand narratives' in history. Instead, they argue, we must be mindful of agency, of cultural specificities, and of the multiple contexts of science and technology. I hope to have shown, however, that such extreme contextualism can be overcome. The vagaries of social theory are such that there are continual swings between theories which focus more on actors, culture and context while others focus on macro-social patterns, comparative-historical analysis and general social theory. When and where the latter predominate, broad patterns of science, technology and social change and their modernity and globalizing force will come into the foreground.

At the furthest extent, the impact of technoscience is how it has transformed the human-made physical or natural environment. As we shall see in the next chapter, in the 21st century the arguments about the 'limits to growth' focus less on population growth and economic growth and increasingly on limits to the exploitation of the natural world. But there are other limits too: science is an autonomous institution with a monopoly on legitimate knowledge, yet most people have little to do with it on an everyday basis. Shapin is therefore right to claim that many people hold views which conflict with science (though not when science needs to be relied on, for example, in life-threatening situations). Even technology, once it has faded into the background, no longer seems to be a transformative force. This explains why Edgerton is also right to suggest that technology has been more transformative in the past than it is today. Yet this is not true in relation to areas where the transformation of nature faces limits: at the broadest extent, in terms of how far humans have extended the 'cage' or 'exoskeleton' of their powers over the natural world, and how this effort is rebounding on them.

6
The Limits to Transforming the Environment

As we have seen, the social implications of science and technology present a number of challenges which the previous chapter began to address.[1] Some of these problems – and solutions – also apply to understanding how society shapes and is shaped by transforming the natural environment. Environmental issues have, for obvious reasons, recently come onto the agenda in sociology. These include energy, climate change and pollution. This chapter provides an account of environmental transformation and how it is rebounding on social change. To do this, it will draw on several disciplines, but above all argue for a long-term comparative-historical perspective combined with the realist sociology of science and technology that was presented in the previous chapter. This chapter will focus on energy – since the foreseeable bounds to using energy sustainably provide the most important illustration of the idea that transforming the environment is confronting limits, even if the argument has broader ramifications. Focusing on energy, however, is one way to think about whether there are potential social forces that may be able to counteract the future tensions arising from environmental transformation. The argument will be that only two of these countervailing forces – namely state intervention and technological innovation – stand a realistic chance of counteracting these tensions, even though these solutions themselves face severe constraints. The chapter therefore concludes with a broader point, echoing the limits discussed throughout the book, which is that only a realistic assessment (in relation to science and technology, 'realist' would also be appropriate) of constraints is a useful way forward in social theory – though this realism also reveals the limited role that social scientific knowledge can play.

This chapter begins with a discussion of why the various disciplinary approaches provide quite different and non-overlapping perspectives on environmental transformations. Next, it will present a long-term historical view which puts recent environmental ruptures into context. These then need to be complemented with a realist account of the increasing power over nature, which has already been developed in the previous chapter with Weber's notion of an iron cage – or rather an exoskeleton. Then the chapter will outline the tensions arising from the depletion of natural resources, and ways to counteract this. The responses to these tensions include growing scientific expertise, shifting public understanding and media representations, and the possibility for civil society to encourage the state's regulatory intervention. Yet states, it will be argued, also have a limited capacity to address environmental issues, as do the various scientific and technological options that are being put forward. The chapter concludes by arguing that the social sciences can play an important, albeit limited, role, in pointing to the increasing constraints upon environmental changes, and the limited possibilities for counteracting them.

Disciplinary fragmentation and lack of realism

Disciplinary fragmentation in understanding the relation between the environment and social change can be explained by the fact that a number of topics, though interrelated in practice, are contained within silos of knowledge (Boykoff et al. 2009). So far, the environment has mainly entered social thought via five routes: one is in theories of society as a whole, such as the 'risk society', where environmental threats influence people's perceptions of society generally. The second is via research on new social movements, and especially 'green' or 'environmental' movements, which exert pressure, among other things, on the state for environmental regulation. Third, the environment is the subject matter of the sociology of science and technology, which has mainly been concerned with scientific expertise and the public understanding of environmental issues.[2] A fourth recent area of research, notable for being completely separate from the other three, is the work of environmental historians. As we shall see, they add a crucial dimension that is missing in the other approaches, which is to chart the massive transformation of nature that has taken place since industrialization, including its acceleration in the last few decades. Finally, fifth, there is research into how behaviour in relation to the environment (such as energy uses) can be changed. But if historians lack the conceptual tools to address changes facing us in the future, research on behaviour change has difficulty with translating micro-level changes into the longer-term and macro context of the difference they can make.

The limits of the sociology of science and technology in addressing macro-social change have already been discussed in the previous chapter. Here it is possible to add one more; the lack of 'realism' in this subdiscipline: since nature or the physical world are not treated as separable from the rest of the social world, the advance of scientific knowledge and progressive mastery of environment by technology cannot find their way into the analysis.[3] This makes it difficult to explain the transformation of nature and the (separate or deterministic) consequences of this transformation for social change.

Accelerated transformations and an uncontrolled experiment

Before discussing these approaches further, it will be useful to take stock of the radical social and environmental discontinuities with the past. Environmental and economic historians agree that the industrial revolution in the 19th century – or its two industrial revolutions – brought with them unprecedented levels of economic growth and resource exploitation. Sometime during the 19th century, in parts of Europe and the United States and for the first time in history, continuous economic growth and the associated belief in constant improvements in living standards came to be taken for granted – a belief that was borne out in practice. This idea has become more deeply entrenched in the 20th century. As McNeill puts it, 'economic growth became the indispensable ideology of the state nearly everywhere', and 'the overarching priority of economic growth was easily the most important idea of the twentieth century' (2000: 335, 336). This accelerated economic growth and transformation of the environment are historically very recent. By Christian's reckoning, 'in the past 250 years . . . global industrial output has increased almost by 100 times' (2004: 406). Or again, 'growth in just the three years from 1995 to 1998 is estimated to have been greater than total growth in the 10,000 years before 1900' (ibid.: 446). Whether we see these as one or more discontinuities or ruptures, the industrial revolution constituted a new – modern – departure.[4]

It is important to note immediately that it is not economically unsustainable activity per se that makes the 20th century unique in the exploitation of non-renewable resources; such unsustainable practices have taken place regionally for much longer. What is new is that this activity takes place on a territorially extensive or worldwide scale – and at an accelerating pace (Radkau 2008: 250). Put more succinctly, it is 'not human behaviour as such' but its 'aggregation' (or massification) that is environmentally destructive (Radkau 2008: 18). A *mass* consumer society, as we saw in Chapter 4, only emerged in the US in the early part of the 20th century (Schroeder 2007: 64–6), and was subsequently exported to Europe (de Grazia 2005) and across the globe (Stearns 2001). Consumption has thus become a systemic part of the global economy: 'The distinctive feature [of twentieth century consumer capitalism] has been the requirement that the mass of the population should consume commodities in ever-increasing amounts for the good of the entire system' (Christian 2004: 446). Note that this shift was partly a technological shift, partly a shift in the infrastructures of mass distribution, and partly a cultural shift in higher standards of living, including leisure activities such as travel. These have become widespread and routine as well as requiring increasing amounts of energy.

Hence there has also very recently been a sea change in thinking about the *level* of economic activity. Christian notes that 'whereas for most earlier epochs of human history scarcity had been the most fundamental problem faced by peoples and governments, now the main issue was' – or is – 'to cope with abundance' (2004: 446). As we shall see in a moment, the problem with abundance is that it is not clear if the extension of the human footprint can continue in the same way indefinitely. But one counter-argument against the limits to this extension can already be noted: Christian says that 'in principle, the recycling of resources or the sale of information and services rather than goods can generate profits as effectively as the exploitation of virgin resources' (2004: 480). Such a shift, according to Christian, could be enabled by governments 'taxing unsustainable production methods' (ibid.: 480). This argument also raises the possibility that a slowing or reduction of the human footprint could also come about by means of technological innovation. Yet as we shall also see, it is not clear where the will to impose such taxes or to foster such innovation on the required scale could come from. Furthermore, looking ahead, it is possible to calculate the difference that this type of shift can make. For example, Pielke et al. have argued that 'only about 20% (+/–10%) of global energy intensity decline can be expected from sectoral shifts in economic activity, such as from manufacturing to services. The rest must come from improved energy efficiencies in individual energy-using sectors, requiring either technology changes or new technologies' (2008: 532, citing an earlier study of theirs for the claim about sectoral shifts).

All this can be put differently: McNeill has called the recent intensification of the transformation of the environment 'a giant uncontrolled experiment':

> The human race, without intending anything of the sort, has undertaken a giant uncontrolled experiment on the earth . . . Although there are a few kinds of environmental change that are new in the twentieth century ... for the most part the ecological peculiarity of the twentieth century is a matter of scale and intensity ... matters that for millennia were local concerns became global. (2000: 4)

The question from a social science perspective is therefore to identify the consequences of this experiment, and how the potential limits (or disasters) arising from this experiment can be handled or mitigated. Still, in view of seeing these radical discontinuities from a longer-term perspective, it is important not to extrapolate the future from quite recent trends. First, future environmental changes will take a long time, as sceptics like Lomborg (2001) have pointed out against the doomsayers. Second, it is not just the natural laws of the environment that play a role, but people are often capable of 'counter-strategies' (Radkau 2008: 8). However, these possibilities for counter-strategies must also be put into a sociologically and technologically realistic frame.

Technology, social change and the environment

Against this backdrop, how should the transformation of the environment be understood? The 'experiment', as McNeill calls it, is an intensification of human mastery over the physical environment that extends our capabilities, but this mastery also imposes new constraints. To recognize these, we need to take into account both the constraining ('caging') and enabling (an 'exoskeleton') sides of the relationship between technology and social change: one side is how the natural or physical world are transformed by science and technology, and the other is how different parts of social life – social institutions and everyday practices – are transformed by science and technology. The more powerful manipulation of the natural environment by means of technological artefacts can be understood by reference to the realist and pragmatist understanding of science that was presented in the previous chapter. Now it can be added that this intervention in – and manipulation of – the environment is limited by the extent to which the human-made environment has been transformed at any given point, and so also has a social side. As Weber argued, the world around us has become increasingly 'rationalized', and the mastery of the world has led, as argued earlier, not only to an 'iron cage', but also to a more powerful 'exoskeleton'. Thus environmental historians speak of the extension or expansion of the human footprint in the environment.

Yet this expanding footprint, based on technologies for delivering permanent economic growth, is also harnessed to consumerism, and especially the expansion of leisure. Here we can think, for example, of cars and other forms of travel for tourism, or of the increasing size of homes and their appliances, and many other artefacts for consumption – all of which require more energy. In addition to new consumer technologies (already discussed in Chapter 5), it is necessary to add the systems – here, energy – which support them. Historians describe them as 'large technological systems' (Hughes 1987) or infrastructures (which also include transportation and communication) which enable the increasing scale and scope of industrial production and of the service industries – and ultimately a consumerist society. The transformation of the human-made environment is not, of course, purely driven by a consumer culture; much of the extension of the human footprint in the 20th and 21st centuries has taken place because it has been necessary to meet the needs of a growing global population with more powerful agricultural technologies and the technological infrastructures for basic human services. But the balance between transforming the environment to meet growing basic human needs as against raising the ever higher standards of living of the most affluent societies – establishing this balance would require a look into the future with a rear-view mirror that is not necessary for the present purpose: in developed societies, the balance is overwhelmingly on the side that consumerism rather than basic needs account for the bulk of energy needs, while in parts of the developing world it is other way around. Both will continue to contribute to greater technological mastery over and transformation of the natural environment, and both contribute to the way that this exploitation of the environment is rebounding on society. The difference between (to simplify matters) the two parts of the world are in any case trumped by the fact that the effects on the environment are global while the social effects are unevenly distributed. We will need to explore this unevenness further below. However, energy uses are the clearest illustration of these changes, so this chapter can focus on energy from now on.[5]

Energy infrastructures and developmental paths

Energy resources are obviously essential for continued economic growth and rising living standards. But from the perspective of the sociology of technology, as mentioned, these power sources can be conceived of as 'large technological systems' (Hughes 1987), or as an infrastructure of society. These systems, moreover, tend to gain a momentum of their own (Hughes 1994). Energy, as Radkau (2008) notes, only became a 'system' with centralized electricity supplies and the supply of fuel for cars, for example. With this, energy became an infrastructure in the sense that it became an essential support system for the whole of society (recalling the 'massification' discussed earlier). Energy needs are still rising on a global level, but energy has also become more effectively produced and used – as well as cheaper (though perhaps very recently this is changing again) over the course of the past two centuries (Pomeranz 2009a: 17). Thus, 'in the world as a whole, energy intensity [ratio of energy use to GDP] peaked around 1925 and by 1990 had fallen by nearly half. This meant far less pollution (and resource use) than would otherwise have been the case in the twentieth century. But this happy trend was masked by the strong overall expansion of the scale of industry' (McNeill 2000: 316). Hence we must focus not just on the technological system, but on the energy use levels it supports – which, again, is a key resource that underpins economic growth and consumption.

To ascertain the potential limits of these infrastructures, we must look at 'demand' and 'supply' simultaneously, both their past trajectory (Nye 1998) and how they will relate to each other in the future: Maddison estimates that fossil fuels as a percentage of total energy consumption will only drop from 80.4 per cent in 2003 to 76.9 per cent in 2030 (2007: 334, Table 7.13). His forecast is based on projections that global GDP will more than double for the period 2003 to 2030 (using purchasing power parity converters) and that world energy demand will increase by approximately a third during this period. Thus Maddison concludes, for example, that 'proven reserves of fossil fuels are in any case likely to be inadequate to sustain the growth potential of the world economy to the end of the current century' (2001: 366). If this applies to fossil fuels, then climate change complicates their exploitation further, and there is widespread agreement among expert groups such as the Intergovernmental Panel on Climate Change (www.ipcc.ch), the Stern Review of the Economics of Climate Change (2007, updated Stern 2010), and others (Rockstroem et al. 2009) that some urgent remedial actions are needed so future energy needs can be met without serious economic and environmental costs.[6]

A key consideration here is the difference that overall higher incomes will make in the future, since these could either mean that people will be able to pay more for fossil fuels (for example) such that these higher prices might reflect the environmental damage they cause (which could also lead to a shift to non-fossil-fuel sources), as against a scenario without these higher prices and whereby there are higher incomes and thus higher levels of consumption and therefore energy use. These two possibilities anticipate an argument that will become relevant later: if there continue to be higher incomes, then economists would argue that higher energy costs (for whatever reason) can be shifted onto consumers. But such a shift would require either that energy supplies are moved from one source to another, or the costs of depleting resources would need to be somehow incorporated – something which cannot be brought about by unaided (or disembedded, see Chapter 4) markets alone: both would require government action to force people to pay more. Put differently, there is no market-based solution to rising energy needs and their foreseeable limits. (Indeed, arguments are being made that economics as a discipline needs to be rethought to take the depletion of natural resources into account Dasgupta [2009], but this rethinking is not yet widely accepted among economists.) Instead, solutions will rely on government and thus on what governments are empowered to do by civil society (or not, in the case of governments that are less accountable to civil society). Hence we must now turn to the different constraints and possibilities for government action.

To do this, we can examine various socio-political paths and how they have fostered the development of technological and environmental infrastructures; for there is no single socio-political path but several – perhaps with different limits. Thus Pomeranz characterizes what he calls the 'liberal developmentalist project' of the last two centuries as 'the idea that useful knowledge creates power that can be mobilized to transform nature in pursuit of material benefit for people. "Material benefit" is measured largely by levels of individual consumption, and to a lesser extent by the political status and security of a national state in which people are presumed to have a stake' (Pomeranz 2009b: 119). In fact, however, this idea is not 'liberal' so much as Western or modern, and rests on the notion of constant and open-ended material progress that we have already encountered. In any event, Pomeranz wants to argue that although the liberal developmentalist project has been partly adopted in China over the past century, and particularly in the recent reform years, there is also a longer-term imperial and state-centred developmental project that placed greater emphasis on overall economic well-being: under the Qing and Ming, he says, 'the market and economic production were not ends in themselves: they helped facilitate the Confucian good life for as many people as possible'

(2009b: 121–2). This project, he argues, remains partly in place, even in recent years of rapid economic growth (ibid.: 119).

China, of course, may only be one example of a different developmental path, albeit one that has recently partly embraced the 'liberal developmentalist project'. But China deserves highlighting first, because it is an example of where the government may be constrained in different ways in meeting rising energy needs and counteracting environmental constraints, and second, inasmuch as it faces environmental problems related to energy needs on a scale that is otherwise only matched by the United States. Further, China is a clear case where, in relation to energy in particular, the current course of economic growth is unsustainable and radical changes to energy needs and supplies will be necessary in the coming decades (Naughton 2007: 487–504). Finally, it has been argued that consumerism is, if anything, more rampant in China than in the US (Gerth 2010).

Counteracting limits

Against the backdrop that it can be foreseen that societies will come up against energy-related resource limits, how are these likely to be addressed or counteracted? If we think of the most plausible candidates here, they can be put into four main categories: 1) changing patterns of consumer behaviour and of economic growth; 2) changes brought about by social movements and via the influence of expert views and how they influence public attitudes; 3) regulation and intervention by the state (which can be placed in the context of the various socio-political development paths that have just been discussed); and 4) technological innovation. Of these, I will argue, only the last two have a realistic prospect of making a difference, and even these two face severe barriers. Thus I will conclude that change is most likely to come from – or, better, be imposed by – the cage/exoskeleton of the physical environment itself insofar as there are limits to transforming it. But before we come to this conclusion, let us examine each of the four counteracting forces in turn.

1) Changing consumer behaviour and reduced economic growth: social science surveys have claimed to detect 'post-materialist values' in recent decades in advanced societies (Inglehart 1990), but if so, it is difficult to reconcile these values with the continuing emphasis on economic growth and rising standards of living. Moreover, it is not clear how the economic behaviour of consumers is changing in response to environmental concerns since, as Yearley notes (2005: 315), 'many

environmental issues – even if real – are plainly remote from everyday experience so that their reality is not apparent to everyday experience' (Hulme calls them 'distant and intangible' [2009:196] rather than 'remote'). To give just one example: although the social sciences have extensively studied people's choices in relation to residential energy, it is unclear how choices at the individual level, even if successful, would add up to larger changes that can have a significant impact, since the inexorable drive for rising living standards shows no sign of abating.[7]

If on the other hand, we think of economics not as consumer behaviour but as markets, then one key problem, as we have already seen, is that higher prices for energy are unlikely to come from markets themselves (even if they may come from scarcer energy sources driving prices up), but must rather be imposed by government regulation (of which more shortly). The problem here is that economic power is diffuse: it does not reside in any particular actors with bounded powers, but in many dispersed actors (see Chapters 1 and 4). Further, the solution of economists, of putting a price on environmental problems themselves, is deeply problematic, as Yearley (2005) points out, and it is unclear whether it can have a policy impact. For example, even when knowledge about costs to economic growth, including their origins in environmental damage, is available within the scientific community, it is difficult to see how this knowledge can be acted upon. Consider the report by McNeill, who quotes World Bank estimates from 1997 that 'China's air pollution cost the country 8% of its GDP' (2000: 107). But the years since have also seen a considerable worsening of air pollution (Economy 2004), presumably at equal or greater costs to the economy, without much evidence that *economic* actors have reacted to this (though interestingly, there are signs that the Chinese government may be responding).

In short, knowledge or awareness of environmental damage and its economic costs has not led to large-scale concerted policy change. This goes for developed and developing parts of the world as much as it does for less developed ones. Pomeranz points out that 'unprecedented economic growth has created unprecedented economic inequality in the past two centuries. It has also created unprecedented environmental inequalities, with the world's poor far more exposed to unhealthy air and dangerous wastes than the rich, and far less likely to have clean water' (Pomeranz 2009a: 13, see also Beck 2010). At the same time, Roberts and Parks say that there is 'an enormous "worldview gap"' (2007) between the developed and the developing world, with only the former being able to push environmental problems into the future

while the latter focus on current problems (though of course rich countries have more power and resources than poor societies). Here we can
also recall Christian's argument (see above, and McNeill 2000: 480), that
it may be possible to shift profit-making away from the use of virgin or
non-renewable resources: again, it is hard to imagine how the balance
between these non-resource-intensive services and resource-intensive
ones can be shifted, if we think only of the growing global demand for
tourist travel and for automobiles.

2) Social movements and expert ideas: to be sure, sensibilities about
nature and about the mastery of nature have changed significantly.
A shift has been charted even for the period before industrialization,
at least in England (Thomas 1983: 330–3). But it is only recently, since
the 1960s and 1970s, that there has come to be a widespread awareness that the effects of the transformation of nature are destructive. As
Radkau points out, what is new about the environmental movement
since the 1960s is not the romantic attachment to nature and the call
for its preservation, which is much older, but rather the awareness that
'in the long run the destruction of nature would threaten the physical
existence of humankind' (Radkau 2008: 270; see also Radkau 2011).

Yet changing sensibilities and ideologies need to be translated into
action, and for this they need organization and visibility. Political parties and social movements with an environmental agenda have made
considerable strides, but their agendas in relation to lower-intensity economic growth and energy consumption have had a limited impact. As
Keck and Sikkink note, although environmental transnational advocacy
networks have often been successful in framing the debate, it is much
more difficult to translate their agendas into action – unless this coincides with national interests and is not regarded as costly (1998:
203–4). Parties and social movements are competing for attention in
the media, their main avenue for influencing policy. Further, they
are competing with other actors in the public sphere in which environmental issues are being debated and which, following Bauer and
Gaskell (2002), can be conceptualized as consisting of three arenas:
policy regulation, public perceptions and media coverage.[8] Within the
triangle of these three arenas, environmental agendas are continually
being pushed hither and thither by different actors, including actors
with economic interests, social movements (including green parties and
non-governmental organizations) and various expert groups.

The last, of course, provide additional input into the public sphere,
in the form of scientific expertise. Science has been quick to respond

to environmental challenges. McNeill (2000: 340) suggests (based on the American National Science Foundation's estimations) that 'global-change science programs . . . by 1998 . . . amounted to the largest research program in world history'. But scientific expertise, too, needs to be translated into action. One example can be used here to illustrate why it is particularly difficult to translate environmental issues into action: in a recent effort to prioritize different global challenges (the 'Copenhagen Consensus'), social scientists (in this case, economists – though a youth forum panel which did not use cost-benefit but rather human ben-efit analysis did not differ significantly) ranked climate change much lower on the list of priorities than more tractable problems like com-municable diseases and hunger and malnutrition – since the rewards for action seem to be so much higher and more immediate (Lomborg 2004: 605–44; also discussed in Hulme 2009: 266).

The relationship between scientific expertise and society is thus an indirect one: experts need to convince the public via media, and get the public on the side of their views. Or, as Collins (1993a) puts it, sci-entists need allies in society. And even if epistemic communities (Haas 1992) of experts can arrive at a consensus view that sways policymakers; again, these policymakers need to be enabled to take action in the form of policy and regulation. Yet, as we have just seen, policy takes place in a field which includes (according to Bauer and Gaskell) not just public perceptions and media coverage (itself constrained by 'balance', which can be biased, see Boykoff and Boykoff 2004; Boykoff 2011), but also other actors that shape the agenda and include economic interests and NGOs. Thus surveys show that the public remains confused about who should act on climate change (Hulme 2009: 318) and experts who have been in this field for a long time say that the preconditions for political action in this regard remain 'weak' (Speth 2008: 72). In sum, scientific expertise and social movements may be able to shift perceptions, but their combined efforts would need to be complemented by large-scale cultural change in relation to environmental transformation to enable policymaking that can translate this shift into action.

3) State regulation and intervention: to examine the role of states, we first need a sense of the different states or regimes have different pos-sibilities for facing environmental challenges. One widely shared view (Josephson 2004) is that pluralist or democratic regimes are better able to cope with environmental problems than authoritarian ones. This is because their open political institutions are more responsive to the concerns and harms experienced by their citizens. Josephson's

main examples here are Soviet Russia and pre-reform China, and he describes how these and other authoritarian states, by pushing through large-scale technological projects (or the 'large technological systems' or 'infrastructures' discussed earlier) and riding roughshod over the views of their publics, have caused enormous environmental damage.

Yet those who argue like Josephson overlook that these authoritarian states also exercise greater control over environmental issues since they can ignore economic interests or public unwillingness to pay for the mitigation of environmental problems. As we have seen, Pomeranz (2009a), among others, argues that *post*-reform China exhibits at least some continuity with a much longer Chinese tradition whereby the government must be responsive for the care of the environment and its beneficial use for the population. It is also possible that scale is an important factor in the possibilities for political steering. In this vein Radkau suggests that environmental policies are easier in 'small manageable countries' like Denmark and the Netherlands that are also able to achieve a 'praxis-relevant consensus' (2008: 290). In any event, Pomeranz concurs with (and summarizes) McNeill's argument (2000) that 'thus far even fairly democratic polities have been much better at addressing environmental problems that are immediately and locally present (e.g., cleaning up the water that current citizens drink) than at addressing problems like global warming which are diffuse and unfold more slowly (2009: 13). This conclusion fits well with the point made earlier about the opposite situation – whereby the distance and intangibility of environmental problems impacts on *not* being able to mobilize the public behind making changes.

The large-scale steering of environmental transformations in any case invariably involves the state – whether in authoritarian or democratic regimes, or in small or large states. This is because state support is required for the largest technological projects. Even if multinational corporations sometimes also play a major part in these projects, they do this only with state involvement. At the same time, states are also responsible for promoting technological infrastructures that improve well-being and underpin economic growth, and so need to instigate large-scale projects in the first place which rely, to a greater or lesser extent, on public support. Finally, it can be added that large-scale transformations increasingly involve not just single states, but coordination among states, since conflicts over resources crossing state boundaries, increasingly move into the foreground. Yet global governance of climate change faces so many challenges that coordination is only likely as part of a process of long-term adaptation (Deere-Birkbeck 2009), aside from the North–South power imbalance and divergence of interests mentioned earlier (Roberts and Parks 2007).

4) Technological innovation: we have already seen that dramatic solutions will be required for how energy needs are met. One solution could therefore be new technologies. However, all the relevant new technologies would necessarily take the form of 'large technological systems', with all that this implies for creating infrastructures. So, for example, there could be new fuels for vehicles which might overcome the foreseeable constraints on fossil fuel reserves as well as the harmful environmental consequences of their uses. Yet the main obstacle to these changes are not so much the fuels or vehicles themselves, but the infrastructures to support them, which include the logistics of distributing fuels over extensive territories and the large-scale mechanisms for switching from one type of vehicle and its supporting institutions to another (and a further feature of infrastructures that is often overlooked is that they need to be maintained, as Edgerton [2006] points out). Other new sources of energy which are less exhaustible – renewable energy like wind, solar, hydro and biofuels – have been shown to have limited possibilities for replacing non-renewable sources (MacKay 2009).

Similar considerations apply to the solutions to environmental harms that have become known as 'geo-engineering', which also involve 'large technological systems'. These solutions, which would potentially allow much higher rates of energy consumption and mitigate the harms that are produced by this, would nevertheless require even larger 'uncontrolled experiments' than hitherto which, even if they are aimed at 'controlling' some of the effects of an intensified transformation of the natural environment, would introduce further 'uncontrollabilities' of their own. In short, all technological options require large-scale and highly coordinated efforts which are supported by states, like all 'large technological systems' – but perhaps more so since they either have high costs without certain benefits in the case of geo-engineering, or they need to displace existing systems in the case of transport or energy – unlike earlier technological systems when they were initially created.

This chapter has argued that the recent and radical transformation of the environment is encountering limits that rebound on society. This rebounding is caused by the combination of increasing resource scarcity and expanding resource use without at the same time having the capacity – technological, governmental or otherwise – to cope with these combined trends. In any event, enhancing technological capacity would also lead to greater instability and further degradation of the environment. In short, there is a narrowing window of possibilities in the face of a constricting cage. Before going on to spell out implications, it is important to note that these constraints do not necessarily point to global resource wars, which is one prognosis. Wars are one possible outcome (though notoriously difficult to foresee), but the resource constraints that have been described are inescapable with more general consequences that *can* be foreseen.

First, the various limits that have been discussed should not be exaggerated: the transformation of the natural environment, or the extension of the human footprint, is still deepening and will continue to do so. Still, these limits will shape the direction of science and technology, the pace of economic growth (and with it the culture of consumption), as well as state efforts aimed at mitigating them. These limits are also bound to require an extension of technological infrastructures and how they support (among other things) energy uses. It has been argued that when the various forces at play are seen in their entirety, these limits or constraints can be recognized as structural, caused by the relation between technological mastery and the physical world, and that social institutions – and especially states – will be forced to adapt to these constraints.

Put differently, these constraints follow from technological determinism which, combined with a realistic assessment of the countervailing forces which have been shown to have limited possibilities of success, leads to the conclusion that there are structural (technological and environmental) constraints which will shape social responses. These responses to the extension of caging and of our exoskeleton will also produce new constraints of their own. The notion of a cage/exoskeleton thus foresees a condition in which technological mastery will require seeking a steady (or steadier) state in which environmental problems no longer rebound on society on such a scale. The alternative is an unstable state in which the continuing expansion of the transformation of nature produces increasing tensions over growth.[9] Second, it suggests that continued instability is more likely because scientific and technological mastery, as we have seen, is two-edged: further mastery, even if it addresses the obstacles of implementation, will also introduce further problems of uncontrollability. Third, tensions are bound to arise, primarily over economic growth, and produce disputes beyond national boundaries. Yet these tensions will also be diffuse, so that dramatic policy changes are unlikely except when their severity forces responses and coordination. Unlike the patterns in the other chapters in this book, the relation between technology and social change poses problems that transcend the nation-state and the control of disembedded markets – though this obvious difference has not been addressed in social theory. The likely outcome in this case is to produce instability and ultimately demand dramatic intervention by the state and by means of technology.

In short, the notions of caging and an exoskeleton allow us to recognize the shape of the bars of our cage or the limits of how far our exoskeleton can extend, given certain foreseeable technological, environmental and social developments and constraints. The focus here has been on energy because that is the motor of economic growth, and thus a crucial technological and environmental determinant. Yet the argument could equally apply to other transformations of the environment (for example, large-scale harmful pollution unrelated to energy, or growing needs for water, or climate change resulting from energy uses) that run into similar kinds of constraints. Thus a policy implication of this chapter is that there should be continuous monitoring of how the various social forces and transformations of the environment are coupled in a single overall constraining feedback loop,[10] which would also pinpoint the resulting tensions and ways to alleviate them. If this seems to be an overly ambitious idea, the counter-argument is that the scale, scope and complexity of the problem demands such ambitiousness.

The transformation of the environment is beginning to rebound on society in the sense that the increase in the mastery of nature evinces limits. These limits can be expected to change the direction of scientific knowledge and technological innovation, towards a focus on knowledge about these environmental constraints, the problems in overstepping them, and how to reign in economic development. Yet, as argued above, scientific knowledge, while it is intrinsically boundless, faces limits in this case of translating into policy and practice. Thus there is a further tension: only further scientific insight, including social scientific insight, and more effective technologies, can, in view of this rebounding, enable the envelope of human mastery to continue to be pushed – and simultaneously ensure continued sustainable growth. Yet as we have seen, the social sciences are ill-equipped to contribute to understanding these changes because of their fragmented perspectives which overlook long-term trends and large-scale transformations and the structural limits they impose. We have also seen that there are limits to this knowledge, quite apart from this fragmentation – not so much in terms of what we know or can foresee, but to putting this knowledge to use in shaping practice. Social science can therefore play a useful role by (realistically) pointing to its own, quite limited, role in shaping practice, and at the same time also weighing the possibilities and constraints in other courses of action and inaction.

These limits and this rebounding thus expose a further tension between the imperative for continued economic growth, a requirement of a culture of consumption and of political legitimacy – and the constraints that this culture and this source of legitimation will face in the future.[11] While the evidence for a rebounding is still weak as it is mainly on the horizon, it follows from realistic forecasts about growth. How these limits to growth can be counteracted – and what the limits are to this counteraction – are thus also foreseeable. Social science leads to the expectation ('prediction' is perhaps too strong) that only large-scale state-led dramatic intervention directly into the technology–environment relationship is likely to have the necessary impact required by foreseeable constraints.[12] Social science should thus also take the next step of theorizing how this dramatic intervention can come about.

7
Three Cultures

The concept of culture is notoriously hard to define, and it is not clear what falls inside and outside of culture.[1] A definition will be provided shortly, but as mentioned in the introduction (Chapter 1), the argument here is that there are three major candidates for culture in modern society: religion, science and consumption. Religion becomes residual, consumption provides diffuse legitimation, and science (Chapter 5) undermines some parts of culture but strengthens others. That leaves one other contender: political beliefs. These can be subsumed under political change or the political order if they are powerful enough to contribute to divergence (as discussed in Chapters 2 and 3). Yet as discussed in Chapter 2, even in this case it is important to put beliefs such as 'individualism' into a broader context – importantly here, how 'individualism' relates to the state. There is also a broader, anthropological, notion of culture as everyday life. In keeping with the overall argument, however, culture only contributes to macro-sociological patterns if aggregate changes in everyday life can be shown to have wider repercussions.

In sociology, the analysis of culture has come to be so prominent that a new label – cultural studies – has been established as a separate academic discipline (Kuper 1999: 229–32). At the same time, there has been little theoretical focus in this area. Consider, for example, debates about the relation between culture and power: for a long time, the view of 'critical theory' (associated with the Frankfurt School) claimed that culture was the key to elite power in capitalist society. Yet this link has often been challenged (see, for example, Gans 1974; Halle 1993: 193–204) and there is currently no push to reassert such an overarching link. Despite the proliferation of analyses of culture, theories that tie culture to larger social changes at the macro-level are missing.

There are a number of reasons for this absence and the resulting lack of cumulation: one is that the concept of ideology, which was central to the study of culture and engendered intense debates which pitted the evidence for and against the notion of a 'dominant ideology' (Abercrombie et al. 1980) – this concept has largely been abandoned since the end of the Cold War. The field of cultural studies has stepped into this vacuum, but unlike with 'ideology', there is no delimitation in cultural studies of the role of culture vis-à-vis other social forces (though implicitly or explicitly, culture is seen as a driving force). A second reason for the lack of theoretical focus that was mentioned in the introductory chapter is that 'grand narratives' have been roundly criticized in the social sciences. Third, it is not clear what the object of study is: high culture or popular culture? Should science should be treated as part of culture or not?

There is no argument (to my knowledge) – in principle – against the conceptual delimitation of culture, nor any a priori reasons why it should be impossible to identify its main components. However, this does not mean that they cannot play completely different roles: consumerism dominates leisure and functions as a diffuse source of political legitimacy, unlike other political ideologies which mobilize groups towards specific goals. The role of religion is highly contested: opponents of the secularization thesis have put forward evidence that religion continues to matter. What is overlooked here is the absence of a *structural* role for religion, and the limits that are set to this role by politics but also by the entrenched autonomy and legitimacy of science. Finally, science is either (mistakenly, it will be argued) seen as part and parcel of culture, and its role therefore underplayed, or its role is inflated and exaggerated with claims about a 'knowledge' or 'information society'. In fact, as we shall see, science is corrosive of some parts of culture such as religion while enhancing (via new technologies) others, such as the consumption of mediated entertainment.

Culture can be defined broadly, as 'the order of life in which human beings construct meaning through practices of symbolic representation' (Tomlinson 1999: 18). Or we can take Fischer's definition: 'the collection of shared, loosely connected, taken-for-granted rules, symbols, and beliefs that characterize a people' (2010: 10). With such broad definitions, however, it is important to delimit culture to an 'an emphasis on meanings as ends in themselves', thus excluding the meanings and symbols oriented towards instrumental economic ends (though the 'culture industries', which are aimed producing 'meanings' and can thus be seen as the supply side of a culturally or consumer-driven part of the economy) (Tomlinson 1999: 18–19). Meanings and symbols oriented towards political ends can also be included, though without adopting organizational materialism (for example, Mann 2006: 345) – that is, identifying organizational forms in which they are mobilized – it is difficult to see how they translate into political change. This leaves one further approach to culture, which is to focus on the social history – or anthropology – of everyday life. This approach has already been drawn upon in Chapter 2. In this respect, it is possible to establish many patterns, such as the stratification of culture between 'cosmopolitans' and 'locals', based on the networks that people have (Collins 1975: 64–5). Or again, stronger and weaker networks may make some parts of culture more durable and exclusive than others (Fuchs 2001). Even with this approach, however, evidence is needed for arguing that everyday life translates into larger social changes. Against this backdrop, we can take the three components in turn.

Religion

Religion undoubtedly played a structural role as *the* culture of *pre*-industrial societies (Crone 1989: 123–43). Equally clearly, it no longer plays such a central role. There are a number of reasons for this shift. First, the separation between church and state has become ever more firmly entrenched throughout the North, and thus there is no longer a politically sanctioned status of the clergy or an institutional base for churches in education. Hence Chaves and Altinordu can say, in their review of research on the secularization debate, that there is widespread scholarly consensus, among other things, that 'ecclesiastical organizations and elites throughout the West perform far fewer social functions than they used to' (2008: 62). The main exception outside the West are Muslim societies, and according to Norris and Inglehart, 'support for religious authorities is stronger in Muslim societies than in the West' (2004: 154). Yet the reasons for the secularization-proof nature of Islamic religion are well-known (Gellner 1992), even if there continue to be debates about the significance of political Islam (for example, Bayat 2007). Apart from Islam, however, it is important not to confuse the still growing number of believers in parts of the developing world with the pattern in the North: as Norris and Inglehart observe, secularization in rich countries in no way conflicts with the increasing number of people with traditional beliefs around the world since the latter make up a growing proportion of the world's population (2004: 231–9).

It is well-established that religious patterns, such as the Protestant versus Catholic divide in Europe and its settler states, decisively put their imprint on the political trajectories of party politics in the 19th century and into the post-war period (Martin 1974). Yet this influence is no longer decisive if we search for patterns among the most developed societies of the North. Even in the parts of Europe where churches are associated with (Christian Democrat) parties, these parties are no longer mobilized by churches per se. The US is an outlier in regard to the role of religion insofar as it is 'exceptionally religious for its level of development' (Norris and Inglehart 2004: 240). Norris and Inglehart say that it is unclear based on survey evidence why this is so, though they suggest a number of factors which *may* account for it. They also, however, provide indicators for a declining role of American religiosity, pointing out, for example, that in the US (as elsewhere) the poor are more religious than the rich (Norris and Inglehart 2004: 108). And one reason for the continuing role of religion in America that they do not mention is that from a historical-sociological perspective, there are important reasons why a diffuse sense of religiosity, a 'civil religion', has continued to pervade America outside of any of the established churches. As Hall and Lindholm (1999: 92) put it: 'lacking a national religion, America has made a religion of the nation'. Churchgoing and belonging to a faith in the US can thus be seen as more of a diffuse social obligation than a purely religious one.

It is true that the argument that religion plays a declining role would fail if, as some have argued, greater religious pluralism, as in the US, would lead to more competition in the religious marketplace and thus to an increase in religious vitality. Yet this argument has been rejected and found to hold, if at all, only in limited contexts (Chaves and Gorski 2001). Or another type of evidence against a declining role would be if religious groups played a distinctive political role, such as promoting political conservatism. But this popular idea overlooks the fact that religious groups have played both progressive and conservative roles in American society and elsewhere, and still do. As Collins points out, 'there is a mismatch between the prevailing organizational forms of conservative religion – localized mass participation communities – and of conservative economy – the dominance of the autonomous, hierarchic corporation' (1993: 144). It could be added that there is also a mismatch between the promotion of the value of the family in conservative religion and the economic individualism of a major (anti-state and pro-market) variant of conservative politics.

Why, in view of secularization, is religion nevertheless a key component of contemporary culture? First, because outside of consumption, religion is unparalleled as the single largest distinctive extracurricular activity (outside of economic and political activity) in the developed world. (Perhaps sport is more popular, but sport can be subsumed under consumption.) This raises the question of whether religion could also be subsumed under consumption? Clearly not: although some of practices of contemporary resemble a supermarket of spectacular entertainment (Lyon 2000), the origins of religion are distinct from consumption even if religiosity contributed – in a Weberian vein – to consumerism (Campbell 1987). Nevertheless, it may be that religion contributes to civic engagement (Putnam 2000: 65–79), though this type of engagement, again, is bound to take many diverse forms.

All in all, it is hard to disagree with Norris and Inglehart who, after reviewing the evidence from a number of sources, conclude that 'the publics of virtually all industrial societies have been moving toward more secular orientations during the past fifty years' (2004: 235). The two exceptions, America with its civically tainted form of religiosity, and secularization-proof Islam with its politicized religion, should not be put in same category: in America, religion is not only much more diffuse and diverse in terms of organization, but also constitutionally barred from influence on political institutions. Arguably, Islam is thus alone among the major world religions with a unique entwining between religious and political authority.

Finally, and in relation to the criterion that all major components of culture should have a distinctive role, religious culture is sui generis in the modern world. Its social organization is primarily aimed at sustaining itself; it has become one of a number of institutional orders or 'subsystems' of culture or society (Turner 1997: 101–26; Luhmann 1977) from an evolutionary or functionalist perspective. Or, from a conflict perspective, religious cleavages overlap and intersect with cleavages of class and ethnicity – which again, make religion secondary from the point of view of macro-social change.

Consumption

Consumption or consumer culture could be taken to indicate leisure generally, and thus include a range of activities such as sport, media entertainment and art. It might also refer to high and popular culture, both of which comprise of 'taste cultures' 'composed of content or products or cultural items' (Gans 1974: 14). Here the term is used in a broad sense to refer to the open-ended accumulation of goods and experiences for the individual's pleasure. However, consumption must be confined to non-essential needs since otherwise, as mentioned, the culture of producing and consuming basic economic necessities would be included, which would make meaningless the idea of focusing on culture as mainly an end in itself.[2]

The cultural roots of consumerism have been located among an elite in 18th-century England, in an 'ethic' which ultimately became a much wider 'spirit' of 'permanent consumption of "novelty"'(Campbell 1987: 94). *Mass* consumerism, however (as we have seen in Chapter 4), only became possible after the American 'system of mass production' (Hounshell 1984) was in place in the US in 1920s and its implementation enabled via a 'control revolution' (Beniger 1986) that provided a feedback loop between producers and geographically dispersed consumers. Once in place in America, it was exported to Europe as part of an 'irresistible empire' (de Grazia 2005).

Why, in view of this export, not consider consumerism as the ideology of (American) capitalism? One reason is that consumerism has taken hold not just in the capitalist world, but also far beyond, most notably in China, which has been ideologically anti-capitalist (see Chapter 8; Gerth 2010). Consumerism has been embraced in modern societies by peoples across the world under a variety of political regimes and throughout the Western world and beyond (Stearns 2001). Put the other way around, there are no societies in the modern North that fall outside the ambit of consumer culture. Further, the legitimacy of all modern states has come to rest on policies that provide the continuous economic growth that is necessary for a steadily expanding supply of consumer goods and services (Gellner 1979: 277–306). Hence, if consumerism is an 'ideology', it can be so only in the sense that it provides a diffuse functional underpinning of all societies rather than one which is imposed on certain groups or which is contested. Yet such an understanding of belief surely comes closer to a Durkheimian notion of culture rather than ideology.

At the same time, consumerism must also be located at the level of everyday life as well as on the level of society as a whole. Schulze (2005), instead of treating consumerism as ideology, treats contemporary society as an 'experience society' in which an 'aesthetization of everyday life' takes place and there are 'markets for experiences'. For Schulze, life has become an 'experience project', a constant search for meaning in the accumulation of novel experiences. This points to the sui generis nature of consumer culture and further clarifies why consumerism cannot simply be reduced to a political or economic ideology: the cultural roots of the spirit of consumerism can be located in religious currents, but as with Weber's spirit of capitalism, once in place, it exercises an inexorable hold over society (the possible exception is Durkheimian 'deviance' in the form of anti-consumerist refuseniks).

Consumerism is dominant nowadays: it dominates high and popular culture, it has industries (advertising, marketing) to promote it, it outweighs all other cultural activities in terms of hours spent (for example, in the uses of information and communication technologies, see Chapter 5; Schroeder 2007: esp. 104–16) and geographically it is almost universally spread around the globe and popular among all social strata. Even if consumerism is costly and deeply embedded in society, it is also shallow and easily exportable. Mann says that 'the most successful globalisation is of cheap cultural consumption goods: clothing styles, drinks, fast food, popular music, TV and movies. The cheapest products are available to almost all the world's population, including teenagers with low incomes, generating a global youth culture' (2001: 9). But he adds that even if this form of consumption penetrates micro-interaction, it does not necessarily translate into macro-politics.

Science and technology

To say that science and knowledge obviously constitute a core component of culture in modern society seems obvious at first, but as we shall see, it is in fact anything but. One of the main theoretical arguments about the role of science in modern society has been made by Weber and his followers (as we saw in Chapter 5). Weber regarded science as the driving force in the 'rationalization' of the world whereby modern culture becomes 'disenchanted'. For Weber, the implication of rationalization is encapsulated in his statement that 'culture's every step forward seems condemned to lead to an ever more devastating senselessness' (1948: 357). In this view, rationalization displaces culture.

Weber's 'disenchantment' thesis of an 'iron cage of rationalism' must be amended since it has been pointed out that a 'rubber cage' (Gellner 1987: 152) is a more appropriate metaphor for the consequences of rationalization: 'rubber', because the consumer devices that surround us in daily life, designed for user-friendliness, in fact leave people plenty of room for human comfort and individuality, rather than imposing cold and impersonal strictures on our lives.

There is, however, a paradox about science and culture (again, this has been partly addressed in Chapter 5): on the one hand, science dominates modern culture, if by this we mean that it displaces religion and other all-encompassing faiths. Yet on the other, science transcends culture since it is universal; true or valid regardless of any particular cultural or social context. This is one reason why science is separate from the rest of culture, the latter (if we recall the definitions provided earlier) being intrinsically bounded to the practices of particular places and times. A second reason why culture and science are distinct is because science is cumulative, which cannot be said in the same way (or perhaps in any way) for the rest of culture.

To be sure, science has its own rituals of legitimation (award ceremonies, status hierarchies, public displays in museums and the like), but these only to serve to highlight that cultural rituals are not essential to the core of science, which consists of intervening in the relation between objects and their representations (Hacking 1983). Something similar applies to technology, though in this case the scope needs to be widened from the objects of science to the transformation of human-made environment by means of artifacts. This provides a link to consumer culture, since much technological innovation is aimed at – and harnessed for – providing an endless stream of novel artifacts for consumption. Hence, too (as mentioned in Chapter 5), the intertwining of culture and technology in a 'technology-culture' spiral (Braun 1994), whereby novel artifacts provide increasingly mediated experiences of cultural consumption, which in turn generate ever more needs for novel artifacts, and so on in a never-ending spiral.

Information and communication technologies such as the telephone and television, but also the automobile and other forms of transport for leisure, provide the most visible examples of this 'technology-culture spiral' in contemporary culture (as discussed in Chapter 5). They also exemplify how technology impinges on the rest of culture insofar as it leads to an increasingly technologically mediated culture. (But note: outside of culture as delimited here, as an end in itself, technology also obviously has functions outside of its role in culture, such as in transforming work practices.) Science is thus separate from culture (as cumulative knowledge) and at the same time mediates culture (in the form of technologies of consumption).

The vagueness surrounding science has meant that a number of other concepts have been put forward to account for this component of culture: For example, 'knowledge', as in the 'knowledge society' (Stehr 1994). Yet this concept only makes sense if we ascribe a powerful role to experts who wield knowledge, which applies not just to this (scientific) part of culture (howsoever conceived) but also, for example, to political and economic professionals (Perkin 1996). Similarly with the 'information' or 'network' society: in this case, changes are driven by the economic mode of production rather than by the cultural 'superstructure' (Castells 2000). Finally, why not 'enlightenment' rather than science? The problem here is that the 'Enlightenment' is a historically bounded period which, if extended into the present day, would become rather vague and contested.

Science is therefore paradoxically outside of culture and yet, in the form of technologies for mediating cultural experiences, partly shapes it. Science clearly cannot be reduced to other social forces (since a realist and pragmatist definition of science has been used, and it is argued that science is cumulative), and yet it has a pervasive influence on modern culture, a major one being to displace religion from its erstwhile dominant role. Science thus can also not be reduced to ideology; it legitimates no particular social arrangement, but nor does it receive legitimacy from any specific social arrangements – unless it is the self-referential one whereby the open flow of scientific communication must be guaranteed (Fuchs 2002).

Patterns of culture

At this point, three arguments are needed to consolidate the claim that these three cultures dominate modern societies: one is to show that culture is distinct from the rest of social life, and in particular that it can be separated from the economic and political orders – or, to put it in the language of alternative theoretical approaches, that culture has become differentiated from other institutional orders or sources of power. The second is to provide grounds for giving priority to the three cultures described above as opposed to other contenders. And finally, it is necessary to identify the different patterns of the three contemporary cultures and their relations to each other and to social development generally. Let's take each of these in turn.

The three cultures have become separate from the other two orders (economics and politics) and from the rest of social life in several ways: first, it is well-documented historically that leisure/consumption has only recently become a separate activity, segregated into a separate part of the day or the weekend and into private households or specialized venues, perhaps for many in the developed world only during the course of the 20th century (Collins 2000: 37).[3] Science has also developed separate institutions and specialized personnel, and the boundaries of valid knowledge have become well-policed. Finally, religion used to be quite closely related to politics and integrated in everyday life, but nowadays only certain groups engage in worship, and public engagement is limited to special occasions and places.[4]

In addition, however, it might be asked how all three components put together, or how a separate order of culture, can be separated: isn't it the case that all aspects of society are, in some way, cultural? Yet putting the point this way immediately allows us to recognize its limitations: sociology must have a means of differentiating culture lest the whole of sociological analysis becomes cultural analysis (again, perhaps this is unproblematic in cultural studies).

Still, there are several other candidates which are often treated under the rubric of (political) culture or ideology: nationalism, political ideologies in the sense of beliefs, and social movement ideologies. There are several reasons not to conflate these with culture: one is that, as Mann has argued (1999), social movements must nowadays achieve their goals via the state. Put the other way around, ideological movements need the capability for mobilization and resources in order to achieve their aims and become organized as political actors. This applies, for example, to the politics of 'cultural identity', which are among the social movements that seek to have claims for social rights recognized by the state. Public opinion (Stearns 2005) belongs mainly to the political order rather than to culture, whereas cultural heritage may be part of a high or popular culture – although it is not clear how to operationalize such cultures within social science. And as mentioned, Gellner (1993) has argued that nationalism – national culture – can only be held in an 'ironic' way once the transition to nation-state has been made.

If we now turn to the relations between the three components, I have argued that science undercuts religion, but otherwise, the three cultures are largely independent from each other. Only religion is a declining force. The authority of science is undiminished, as is the contribution of technology to mediating consumption. Consumerism may be unsustainable, but as yet, as we have seen in Chapter 6, the rebounding of the natural environment has not yet led to a general diminution of consumerism. One notable feature of modern cultures is thus how little conflict there is between them. The same obviously does not go for contemporary political beliefs or ideologies (if the term is preferred). But religion (again, Islam is an exception), science (not as a whole at least, there are some areas of contentious science such as stem cell research or climate change) and consumerism seem to evince little strain in society or social movement mobilization which mobilizes culture for conflict.

The limits of culture in everyday life

One criterion for the importance of cultural forces, as mentioned earlier, should be the extent to which they translate into everyday life – on the ground, as it were. Culture is typically seen in this way in social history or historical anthropology. However, in these terms, among the three cultures, only consumerism penetrates deeply into the everyday life of most people in modern societies (though, as mentioned, the penetration of consumerism may be shallow in the developing world). Science is not part of everyday life for most people, so that even though its own separate institutions have become global (Drori et al. 2003), it is precisely the autonomy from the rest of society which also ensures that it has exclusive authority within the realm of knowledge and expertise. Religion *does* enter into everyday life, but only among ever smaller groups within pockets of the population (barring the US exception in the North). Moreover, these groups are heterogeneous and even where there is a single group which dominates nationally, the beliefs of this group have no general authority or legitimacy, though again, this is not to deny that there remains a more widespread penumbra of religious belief in modern culture.

If, on the other hand, culture is preferred as 'grounded' or embedded, in the way that anthropologists might prefer – culture as a 'way of life' that is instantiated in everyday practices – then this does indeed prevent an 'idealist' or 'free-floating' account of culture. Yet 'ways of life' are also elusive in relation to social development: they are bound to local practices and routines rather than to contributing to large-scale changes. Mann's conception of ideological power can illustrate this contrast (where ideology can stand in for culture for the moment): Mann has argued that ideological organization comes in two types – sociospatially transcendent, and immanent morale (1986: 23–4). An example of immanent morale is the fighting spirit of troops in battle, or the solidarity among groups of protesters. This type of ideological power reinforces existing power relations, maintaining the cohesion among (for example, military and political) groups. Sociospatially transcendent ideological power, on the other hand, is exemplified by the world religions and by political ideologies, providing an appeal beyond existing boundaries and promoting a vision beyond everyday realities. Yet in the latter sense, fascist and communist ideologies are perhaps the main examples of new beliefs that have embodied this kind of power in the 20th century. This makes it possible to contrast culture on an everyday level as against the mobilizing nature of cultural forces: if they reinforce the solidarity of socio-spatially bounded groups in the manner suggested by Mann, then their effects are also bounded or limited. If, on the other hand, culture is transcendent in the manner of the world religions – culture as transmission on a grand scale – then we need, in addition to everyday practices, some institutions beyond everyday life which facilitate this transmission. These institutions are available and have been described for the case of global scientific institutions, and they can also be evidenced (though with relatively reduced authority) for some contemporary religions. Consumerism, the culture which, of the three, is strongest on a widespread scale in everyday life, lacks these institutions except for the cultural industries which reinforce it. Consumerism thus illustrates that this part of culture is closer to what anthropologists have in mind; mundane everyday practices, rather than ideologies (including in some cases religious beliefs) which can be mobilized for transcendent political goals, for what 'ought' to be rather than what 'is' (Snyder 2006).

This contrast between mundane culture as against non-everyday cultural mobilization largely overlaps with the contrast between the sociology of micro-interaction in everyday encounters as against the macro-sociology of comparative-historical patterns. Culture can be analysed on both levels, but the link between micro- and macro-sociology is notorious for its elusiveness. One potential bridge between the two in this case could be surveys, whereby individual daily practices or values that people espouse are aggregated on a large scale and over long periods, covering post-industrial societies, for example (Inglehart 1990). Such value shifts over the course of time can then be integrated with comparative-historical analyses. Yet even these will need to be put into analytical categories which make sense of culture as a whole (for example, in Inglehart's case, a shift towards 'post-materialist' values has arguably failed to become established as a general way of characterizing contemporary culture, or to result in larger patterns of social change).

Cultural movements on a larger scale, vis-à-vis the state, can contribute to lasting political change. Collins' summary of Mann's position is one way of identifying an overall pattern: 'In the late twentieth century and into the next,' Collins says, class conflict movements as

> forms of group mobilization have not been superseded, but they have been joined by many more movements: race and ethnicity (construed in various ways), gender, sexual preference, student, environmentalist, animal rights, anti- and pro-religious movements. All these operate under the umbrella of the overarching, society-penetrating state, and thus make an appeal to the same large public consciousness and to state enforcement of their demands. (2006: 30–1)

At a larger level still, we can find wider geopolitical (in this case, ideological) or 'civilizational' shifts (but in this respect, it is preferable to speak of converging or diverging cultures, as here). Yet after the Cold War, as we have already seen (in Chapter 2), Americanization is also waning, and culture is bound to adjust to a shift away from a hegemonic American empire towards a culture embedded in a multi-polar world (or a multi-power-actor-civilization; Mann 1986: 533–8).[5]

Why these three? Why not four, or a larger number? After the three that have been described here, it is difficult to think of other components of culture that come close in scale, scope and significance. The question can be put the other way around: why not none? Is culture really a separate order of society? Yes, because, as argued earlier, it has become differentiated out as a separately functioning order, as a set of effective institutions, and (occasionally) as a separate source of structural change (or power, if that is preferred). All three cultures, or components of the cultural order, can be shown to be effective (or becoming less so), but in different ways:

- Religion is residual; its encompassing and dominant power is fading, even if it has the deepest (in the sense of the most long-lasting) roots among the three;
- Science transcends the other two orders, and society as a whole, but affects only nature in the first instance (and is only affected by it, in intervening in the natural world). It is not integral as a world view to everyday life for most people (apart from scientists and researchers), but can nevertheless claim to be the exclusive source of legitimate or authoritative knowledge in society;
- Consumerism has become dominant, shows no sign of waning (except perhaps at the margins, in 'deviance'), and although it interacts with the political and economic orders (driving economic growth which is required for political legitimacy), it is still becoming further entrenched throughout contemporary societies.

We have already encountered culture in terms of convergence (Chapter 2). Convergence has been part of modernization theory, with an implicit idea about the West (or Western culture) versus the Rest (implying zero-sum or direct competition). Postmodernism supposedly put an end to these ideas, with multiple cultures without any 'grand narrative'. But if cultures are multiple, it must be possible to say how many multiple modernities (Eisenstadt 2000) there are. And if several, this should not rule out contrasting specific cultures in their converging or diverging contexts (as in Chapter 2). Whether science and consumerism, wedded to an expanding economy, is reaching limits in terms of environmental constraints, has been addressed in Chapter 6. Religion has declined for some time. Everyday life offers a cultural redoubt, of interest to social historians and anthropologists, though within these limits there is ample scope for consumer activity, including a niche market for the consumption of academic interpretations of culture.

8
Modernization and the Politics of Development

This chapter will examine two countries outside the Global North: China and India. The main reason for doing this is to ask to what extent the arguments about developed societies that have been made so far also fit here – or if these two depart from them in ways that shed light on globalization and other processes that have been identified in previous chapters. There is another reason for examining these two cases, which is that they are bound, by virtue of the size of their populations and economies, to affect countries elsewhere, and so offer important models of development. In any event, the question of how developments outside the global North mirror those within it – or not – will be central here.

The puzzle of China

Social change in China presents a puzzle for social theory: given that China is rapidly emerging as a first-rank economic power, how should we understand its developmental trajectory, since there are as yet few indications that China is moving towards pluralist democracy. This is a puzzle because it means that China does not fit modernization theory, which requires (among other things) an advance beyond authoritarianism. Moreover, even if modernization theory is regarded as outdated, China does not fit other macro-level theories of social change either. For example, it sits uneasily with the distinction between a democratic North and other kinds of regimes in the global South – with none (such as 'post-communist' regimes) that jump out as fitting the Chinese regime (since it is not clear if China is 'post-communist'). Other categories, such as emerging markets or BRIC countries (Brazil, Russia, India, China) are also unhelpful as they relate only to economies. Finally, even if China fits with the theory or idea of economic globalization in the sense of the spread of capitalism – and whether China is capitalist is still debated, as we shall see – this still leaves the puzzle of where it fits into the global political landscape.

Before we tackle this puzzle, it can be recalled that modernization theory was tied to the debate about 'the rise of the West'. We shall see shortly (this has already been discussed in Chapter 1) that this debate has recently taken a new turn. However, one reason why 'the rise of the West' and 'modernization' theory are no longer so central in social theory is because they have been displaced, as already indicated, by the concept of globalization. But is it possible to limit globalization to the spread of capitalist economies? This would imply an economic determinism which leaves out questions of political development. A recent alternative in these debates has been to posit 'multiple modernities' (Eisenstadt 2000). Yet this way of thinking about modernization or globalization only raises a new issue (as mentioned at the end of Chapter 7), which is that even if these multiple paths lead to more than a single Western modernity, it is still necessary to spell out how many other routes to modernity (or globalization) there are. It is therefore important to gauge whether China constitutes or falls within one of these 'multiples'.

A way forward here is to decompose the puzzle of China into several interconnected questions: first, how does China relate to 'the rise of the West'? Second: how has China managed to become capitalist (or has it?) and embraced a market economy but failed to develop democracy? And finally, is China a stably non-democratic society? And if the answer to the last question is affirmative, should China be relegated to a category of post-communist transition economies with quasi-authoritarian states, alongside Russia and its ilk, or as a lasting and peculiarly Asian regime form? To tackle these questions, we shall have to briefly trace China's political and economic developments – or rather, for brevity's sake in covering a vast area – review the debates about these developments. Before we do this, it will be useful to start with a broader question, which arguably needs to be settled before the others can be addressed, which is about the extent to which China's modern history was influenced by outside development, as opposed to ploughing its own autonomous path.

Openness to external influences

To start with, then: how open has China been to influences from the rest of the world? This question has been addressed from a long-term perspective by Osterhammel (1989) who argues that this relationship has undergone a number of cycles of openings and closings, political and economic: its incorporation into the world of states and into the world economy. He traces a number of these cycles – sometimes overlapping, sometimes separate – up to the Cold War period, with its closing off of China within the Communist 'bloc' of states and its shutting itself off from the world economy. Without going into the details of his analysis of the earlier cycles, the economic 'closing' during the Cold War combined with being part of a communist bloc has been followed by the reform period in which the economy has been increasingly open.

Importantly for the present argument, Osterhammel points out that the course of Chinese history has never been primarily determined by external forces. The 'highest point of influence of foreign powers on the economy and society of China' (1989: 403; cf. xiv) was the Sino-Japanese war 1937–45, but even the Chinese Revolution which was fermenting at that time was primarily caused by internal forces (ibid.: 405). Furthermore, China has also hardly had any ambitions to enter the world-political stage or expand its influence into other parts of the world (ibid.: 7), at least not until quite recently. The implication is that, unlike with other countries whose developmental path has been decisively influenced by colonization (India obviously falls into this category), this does not apply to the relatively isolated Chinese path up until the post-war period.

In any event, the 'opening' to the world economy during the reform period has been accompanied by an at best tenuous political opening. It can be noted that one reason that 'openness' matters more here than elsewhere (from a comparative perspective) is not just because of the potential outside political influences that might have influenced China if it had been within the colonial orbit. This relative isolation is also important because of China's economic relative and (almost) absolute decline during the 19th century, during the height of colonialism, and relatively recent economic resurgence, all the while pursuing a distinctive political path. This makes China into an important 'test case' for the much debated association between capitalist economic development and political democratization (Rueschemeyer et al. 1992; Acemoglu and Robinson 2006) and political freedom (Friedman 2005: 314–18): here we see the waxing and waning of economic growth, almost independent of colonialism, as well as rapid economic or capitalist growth, without the democratization or freedoms which are often thought to be associated with it.

Fast forwarding to current debates within China, it is interesting to note briefly how the debate about 'openness' is engaging – not just academic social scientists – but also Chinese intellectuals more broadly. Fewsmith (2008) has dissected the various camps among intellectual elites in China, including those that are critical of 'the West' and of globalization (which, in turn, can be divided into nationalists and left-ists) as well as pro-Western and pro-globalization liberals. The influence of these camps has varied, as has their relation to the state and to an ever more educated political elite. Despite a diversity of viewpoints, Fewsmith concludes that 'after a quarter of a century of looking to the West for inspiration, one senses that there is a turn inward to find a more "Chinese" model of development . . . because ideological issues are not as contentious as they were and because the political elite seem more aware of their collective vulnerability to political breakdown, elite politics appears to be more institutionalized than in years past' (2008: 275–6). Put differently, a more cohesive and independent (vis-à-vis the West) worldview may be emerging. Against this background, we can return to the path of 'modern' or 'global' Chinese development, starting with economic development.

The pattern of the Chinese economy

The key starting point in positioning China in relation to the 'rise of the West' and globalization is not so much in ideological debates, but in debates about the pattern of Chinese economic growth. Here there has been recent challenge to the established view by Pomeranz (2000), who has argued that Chinese economic growth only diverged from the pattern of the West in the 19th century, much later than had been previously thought. This argument (discussed in Chapters 1 and 4) has important implications for the 'rise of the West' since it suggests that the decisive European take-off also only occurred during the 19th cen-tury, far later than the distinctive early modern European path that had often been regarded as the baseline for debate.

An extensive discussion about when to locate the European and Chinese growth take-off is not necessary here because, even if Pomeranz's arguments are accepted, there is still a divergence between China and the West. However, an additional implication of Pomeranz's argument (not spelled out by him) is that the European take-off was only possible on the basis of European colonial expansion in the 19th century, and so not 'self-propelled', and that the underdevelopment of colonized powers can possibly be explained by this external factor. This argument could have an important bearing on China – if China was among the countries that had its economic growth adversely affected by the impact of being subject to the colonial powers.

Now there is of course an enormous literature on colonialism and its economic impacts. However, as Bryant points out, one decisive fact for arguments about the rise of the West is 'the preponderant role of intra-European trade, which dwarfed in volume and value all colonial exchanges. Even for England, the world's foremost trading nation by 1800, commerce beyond the bounds of Europe contributed less than 10% of the English total' (Bryant 2006: 434; reviewing recent work by economic historians). He goes on to say that 'it was not the comparative cheapness of colonial resources that provided Europeans with their decisive advantage, but the astounding productivity gains that came with mechanization and the factory organization of labour' (ibid.: 434), again, referring to the extensive work by economic historians on this issue.

As for China, the 19th century, the period of European or Western take-off, was a period of a steep relative decline: from 32 per cent of world GDP in 1820 to 9 per cent in 1913, and from 90 per cent of per capita GDP in 1820 to 40 per cent of the world average in 1913. Even if in absolute terms, China 'declined only slightly . . . this was the period when the economies of Europe and the United States surged ahead' (Naughton 2007: 42–3). In short, and summarizing how an enormously complex debate bears on the argument made here: China, without being 'underdeveloped' by Western colonialism, nevertheless (independently) did not experience the economic take-off experienced in the West.

Take-off and leap ahead

At this point we can again jump ahead to the present day since, as we shall see, the 'decline' of China in the 19th century is also relevant to the explanation of current Chinese economic growth. Anderson has neatly summarized the three schools of thought on the question of how the recent Chinese economic take-off relates to the past – or not:

> 1. millenial legacies of the imperial past . . . knocked off course for over a century by foreign penetration and internal disorder . . . now reverting to its natural position in the world; 2. contemporary high-speed growth is the product of the belated integration of China into a world capitalist economy from whose formation it was historically

absent'; 3. the key to China's economic ascent lies . . . in the Chinese Revolution . . . central to this legacy were the creation of a strong sovereign state for the first time in the modern history of the country. (2010: 91–2)

We will come back to all three, but before we do so it is worth adding that Anderson points out that the first explanation is popular among historians, the second among economists, and the third among sociologists.

There are of course some who think that China's economic growth will soon become a train wreck. Perhaps. All that can be done in regard to this imponderable is to rely on available prognoses. Maddison (2007: 340) says that the economies of Asia as a whole will continue to make gains in the coming decades relative to other parts of the world in per capita GDP and share of world GDP, producing more than half of the world's GDP by 2030. He also forecasts that China will become the world's largest economy by 2018, ahead of the US and India in second and third place, and its per capita income will be near a Western European level of 1990 by 2030 (ibid.: 338–40). In short, China's recent 'rise' indicates that it is joining the advanced economies – if it has not done so already (at least outside the rural hinterland).

What has caused this recent take-off? Naughton points out that the central state has traditionally played a relatively small role in China. There was only a thin layer of state civil servants compared with Europe and government extraction of GDP was only 2–3 per cent in imperial China, far less than in Europe (ibid.: 39). By the mid-1950s, however, the level had risen to more than a quarter of GDP (ibid.: 60), comparable to Western states. Yet in the recent reform period, the state has – at least in fiscal terms – retreated: 'During the course of more than 15 years of reform, China's fiscal position had eroded significantly, dropping from 33.8% of GDP in 1978 to only 10.8% at the low point in 1995' (ibid.: 101). Even if since then there has been some 'recentralization', it is also the case that – at least during the first phase of reform – there was a laissez-faire type retreat on the part of the central government.

The reason for the shrinkage of fiscal capacity can be delved into a bit further: a key reason why this shrinkage occurred is because the state did not have the capability to raise taxes to begin with, at least at the national level: the central government did not really raise taxes (most taxes were raised by local government) or have an effective tax policy until the late 1970s.[1] If government revenues and expenditures since then came close to the average for developing countries (at above

30 per cent), nevertheless they dropped again with the reforms, more than halving by 1994. In short, a dramatic reduction in investment and social expenditure by the early 1990s was recognized by the leadership as leading to a crisis. Thus a drastic tax reform was implemented in 1994, since when revenues and expenditures have crept up to between 15 and 20 per cent by 2005. The share of revenue going to the central government has also more than doubled as part of the same 1994 reform, though central government then passes much of this back to local government to spend, giving it greater control. The Chinese system of government spending is thus still comparatively decentralized compared to India's, where local government spends approximately the same proportion of GDP as in China (around 14 per cent), but the central Indian government spends roughly the same proportion again, while the Chinese central government spends much less (4.8 per cent in 2005). Again, in short: there is a small central state in China, plus a more powerful one locally.

To be sure, the state played a major role in economic development, but a distinction can be made between industrial development and the development of capitalist markets. Andreas (2008: 126) notes that although China has had a market-based economy for a long time, the capitalist sector (relying on wage labour) was 'tiny' up until the Communist revolution. After 1949, the state tried to build on what was only a modest industrial base that was restricted to the private sector and to certain regions – and to widen it (Wong 1997: 181). During the 'big push industrialization' of the Communist regime (1949–78), 'consumption was squeezed' and 'most investment went into industry, and of industrial investment, 80% went into heavy industry' (Naughton 2007: 56). More recently, there have been changes towards a fully fledged capitalist (services or consumer-led) economy, even if many have continued to work in public-sector employment in urban areas and as family units on non-privately owned farms until the early 1990s.

Still, there are different views on the state's role in very recent economic development. Whyte says that although the Chinese state and party have actively shaped economic development, this has been done to 'promote markets, foster competition, and stimulate market-oriented incentives, rather than to try to pick winners and favor investment in those firms with the closest ties to the state' (2009: 383). Andreas argues differently, saying that the state does want to promote 'winners' and that the close connection between state and capital at all levels means that 'it is difficult to distinguish, conceptually or empirically, state development strategies from the pecuniary interests of government officials and large-scale entrepreneurs, who are linked by myriad family and other ties' (2009: 140). Similarly, Shambaugh says that there are close links between the party and those in private business such that the party can be seen as providing the necessary political protection for business (2008: 114). Note, however, that the latter arguments are not so much about the state's role vis-à-vis economic or capitalist development, but more about the extent to which the political elite benefits economically.

It is clear in any event that China has gone from being one of the most equal societies at the onset of the reform period to being among the most unequal in recent years, surpassing the US in inequality (at least in 2006, according to Andreas 2008: 136; 2009: 256). This inequality is a result of reform towards capitalism, though Whyte has argued (2010) that the Chinese population does not feel aggrieved by the last quarter century of rising economic inequalities – and no more so than the populations of other countries (though other countries, of course, may have more of a political outlet for grievances about growing economic inequalities, and economic change may have been much slower there). Hence he calls the idea that the legitimacy of the regime is threatened by growing inequalities 'the myth of the social volcano'.

Whyte's findings about attitudes to social inequality are based on surveys. Equally or more important are the changing fortunes among different classes in China 'on the ground', which have also been documented. So, for example, the ethnography of a village (now town) by Chan et al. (2009) charted how reform transformed lifestyles in an area experiencing rapid economic growth in the Pearl River Delta on the Chinese coast near Hong Kong. This transformation has increased inequality, and especially the growing contrast between a prosperous middle class and a much larger grouping of poor migrant labourers. In any event, this transformation has made the region into a powerhouse of capitalist production. More broadly, Dabringhaus comments that with the strengthening of the capitalist economy, 'the spheres of the political and of private life have become separated' (2009: 234) since the state no longer tries to mobilize the masses or interfere in everyday life. Others (such as Perry 2011) have argued that mass mobilizations for social goals still take place, having shifted their techniques and aims but also evincing a continuity with the period of Mao's rule: perhaps nowadays these mobilizations are no longer aimed at industrial transformation but rather at stimulating faster and more evenly spread growth.

How capitalist?

Whyte (2009) argues that Chinese development is paradoxical because it has been economically successful even though – despite reform – it has not implemented secure private property rights.[2] He says that there are a number of factors which can explain this paradox, including the long-term political stability of the country and improvements in social conditions, but also the short duration of Communist rule (only one generation, and lasting from 1955–78, unlike the much longer Soviet period) and the ties to an extensive Chinese diaspora. Still, it seems as though the institutionalization of legally guaranteed private property, often seen as a precondition for the emergence of modern Western capitalism – or disembedded markets, as here – has not been necessary in this case. Guthrie argues that although business organization might not fall under the definition of private enterprise, nevertheless Chinese firms operate like capitalist firms (2006: 130). Whether a liberalizing capitalism should be regarded as positive or negative (steeply rising inequality has already been noted), and how it has affected rural and urban China differently during different periods of reform, can be left to one side here.[3]

Formally free wage labour is also often seen as a necessary precondition of capitalism, and in this respect China has gone some way towards a contractual labour force, though the large-scale movement of labour from rural to urban areas has been dramatic but also politically fraught. Guthrie (2006: 61) notes that the growth of labour contracts has entailed the end of lifetime employment, with all that this implies for workers' entitlements. Lee writes: 'market reform in the past quarter of a century has entailed a transition between two systems of labor regulation: from one based on social contract to one based on legal contract' (2007: 22). On this basis, workers have begun to resort to legal means to assert their rights (at least in some parts of China), paralleling the assertion of rights by an emerging middle class of home owners who feel they have been wronged or that their interests are not being protected.

At this point it can be added that since the onset of the reforms, economic power has devolved from the centre to a more local level. Guthrie argues that decentralization of economic decision-making, not just in the private sector but also in devolving power from central government to the local level, has been one key to the reforms (2006: 116, 126; 1999: 30). At the same time, this decentralization has arguably become problematic. Wong, for example, says that the decentralization of economic power, with local government gaining control over but also being dependent on local industries, has become a particular problem for the Chinese state (1997: 188–90). We shall need to return to this point shortly – when dealing with the new challenges facing the state.

Finally, in terms of the education of business and political elites, too, China has moved towards a market economy. As Andreas (2009) shows, the political elite in China has come to consist of technocrats with an education and worldview that are similar to those of Western business elites. Importantly, this was not the case until the reform period, since before that time, elite education was riven with ideological conflicts over communist ideology. Nowadays, in contrast, elite education like that at China's top Tsinghua University (the university studied by Andreas, and attended by many of the most prominent Chinese political leaders today) is ideologically similar to the education provided in the bastions of Western capitalism – its business schools – even if this elite has also been able to insulate itself from a Western capitalist political agenda as well as from forces from below (Andreas 2009: 255). As for the political elite, Pieke (2009) argues that party cadres are still educated to maintain the esprit de corps of an elite leadership, though he also details how the content of this training has moved in a technocratic direction even as this leadership remains ideologically committed to what Pieke calls 'neo-socialism'. Yet although Pieke contrasts 'neo-socialism' with the recent 'neo-liberalism' of the West, he also says that it (albeit cautiously) embraces marketization, which many (including this author) would see as 'capitalist' (or as part of the disembedding of markets, as discussed in Chapter 4) rather than 'neo-socialist'.

Political domination and legitimacy

How should China's political regime be classified? Lupher (1996: 10–13) argues that China fits Weber's ideal of patrimonial domination, whereby political elites use their position of unlimited power to gain economic advantage. China (like Russia) created a new political elite by mobilizing the masses during its revolution and has therefore since been able to keep control of centralized power: 'Unlike their imperial predecessors, the communist state penetrated society more deeply, established its authority on an unprecedented scale, and effected the structural transformation of China and Russia' (ibid.: 302). This transformation continues to leave its mark on the reform period: 'On the one hand, China's post-Mao rulers made economic development and the raising of mass living standards their key goal and the means by which they legitimated their power, and on the other, they backed up their hold on power with expanded and modernized coercive mechanisms' (ibid.: 257). The implication for Lupher is that even if the reform period has also unleashed decentralizing forces, which has meant yielding more power to regional and local levels, the communist state's structural transformation ensconcing a centralized political elite seeking legitimacy via growth is likely to continue to shape Chinese society.

At the same time, an increasing reliance on economic growth for legitimacy raises an important issue about democratization: if the Chinese population has supported a single-party state as long as it has produced high rates of growth, then failing to maintain this growth could pose problems for the prospects for democracy and stable rule (but recall Whyte's 'myth of a social volcano'). The issue – or question – then becomes whether the elite and/or the population would have too much at stake in continuing to enrich themselves such that ceding power or causing political upheaval are unlikely. In fact, it may also be too simple to tie economic growth to democratization: first, because China has had a different political tradition from Western democracies. Mitter points out that 'ordinary Chinese did not, for the most part, identify with political parties in the way that mass populations did in the west over the decades in the late nineteenth and early twentieth centuries' (2004: 105). This is an important comparison because in the West, despite different paths, one important commonality among Western democracies is that they have had competing parties engaging mass support while in China, success in mobilizing mass support has been achieved by a single party.

Second, the absence of political contestation can be seen as part of a longer tradition whereby, as Wong puts it, the political order was 'imposed through moral suasion, provision of material benefits, and coercion' (1997: 200). Wong says that this is not just paternalism, it is also 'a kind of "contract"' whereby, 'should the state fail to meet its obligations, peasants have a "Mencian" right to rebel' (1997: 195, after the Confucian philosopher Mencius who elaborated the idea of a 'Mandate of Heaven' which is the basis for the legitimacy of the ruler). Thus, during the 20th century up to the reform period, in times of upheaval, 'when claims were made in China, they were more likely to be substantive rather than procedural, to be claims on what leaders do rather than claims about how decisions are made or who is to make them' (Wong 1997: 257). Hence there is a continuity between Confucian and Communist state policy in creating an egalitarian society that provides for the people's economic and social well-being (Wong 1997: 194; see also Pomeranz 2009b: 121–2), in addition to political order and stability.

Third, as we have already seen in relation to fiscal and economic policy, there has always been a stronger divide between centralized and local power in China such that this divide cuts against a straightforward idea of democratization: there is a long-standing Chinese pattern whereby the central state is regarded as protector against corrupt local officials. And although this tradition was arguably not maintained or overridden from 1949 up to the reform period, the current regime is once again trying to counteract local corruption. But if the centre wants to legitimate itself by reference to maintaining the order and stability that are required for continued economic growth, as Shue argues, then this strategy may undermine itself insofar as the centre also tries to make local officials more accountable:

> If, as they wave the banner of more democratic accountability, these central power-holders perpetually resort to calling into question the dependable legitimacy of their own agents in local offices around the realm, to the point eventually of hollowing out the perceived legitimacy of those agents, they may ultimately rob themselves of the capacity they require to govern China's modern society in the orderly manner they so desire. (2010: 60)

In short, there may be increasing tensions between central and local power.

Thus Chinese political leaders are nowadays aware of the need to adapt and perhaps to democratize. Wong notes that whereas the party was once the source of status and power, nowadays, this has been replaced by economic power (1997: 201). Communist ideology has been almost entirely replaced by the ideology of economic growth, and the main question has become to what extent this growth reflects on the prowess of the party. At the same time, as Shambaugh (2008) has noted, the Chinese regime has been deeply worried about the almost complete collapse of communism around the world, and has spent much effort learning the lessons from this collapse and figuring out how to keep itself in power.

Nascent democracy?

Against this background, we can ask: are there signs of democratization in China? If democracy means competition between parties at the national level, it seems not: Shambaugh says 'the CCP [Chinese Communist Party] has zero interest in transitioning to a Western, or even an Asian, democratic system of competitive parties. Its principal goal is to strengthen its rule and remain in power as a single ruling party . . . the CCP is definitely *not* awaiting the eventual collapse of its power' (2008: 3, see also McGregor 2010). Without oppositional parties which would provide a legitimate vehicle for political input, in China this input is therefore often expressed through political protest. Whether this protest is squashed or not depends on organizational strength (if it seems stronger, the likelihood of squashing is greater as there is a bigger threat to the government), but it may also be a sign of strength on the part of the government, as Wasserstrom (2010: 80–1) puts it, 'to allow people to let off steam without responding harshly'.

Much has been written about the extent to which the Chinese leadership is or is not taking political expression outside of formal political institutions into account. The internet, for example, is often thought to provide an alternative channel for public debate. Zhou Yongming (2006: 16), who has traced the media and politics from the 19th century to the present day, says that the internet has led to 'an expanded space with more refined control'. Even more important than the public sphere of the media, perhaps, is how the political leadership has responded to the public, and it seems that this response has waxed and waned. Shambaugh says that 'there are some indications . . . that the Hu Jintao-Wen Jiabo regime . . . is incrementally expanding the "democratic space" between state and society . . . Hu and Wen are not opening the system to competition, but they are definitely attempting to increase consultation' (2008: 180). Indeed, the concept of 'consultative Leninism' has been applied to contemporary China (Tsang 2009), though apart from increased consultation, it is not clear why 'Leninism' should be preferable to 'authoritarianism' since, as noted earlier, the ideology of communism has been almost entirely abandoned.

As we have seen, the tradition whereby the central government is seen as responsive to the needs of the population dates back to imperial times. This Confucian tradition, however, has also been used to argue that a Western democratic form of government is foreign to China and unnecessary. Yet the idea that a tradition of two millennia of Confucianism is incompatible with Western political ideals, which is promoted by some Chinese leaders themselves (and by scholars), can be dismissed on the grounds that Taiwan has become a pluralist liberal democracy and at the same time more strongly Confucian than the mainland (Mitter 2004: 307).[4] The most likely scenario for China is therefore a continuing problematic role of the party, including its efforts to maintain order within the political system: 'the existing situation of atrophy and adaptation will coexist and be sustained indefinitely' and there is not a 'zero-sum situation' between the two (Shambaugh 2008: 177). At the same time, as Goldman (2005) argues, among a small minority of Chinese intellectuals and other groups, there is a growing assertion of citizenship rights, creating an expanded public space, even as the authorities have kept this within strict limits.

Spectacle and predicament

This is only a brief summary of the debates about Chinese economic and political development, but this chapter has concentrated on globalization and modernization and the puzzle of the convergence or divergence of the political system. As we have seen, China has converged on a capitalist or market economy and even if it is incomplete, the direction of travel is clear. A number of caveats are needed, but the main one is the absence of private property, which is a key remaining difference to Western market or 'capitalist' economies – though it is unclear how fundamental this difference is.[5] Disembedded markets require commodified exchanges, including of private property, as well as firms maximizing profit. It seems that, in this respect, 'capitalism' adds little to free or disembedded 'markets' – except ideological backing, which is also less pronounced and more contested in China, as lip service is still paid to anti-capitalist ideology.

As for political divergence or convergence, it may not be possible to solve this puzzle, but at least the various options can now be laid out more clearly: it seems obvious, but also misleading and unhelpful, to say that China is a unique case. It is not a 'transition' society, like other ex-communist societies, yet China is also (as we have seen) orienting itself to avoiding the mistakes of the collapsed communist societies. There are also parallels with other authoritarian Southeast Asian states like Singapore and Malaysia (Slater 2010). And while we have seen that the idea of continuity with a uniquely Asian political culture as responsible for China's patrimonial or paternalist style of rule is misleading, there are similarities with other forms of 'benevolent' paternalist rule and there is growing support for reviving Confucian ideals.

An important additional consideration is that unlike during the end of the Cold War, there is no competing imperial power to put pressure on the regime's material (including military) or ideological resources. The single remaining geopolitical hegemonic power, the US, is no longer able to exercise the same threatening force, as it is declining. Nor does China have its own imperial ambitions or global geopolitical interests which might put a strain on its regime, unless we count relations with Taiwan (though here the trajectory seems to be one of rapprochement) or other near neighbours. Unlike in the former Soviet Union (Collins 1986: 186–209), international competition is therefore unlikely to delegitimize the regime or cause it to collapse since geopolitical conditions have become more favourable to China since 1989–91 (Li 1993).

Thus a stable reformist path seems likely if China's economy continues to grow. While China had an attempted 'velvet revolution' moment (Tiananmen Square), the differences with other formerly communist states are important: the states within the Soviet bloc engaged in cultural and liberalization first (*glasnost*) and economic reform only came after political collapse. In China, economic liberalization has already largely taken place, and now adaptation continues to be the main political direction (unless external forces intervene). To be sure, the transformation of the economy has created inequalities and these have been 'politicized' insofar as government officials benefit. Yet, as Whyte (2010) argues, compared with the pre-reform period, when economic injustice was seen as resulting from political power, current inequalities, even if they have grown, are regarded as a result of how people take advantage of economic opportunities.

The challenge to social theory that we are left with is whether China's single-party state in this case (among other, though different, authoritarian and/or less economically developed, cases) is sustainable. The state in China has already played the role, as elsewhere, in promoting economic development, first state-led, and then towards a more hands-off market or capitalist economy. Other 'modernizing' or 'globalizing' developments, such as a consumer culture, have become well-entrenched (Gerth 2010). The potential inability to maintain rising levels of consumption has become a threat to democracy, but also a potential boon to democracy if prosperity creates a constituency demanding a political voice. In terms of culture, the role of religion, too, is increasing. Goossaert and Palmer (2011) chart its course in modern China, including its Confucian and non-Confucian (Buddhist, Christian, Islamic and various sects) varieties. It emerges from their account that while the government has recently even partly encouraged religious expression, it has also forced churches and sects to register (and thus be controllable). At the same time, the regime has kept religious expression that does not submit to this official control within strict confines.

The main question is therefore how China's rulers will be able to adapt to the tension between continued economic advance and lagging political development. From the perspective of social theory, then, it is useful to distinguish between seeing China as a 'spectacle', as an interesting specimen among regimes that will somehow need to transition away from authoritarianism towards elements of more democratic rule, as against the 'predicament' that Chinese party leaders find themselves in – in making this transition in the face of economic pressures on the one hand and demands for political input on the other. Tensions will remain in practice for this latter project, but researchers have the possibility to conceptually contain them within the fixed bounds of theory: authoritarianisms continue to coexist in the modern global political order, but they also need to adapt to it. How they do so is one question, but not one of multiple modernities: even if they remain non-pluralist democracies, modern pressures for political input from civil society (again, in the wider sense of 'people' elaborated in earlier chapters) remain. Put differently, the process of adaptation to modern conditions, to participating in a modern global political order of input from society, is ongoing. Whether there will be other paths therefore remains to be seen in practice, but there is no need for positing a 'developmental alternative' or a 'multiple' modernity from this theoretical perspective.

India's fragmented populist democracy

India is the world's largest democracy. Along with China, it is also regarded as a recent economic success story. Yet its democracy is so corrupt and manipulated by elites that some have called it a sham democracy (see Guha 2007: 749; Varshney 2000: 13). And in India more than half the workforce still depends on agriculture for its livelihood (Adeney and Wyatt 2010: 195). There are a number of perspectives on India's modernization and its shortcomings. Corbridge and Harriss provide a useful summary of these perspectives when they contrast the ideals of the founding of independent India (in 1947) with the subsequent realities. The 'invention' of independent India, they say, entailed aspirations to 'sovereignty, democracy, socialism, secularism and federalism'. They also call these 'the mythologies of rule in Nehru's India' (2000: 22), and argue that India has fallen short with regard to all five of these modernizing aims. They mainly blame elites – business, religious, rural landowners and populist politicians – for the failure to reform India in the direction of these aspirations, a Gramscian theory which ascribes hegemonic power to conservative and conjoined political and economic elites. Nevertheless, they also regard these modernizing aims as still hanging in the balance.

These developmental aims will need to be weighed here in relation to the three (political, economic and cultural) modernizing patterns discussed in earlier chapters. As with China, a further question needs to be raised: to what extent has India pursued a Western or Northern model of development – or charted its own course? An important perspective that will have to be addressed in relation to the idea of an independent course is that of post-colonial theorists, who argue that the modernist project imposed by colonialists and Westernizing Indian elites (such as the Nehruvians) has not enjoyed popular legitimacy. This argument partly overlaps with Corbridge and Harriss's view that the five modernizing aspirations have partly failed to take hold. But post-colonial theorists regard this partial failure not as a shortcoming, but instead suggest that on the ground, there are various local cultures that continue to resist the hegemonic project of modernity. Their view is that spaces should be opened for the local everyday lifeworlds of Indian culture (and perhaps other cultures) against the secularizing impulses and centralizing political tendencies that are imposed on this culture from the outside. These are arguments on behalf subaltern populations ('subaltern studies' is another label closely associated with post-colonial theory) asserting 'difference' against homogenizing elites and their universalizing rationalist culture and governance.

Post-colonial theory raises a more fundamental challenge to the idea put forward here that it is possible to identify various paths within the modern world, both converging and diverging – but within certain comparable bounds. Post-colonial theory challenges this idea, as does the theory of multiple modernities encountered earlier. Ultimately, as with the question of China's lack of democratic governance, it will be necessary to see how India fares in relation to the three modernizing and globalizing processes that are central to the analysis of the North and West here: does India represent a departure from these? In fact, I shall argue, the key to understanding Indian social development is not how elites have failed to realize modernizing paths (as both Gramscians and post-colonial theorists argue, though the former see this as negative and the latter as positive), but that there has been a lack of differentiation which continues to entrench religious groups politically and political groups economically (the latter, as we have seen, is also characteristic of China). This lack of differentiation is a greater barrier to social development within a globalizing modernity than the 'project of modernity'.

To make this argument, it will be necessary to examine the legacy of colonialism in India and the extent to which the modernizing project after Independence is continuous with this legacy. The post-Independence period can be further broken down into the periods dominated by the prime ministerships of Jawaharlal Nehru and Indira Gandhi, from 1947 until 1977, with Nehru associated with relatively stable rule by the Congress Party while Gandhi shifted to populism and began bypassing the Congress Party. From the late 1970s until the early 1990s, politics became more fragmented as parties began to appeal for support on the basis of religious and economic cleavages. During the period from the early 1990s to the present, this fragmentation has continued, but economic policy has also shifted away from a strong role of the state in the economy towards liberalization. In charting this course in greater detail, we can begin with a discussion of the impact of colonialism, and then take political, economic and cultural developments in turn.

Colonialism to independence

There is a growing consensus among historians that the legacy of British colonialism was mixed: the state and administration that the British created and left behind was weak and industrial development was only fostered during the tail end of British rule in the interwar period. How is it then, Kohli (2004: 232) asks – like many others – that 'a relatively small group of Cambridge and Oxford-educated elite civil servants – backed by a significant armed force – could run a colony the size of India'? Part of Kohli's answer is that:

> British India saw no close, systematic cooperation for economic growth between the colonial state and private producers . . . this limited role of the state, in turn, came to be reflected not only in the design of tax collection (mainly indirectly) and expenditures of the limited public monies (most on financing an army and bureaucracy), but also in the limited types of activities that the state learned to master and in the generalist nature of state bureaucrats. (2004: 232)

The main legacy of colonial rule could thus be said to be an administratively weak state which had not penetrated deeply into society, even if the small elite Indian Civil Service has continued to provide a cohesive but thin national layer of rule to the present day.

While it is agreed that the British did little actively to develop the Indian economy, a separate but related question is: did colonialism actively underdevelop the Indian economy? This question, it seems, has become too sweeping for historians and sociologists: the British economic take-off did not, as has sometimes been argued, depend on empire (Mann 2012: 17–57, esp. 33), even if India was the 'Jewel in the Crown'. Tomlinson says that 'the chief reasons for economic stagnation were usually present before the British arrived, remained in place during their rule, and have stayed there after its ending' (1993: 21). How the British helped or hindered agriculture and industry depends on which period and which sector is being considered (argues the historian of South Asia, Michael Mann [2005: 291]).

Colonialism nevertheless had a rather skewed effect on social development, if we consider the following combination of circumstances before, during and after colonization: in the 17th century, India had been more urbanized than Europe (at 15 per cent of the population), while at independence India's level of urbanization was practically unchanged at 17 per cent (Mann 2005: 279, 310). But although the British colonial government was confined to urban centres and preoccupied with trade, 'tax revenues had been derived almost exclusively from agriculture' (Mann 2005: 145). However, as Mann also points out (2005: 99), 'although British rule was experienced on the village level, if only through taxation, this was only indirect, as many peasants in the mid-20th century did not know that the country had once been under British colonial rule'. He also notes that 'living standards of the rural population in the 18th century were higher than those in the mid-20th century' (2005: 99). In short, colonialism affected large parts of the country and of the population, but often indirectly.[6]

Kohli (2004) has argued that it was precisely the weakness of the state that the British left behind, its lack of autonomy and failure to foment a cohesive elite, that prevented Nehru's rule and subsequent governments from being able to carry out its developmental agenda. The state in India, as we will see shortly, is fragmented, since party elites in particular have been captured by different societal interests. From a comparative perspective, Corbridge and Harriss say that the 'developmental state' under Nehru differed from other East Asian developmental regimes insofar as it came to depend on clientelism:

> In the 'Tiger' regimes . . . the historically dominant classes were all in disarray, in the context – variously – of military defeat and the outcomes of armed revolutionary struggles, so that their ruling elites did not need to compromise with local power in the way that was characteristic of the Congress regime in India. (2000: 58)

Added to which, of course, is that the Congress regime was forced to compromise because it was democratic. All of this can be put differently: after Independence, the strength of the Congress regime lay in the legitimacy derived from its nationalist struggle (though without a military struggle against colonial rulers); its weakness was the lack of a coherent state apparatus that reached down into society. That has remained its weakness ever since.

From successful to populist democracy

During the final phase of colonialism, as nationalist opposition grew from the late 19th century onwards, the colonial regime kept this opposition at bay with a 'divide and rule' strategy. It yielded a limited amount of power to different groups, for example, providing greater scope for Indians to elect Indians at the level of local government, or favouring Muslims over Hindus when this was opportune for maintaining stability. This strategy of selectively incorporating some groups was combined with repressing the more militant groups and strengthening the grip at the center. Again, this meant that there was only a weak state left when democracy came soon after Independence in 1947. Congress, the party which could derive legitimacy from its anti-colonialist struggle, won the first elections in 1951–2.

Yet despite the state's weakness, India's democracy has been a success in comparison with other post-colonial regimes that started off democratically but slipped back into authoritarian rule because of elite schisms. In India, in contrast, Congress stably dominated politics at the national level until 1977 because of the number of seats it gained in parliament. As Adeney and Wyatt (2010: 31) note, while neither Congress nor any other party has ever had an outright majority of the votes, the legitimacy of the democratic system has never been challenged. Still, the 1980s marked a shift, with no single party winning a majority of seats since 1989 and the number of parties contesting national elections rising steeply, from 36 in 1980 (or 35 in 1984) to 113 in 1989, 209 in 1996 and 230 in 2004 (ibid.: 70, 128). Many of these have a narrow regional base. Congress – and during the 1990s the Hindu-nationalist Bharatyia Janata Party (BJP) – have been the main national rival parties, and both have alternated with a third or more share of the seats in parliament (even with a lower percentage of the votes) since the late 1980s (ibid.: 141). So the overall workings of the democratic system and its legitimacy in India have remained intact, and coalition governments have by and large also been stable (the state-of-emergency period

1975–7 is an exception). What has changed is the way in which parties have become increasingly populist, deriving support from religious and ethnic groups.

This shift has been interpreted as a decline in the appeal of Nehru's statist (or socialist) and secular agenda, or the loss of the authority of the traditional religious elites (Brahmins) which traditionally dominated politics at the national and local levels. But the shift can also be seen as the result of Indira Gandhi's and her son Rajiv's increasing turn to populism because she (and Rajiv, who stepped into her shoes after her assassination in 1984) did not receive support from a fractured party. Indira Gandhi abused the Constitution by implementing emergency rule, but to compensate for a lack of party support, she also made promises especially to poorer voters that led to the massive subsidies, especially for rural voters (though these subsidies often wound up with well-off landowning farmers), that have remained to this day.

With the continued weakening of Congress and growing party competition, Corbridge and Harriss say that:

> elections became more and more like populist referenda, or plebiscites on the performance of particular leaders. And lacking local organization, come election time, politicians had (and still have) recourse, often, to 'black money' derived from the informal and illegal economies in order to fund their campaigns. This, in turn, contributed to the criminalization of politics. (2000: 77)

But they don't want to go as far as Bardhan when he says that 'some of the new social groups coming to power are even nonchalant in suggesting that all these years upper classes and castes have looted the state, so now it is their turn' (2010: 154; Kohli 2012: 172 says the same for Uttar Pradesh), and who characterizes India as 'less a legislative or deliberative democracy than one of popular mobilization' (Bardhan 2010: 145). In any event, there is a consensus that while the form of India's democracy remains, much of its substance has drained away.

Economic development and social divides

As we have seen, Nehru's agenda of state-led economic development had limited success. For the decades after independence, Bardhan (2010: 85, 86) and Kohli (2012: xi) differ in how they describe state and bureaucratic elites as not being particularly pro-business or not being anti-private enterprise during its early statist decades when there was much socialist rhetoric, but by the 1980s, the political culture had in any case become increasingly market-friendly. Growth continued to be sluggish until the 1970s (some would say the 1980s), but picked up with liberalization in the 1990s.[7] Liberalization has mainly consisted of removing bureaucratic obstacles to business (the 'licence raj'), reducing tariffs, and privatization, but the reasons why it was initiated are still debated. Corbridge and Harriss argue that it was primarily a product of problems in financial markets, rather than being related to any fundamental problems in the real economy of the agricultural or industrial sectors (2000: 121), though Kohli (2012) argues that its roots can already be found in the business-friendly culture of the 1980s. Equally debated are the effects of liberalization apart from growth. The period of the greatest poverty reduction was from the late 1970s to the early 1990s. Corbridge and Harriss cite official estimates according to which 'rural poverty declined from 51.2 per cent of all rural households in 1977–8 to just 20.6 per cent in 1990–1 . . . a similar decline has been charted in urban India' (2000: 147). We can already note the similarity with China, where poverty reduction also made the greatest gains until the period of market liberalization (though it needs to be added that the poverty reduction in both countries also coincides with the Golden Age of economic growth in the global North and beyond, so the coincidence with Nehruvian socialism and Maoist communism is not straightforward).

Kohli (2004, 2012) argues that the Nehruvian legacy of support for heavy industry and discouragement of foreign investment lingers, though there are considerable variations between the Indian states in this regard. But an even greater divide remains between the rural and urban Indian economies: although the contribution of agriculture to GDP has fallen from over half at Independence to less than 20 per cent, over half of the workforce (as mentioned at the outset) still depends on the land for a living (Adeney and Wyatt 2010: 195). Most of the export growth has taken place in the information technology services sector, though this sector employs only a tiny fraction (0.25 per cent, according to Luce 2011: 48) of the workforce. And outside of the (heavily subsidized) agricultural sector, most employment in India is in the 'informal sector' (a term popularized by Harriss-White 2003), economic activity that is not taxed and not regulated by the state. Estimates of the number of workers in the informal sector are upwards of 80 per cent and in some cases more than 90 per cent and it has been said that it contributes 60 per cent of GDP (Adeney and Wyatt 2010: 193; Corbridge and Harriss 2000: 168). Finally, it should be noted that this part of the labour force does not consist of an undifferentiated mass of slum dwellers, but is rather highly structured and self-regulated and well-organized (Mann 2005: 333, Harriss-White 2003).[8]

The economy thus remains mixed: wealthy landowners have not been dislodged in the countryside, state-owned companies continue alongside the private sector, labour is largely informal and regulated locally but has little power at the level of national politics, and there are large variations between states in terms of the success of their economic policies. Meanwhile, despite accelerating growth rates, the gap between rich and poor has widened. Bardhan says that 'in contrast with inequality of *outcome* (reflected in income or consumption), inequality of *opportunity* (reflected in inequality of education, land distribution, and social inequality) is much greater in India than in China' (2010: 131). In other words, although China's gap between rich and poor has become much larger than in India, where consumption is still constrained for a large part of the population, the earlier successful intervention of the Chinese state in agricultural redistribution (though the disastrous social costs also need to be factored in) and deliberate levelling in the education system had a stronger effect, reaching down into contemporary Chinese equality of opportunity, compared with India's efforts (though there are examples of Indian states, most notably Kerala, which have had much greater success than other states in promoting wider access to better education).

Cultural conflict and diversity

One possible explanation that immediately comes to mind when comparing India's and China's economic fortunes in recent decades is between the homogeneity of the Chinese population and the religious and ethnic heterogeneity that have fragmented Indian politics, often resulting in violence. Perhaps a diverse population could be a factor in preventing a more even society-wide sharing of economic growth, as has been argued for developed societies (Alesina and Glaeser 2004), or rather, this heterogeneity has prevented the formation of a cohesive elite in India which, in turn, entails a lack of consensus about developmental goals. Yet there are conflicting views about the impact of religion and ethnicity on democracy: on the one hand are those of Snyder, who argues that voting without strong civil society institutions being in place exacerbates religious and ethnic cleavages (2000: 294). Others (Manor 1996, is an example) have argued that the many cross-cutting ethnic, religious, caste and other cleavages in India lead to mutual accommodation. Snyder's argument is relevant to the continuing threat of violence. Yet even if Manor's arguments point to the continuing stability of democracy, populism has also meant that the state is fragmented because the interests that support parties have pulled the state in different directions. Some commentators therefore say that India is closer to an Anglo-American pluralist model rather than a continental European model of state–society relations (Rudolph and Rudolph 1987: 252).

We will return to the relation between political fragmentation and economic and social development in a moment, though it is difficult to draw any conclusions for a period as brief as the recent decades of liberalization. Nevertheless, it is important to put continuing conflict concerning certain regions and groups into a larger context of overall political stability. Some of the conditions for religious and ethnic violence have persisted throughout India's post-Independence history, especially on the periphery: strife in Kashmir, tensions with Pakistan and conflicts in separatist border regions. At the same time, the fact that the Muslim population is a minority (9.99 per cent in 1951, 13.43 per cent in 2001; Adeney and Wyatt 2010: 54) prevents this group from posing a threat to the Hindu majority. Metcalf and Metcalf note that Muslims have not had a party to represent their interest in post-independence India, and while Muslims traditionally supported the secularism of the Congress Party, this support waned in the increasingly fragmented political climate since the 1990s (2002: 276). Nevertheless, Muslims have also developed organizations outside of formal parties, just as Hindu nationalism has developed non-party organizations such as the Sangh Parivar 'family' of organizations associated with the BJP.

Debates over the link between politics and ethnic factionalism continue. Varshney's analysis of ethnic violence between 1950 and 1995 has revealed that riots have been highly concentrated: 46 per cent of deaths in this period occurred in just eight cities (which constituted 18 per cent of the urban and 5 per cent of the country's total population) and only 3.6 per cent of deaths were rural (Varshney 2001: 371–3; see also Mann 2005: 475). He argues that places with stronger networks of civic engagement have been able to contain rioting and violence better because they serve as bridges between Hindus and Muslims.[9] The future of ethnic politics thus hangs in the balance: the main aspect that needs to be taken into account here is how the waxing and waning of ethnic conflict exacerbates the populist politics that have already been described.

Apart from national and violent politics, the influence of caste and of religion is to be found to a large extent at the local level. Caste should certainly not be ignored, though it plays a much stronger role among rural as opposed to urban Indians.[10] Religion is nevertheless not confined to rural or lower-class groups: Fuller and Harriss describe how Hindu businessmen in Chennai 'have become increasingly assertive about celebrating their religion publicly', at the same time that they do not see this as anti-Western or as anti-American: they 'display none of the anxious antipathy towards the west and its capitalist lifestyle found in many less-favoured sections of the Indian middle class' (2005: 227). Intellectual or 'cosmopolitan' elites, who were the carriers of Nehru's socialist ideals, have become more hostile to America and its foreign policy than to the British erstwhile colonizers, and yet they have mixed attitudes to American culture and favour an English-speaking education for their children (Bayly 2007: 14, 113). These mixed attitudes can be attributed partly to the connections with large Indian diasporas in the US and Britain.

Caste and kinship exercise a powerful influence in everyday life and, as mentioned, in the informal sector of work. But 'most agricultural work . . . is not specifically assigned to particular castes' and 'almost all occupations in modern sectors of the economy are caste-free in the sense that members of any caste can take them up' (Fuller 2004: 14), and even those who ascribe a powerful role to Hindu practices in everyday life nevertheless recognize that Hinduism is becoming a more distinctive or separate part of social life (Fuller 2004: 257–8; 288–9). And although it used to be argued that Hinduism imposed an all-pervasive ideology of hierarchy on traditional Indian society (Dumont 1970), nowadays, despite the continuing influence of religion on politics, a strong political thrust to rectify past inequalities has also taken hold, though with mixed success – as we shall see.

A fragmented state?

India's culture is diverse and continues to influence politics, but we can now see that it is more important for theories of social development that the state has remained weak and not autonomous enough from popular pressures (including when cultural groups organize for political ends). Nor have political elites (including those representing different cultural groups) engaged enough with landowning and business elites to effect social change. Kohli says that 'central to this incapacity is its fragmented authority, characterized by both intraelite and elite-mass schisms and ruling coalitions that are generally multi-class' (Kohli 2004: 286). The period of Congress Party dominance and the attempts at socialist reform were ultimately 'captured', and 'more egalitarian ambitions, such as land redistribution and the capacity to tax the agrarian sector, were undermined' (ibid.: 261). Thus India has become a 'fragmented-multiclass state': 'trying to reconcile political preferences of both left and right in the context of a fragmented state, the Indians failed both at a radical redistribution and at ruthless capitalism-led economic growth' (ibid.: 238). Kohli has made a similar point more recently (2012), arguing that despite the strong performance of the Indian economy, the poor are being left behind and governance is weak because leaders are oriented only to the short-term goal of getting elected. But while populist pressures dominate the electoral agenda, he also notes that policy-making is increasingly confined to narrow political and economic elites.

Yet these elites are also fragmented, and this contrasts with the cohesive elites among Asian tigers: 'the tightly knit links between business and officialdom of the East Asian type were difficult to forge in India, where elite fragmentation in an extremely heterogeneous society and the exigencies of populist electoral politics make such tight links politically suspect' (Bardhan 2010: 86). 'In India,' he says, echoing Kohli's arguments,

> the large proportion of the poor in an assertive electorate has not always succeeded in focusing the attention of the politicians on the sustained implementation of programs to alleviate mass poverty or to deliver basic services such as education and health care . . . in a more homogeneous and less conflict-ridden society, China's leadership can be more decisive and purposeful in pursuit of economic reform and long-term strategy. (Bardhan 2010: 126)

However, in China, with a strong state without democracy, the danger is of 'going off the rails' (ibid.). Kohli (2012) argues similarly, though he also points out that there are major differences in how elites have been able to govern well or poorly in different Indian states, and whether they have been reined in by well-organized interest groups or more interested in pursuing their own short-term electoral or economic interests.

Is the elite fragmented, or do the popular forces from below make it so? India is unique inasmuch voter turnout is higher among the poor rather than the rich, the less educated rather than the more educated, and the rural rather than the urban population (Varshney 2000: 20). Also, voter turnout for national elections is consistently high (60 per cent and even higher for local – village – elections) and elections have also become more free and fair over time (Banerjee 2011). The thrust for increasing equality has therefore come from two sides in India: on the one hand, the constitution's reservations (which could also be labelled 'affirmative action') for lower castes and so-called Other Backward Castes/Classes (OBCs) in government positions, bolstered by various other affirmative action programmes at the state level and going all the way down to the village level. On the other hand, parties have catered to and come to rely on supporters from a variety of lower caste groups, and provided them with the benefits of affirmative action in return. It is therefore not just lower castes that have exerted this pressure, and it would be strange to see the thrust from the electorate as only benefitting political elites. To be sure, Brahmins have tried to keep hold of power (especially in certain parts of the country), and politicians of all stripes have materially benefitted from the cronyism that gaining power in government brings. But this is not just a 'passive revolution' of the elites, a clinging on to power by ruling classes that have not been displaced, as elsewhere, by political pressures from a large middle or from working classes, as Corbridge and Harriss (2000) among others argue. Rather, it is a spoils or patronage system in which the spoils accrue not just to bosses or local baron clients, but also to political elites who keep themselves in power by channelling advantages and resources to various groups – while broader infrastructural social development suffers.

Varshney calls the populists 'a new plebeian elite', and says

> their most striking national success is the addition of an extra 27 percent reservation for the lower castes to central government jobs and educational seats. In the 1950s, only 22.5 percent of such jobs were reserved, and more than three fourths were openly competitive. Today, these proportions are 49.5 and 50.5 percent, respectively. At the state level the reserved quota has been higher for a long time in much of southern India. (2000: 7)

However, there are also limits here since 'affirmative action concerns only government jobs, not the private sector. In 1992, of the nearly 300 million people in the work-force, only 20 million were in the public sector' (ibid.: 18). Varshney goes on to point out that the fear among commentators, that the shift of political power downward (to the political elites that have instigated this affirmative action, and its beneficiaries among civil servants) leads to poor quality or less democratic government, is largely misplaced, especially as there is widespread agreement that southern India (where this change was implemented much earlier and has had a much deeper effect) is governed better than northern India. If we combine the gains by lower castes in political and educational positions with the large proportion of economic spoils that go to corrupt politicians rather than to their intended destination for infrastructure and economic development, it is easy to see why the notion of a 'weak-strong state', put forward by Rudolph and Rudolph (1987) even before the period of liberalization – strong in being governed by plural interests, but weak in terms of penetration of society – remains an apt description. Nevertheless, these plural interests, according to Rudolph and Rudolph, are 'demand groups'; they are more mass-mobilized and less organized than, say, in the US, and thus lead to movement and issue politics rather than stable institutionalization.

This characterization allows us to return to an idea encountered at the outset, that the state is a modernizing project imposed on society by the colonial regime and its subsequent Nehruvian inheritors. It is now possible to see that the problem is not the imposition of such a strong state, but rather that the state has not been strong enough. Fuller and Harriss thus argue against the idea of a modern state at odds with local populations: they assembled the studies by a number of anthropologists who examined the perceptions of Indians of – and their dealings with – the state 'from the ground up', and their conclusions go against the ideas of post-colonial theorists that local Indian culture and politics are 'incompatible' with the modern, impersonal, bureaucratic Weberian state. Rather, these studies show

> an everyday understanding of the workings of the state and its administrative procedures among ordinary people which could hardly exist if there were such a profound incompatibility . . . given the obsession with 'resistance' in so much current scholarship, it is striking that the ordinary people described . . . are mostly not resisting the state, but using the 'system' as best they can. (Fuller and Harriss 2001: 24, 25)

Bardhan is therefore right to characterize post-colonial theorists as 'anarcho-communitarians' (Corbridge and Harriss 2000: 194). The problem in India is not that the state is imposing a Western or rationalist programme on society, but that it is not Weberian – in the sense of being an impersonal bureaucratic apparatus – enough (see Evans and Rauch 1999).

One implication is that the attempt by the state to incorporate citizens by extending and deepening rights – which has in India often proceeded along the lines of ethnic, caste and religious groupings, rather than an incorporation by class, as in China – has also stalled: not, as in China, because of an abandonment of egalitarian ideology, but because the demands of affirmative action have run up against the buffers not only of liberalization, but that these demands have become locked in at various levels of the state, including the national centre which continues to dispense these rights and benefits in particularistic ways. Populist democracy ensures that these demands continue to be deeply entrenched, but this pluralized entrenchment also means that, outside of elections, the power of elites is less constrained by a coherent civil society than it might be.

India, China and modernization

If, as in Chapter 3, we regard civil society and class-citizens as synonymous for a moment (as separate from, but engaging with the state), then for India it is clear that civil and political rights have deepened, whereas in China they exist mainly on paper and otherwise only in embryonic form. In terms social citizenship, the attempt to provide benefits to peasants and working classes in China – its 'affirmative action' (to use the terminology for India) – remained a major effort of socio-political development into the 1970s, but it has since stalled or become eroded. In India, the main thrust of extending social rights has not been by economic class, but by religion/caste/ethnicity (and language), but again it has become largely frozen. India nevertheless has a vibrant civil society in the sense of social movements making claims on the state (Katzenstein et al. 2001), unlike China where, again, such movements are either embryonic or suppressed.[11] The Chinese state, authoritarian and paternalistic (or 'from above') in its incorporation of citizen-classes, is strong compared to the Indian state in its ability to shape (civil) society, but weak in its base of support from it (or shaky because of its lack of support). The Indian state has perhaps an all-too strong but fragmented anchor of support in (civil) society, but is therefore weak in being able to bend or push its elites towards coherent developmental goals. And while both societies have embarked on a course of giving free reign to markets, the state continues to have a strong role, especially in the industrial and agricultural sectors of both economies.

A question that can be raised in the light of the comparison between India and China is how to separate economic growth from broader social development: in the past two decades, China has powered ahead of India, so that a key question for the foreseeable future will be how an extractive/redistributive state can encourage strong social development as measured primarily by a combination of avoiding unstable economic inequalities and universalizing the extension of civil, political and social rights. It can be noted that a number of commentators have pointed out that a key problem for both countries is that with liberalization, the opportunities for political elites to benefit economically have grown (Jaffrelot 2011: 620–59; Andreas 2008). The problem is thus in a sense that the two economies have not become disembedded enough: economic opportunities remain embedded within these political systems so that political and politically connected elites can benefit from them, though regulation to separate and ensure legally transparent and fair markets and universal property rights could potentially overcome this problem.[12]

There is therefore no need to 'essentialize' the East, to use different concepts or identify separate patterns of development in a comparative-historical analysis of modernization and its current limits: Chinese authoritarian paternalism and Indian captured populism entail that social development is still more subject to the control of a political elite than in advanced democracies, but the pressures – limited though their expression has become – from society within the (self-imposed) constraint of disembedding markets are similar for social development across developed and in these two developing societies. The problem that demands for social rights have come to overload the political system and threaten its stable future are also, as we have seen, evident in Sweden, the US and beyond, even if the root causes of this problem (financialization and the cost of social rights provision) are quite different than for China and India (weakening commitment to social rights in China's case, particularist demands for social rights fragmenting the state in India).

Put differently, how can the two states foster social development without distorting it towards the capture by a political elite that derives its authority from a single party at the centre (China) or by a fragmented elite that derives its authority from populist support (India)? These are questions with echoes in the gridlocked politics of the US and in the political stalemate between demands on the state and the embrace of the market in Sweden. The roots of these politics are different: a centralized state that has been exerting control, including ethical paternalism, over society in China for many centuries, whereas a decentralized political system in which central rulers never gained the upper hand over religious and local kinship and caste-based authority pre-dates and continued through and beyond colonialism in India. These political and social traditions are still relevant, but they do not represent an entrenched pre-modern culture that specifically counteracts the three modernizing patterns that have been identified in earlier chapters. Instead, and turning the ideas of post-colonial theorists on their head, the persistence of these elite political legacies – and not the modernism of these elites – are now obstacles to social development. And from the other side, the erstwhile nationalist or peasant and other pressures from below have, as in the West, also become exhausted or frozen. Thus they provide different preconditions for further democratization (in the sociological sense of democratization from below discussed in Chapter 3). Yet given similar trajectories of liberalizing economies and increasing competition, particularly in innovative market niches, against the backdrop of a variety of different political options or models in shaping economic and social development, it is hard to ascribe a central role to different cultural traditions. There are no longer any Western or Northern 'models' that are being exported or imposed as political ideologies, as before 1989–91 (with the possible exception of the ideology of a military empire on which the sun is setting). India and China themselves now provide different 'models' to the global South, but there are three aspects to thinking about these models: the first is that both countries have yet to achieve full differentiation. Markets have become disembedded, but they are also still subject to the developmentalist goals of the state. 'The people' or civil society have been incorporated into the state, but this incorporation remains incomplete with the selective or particularist 'affirmative action' nature of this process in India and the party-elite putting the lid on or shaping this process from above in China. Thus there is potential for further disembedding and democratization. An authoritarian state imposing stability and a logjammed pluralist one may therefore provide alternative models for social development in the global South, but when they do so, these potential trajectories of social development are not characterized by lessons that are unconnected from those that can be extracted from those of the global North (which will be discussed in the next chapter).[13]

Post-colonial and anti-modernist thinkers hark back to an era before these 'Western models' (including, for China, the Japanese model when it embarked on modernization in the late 19th century) and before the imperial ventures during hot and cold wars. But such a more East and South Asia-centric culture does not need to be wrested away from modernizing elites and restored to local cultures below them: within a generation, the consumerism of subaltern populations and their affluent and increasingly cosmopolitan elites will pull the centre of gravity of globalizing modern culture eastwards in any event. And this geographic shift will hit the same buffers of differentiation in an Age of Limits as they have already done in the global North until, as Weber put it (1948: 113), 'the light of the great cultural' – or rather social – 'problems moves on'.

9
Social Theory in the Face of the Future

This book has argued that we can identify dominant social structures (here: 'orders') and how they interrelate in the global North and for two major developing societies. It is now time to draw the argument together to show how the various limits of these social structures determine social development. Before we do so, it is worth considering whether there are any intrinsic limitations to social theory itself – after all, 'limits' could imply that there are constraints not just on social change, but also on what knowledge can contribute to analysing it. One question that is raised immediately in this connection is whether social science should be driven by problems. This idea is in keeping with the conception of science that has been put forward here, which revolves around science as a means of intervening in the world. Alternatively, if a philosophical or normative justification for focusing on problem-solving is preferred, we might adduce Popper's view of science whereby knowledge should devote itself first and foremost to eliminating suffering or social ills (see Magee 1973: esp. 84–6). From these scientific and philosophical perspectives, what problems should social theory address?

First, it should address the – not very practical, in an everyday sense – problem of structuring social science knowledge itself. In relation to macro-social orders, this means giving shape to the long-term historical comparative patterns of social change. Thus social theory consists of an edifice, at the apex of which is a hierarchy of concepts that organize those below. For example, the 'state' has been defined here in a particular way, and this has allowed us to categorize the varieties of states and the relations between citizens and democracy, arriving at a small number of types or extremes within a range. Along the same lines, this framework (or the top of the edifice) has meant that it is possible to arrive at a coherent synthesis of theory and substantive patterns of social change which also highlights – to stay with the example of politics – the overlap and divergence between liberal and radical interpretations of the development of the state. This synthesis in turn provides a means of foreseeing the options and constraints in resolving urgent social issues (how do the types of state compare in extending social citizenship rights, and what are the limits to this extension?). This 'apex' therefore primarily intervenes in social science knowledge itself, providing a link to applications of this knowledge in more detailed research on the one hand and – and as we shall see in this chapter – it can also inform normative questions on the other. The latter link will be made shortly, the former depends on the usefulness of the frame that has been developed here.[1]

With this, we can turn to how the different orders in contemporary society constrain each other and leave limited room for maneouvre. The chapter can thus also return to issues raised in the introductory chapter about modernity and globalization and the scope for the validity of knowledge: to what extent do the limits identified here apply across the globe? This generalizability can inform the normative questions pursued later, even if there is no intrinsic connection between them: we can extract from the past certain patterns of social development – for example, deepening democratization – which can then inform our understanding of where (normatively) social development could be going in the future, within possibilities and constraints. These options can be linked to enduring normative questions in social thought: the relation between freedom and equality, which, I will argue, is fundamentally about 'capabilities', or the capacity for self-determination.

The argument has so far been couched in terms of the example of the political order, but it could equally well be made, and will be made, in relation to social development in the cultural and economic orders. These were distinguished in Chapter 1, relating them to classical and contemporary social theory. Drawing on and departing from these theories in certain ways, I argued that we can trace how the three orders became separated in a novel and distinctively modern way during the 19th century, gaining an unprecedented institutional autonomy from each other. From this point onwards, I argued that the institutions dominating these three orders have operated in different ways: the economy is dominated by free markets, and markets are diffuse, divisible and atomized. The economic order experienced a sea change with industrialization, such that permanent growth became entrenched and the exchange of commodities increasingly disembedded. In the realm of culture, science became institutionally autonomous and has since been dominant in terms of its exclusive claim to valid knowledge. Finally, we saw that when the state became legitimated by 'the people', it then becomes possible to chart the subsequent trajectories of how the people were incorporated as classes-citizens. Despite different paths, pluralist democracies continue to be defined not just by the exclusive monopoly of legitimate violence, but also by how political interests have become represented and entrenched within the state.

The dominance of these institutions – they could also be described as social cages – has implications not just for the processes inside them, but also for what they *exclude*: as we have seen, the monopoly of science excludes (if not in a zero-sum manner) other modes of belief, markets exclude and otherwise displace non-market transactions, and pluralist democracies exclude single-party authoritarianisms. These limits in the global North constrain options, but to anticipate, one implication of these three cages (leaving out a fourth, military power or global govern-ance, for the reasons given in Chapter 1) arises from the fact that they are *not directly* interconnected: the absence of direct transmission belts between them constitute one further limit. To give just one example, during the Golden Age, the state's resources were bolstered by unprec-edented economic growth. Now, in contrast, there are limits to this mutual reinforcement between the two orders.[2] Or again, science and technology were yoked in an unprecedented way to economic growth during the Golden Age, but this coupling is now problematic from both sides (as we saw in Chapter 6). In short, during the Age of Limits, the autonomy between the three orders – and, as we shall see below, the dynamic within each order – has become frozen. Even if resources still flow from the increasing intervention and manipulation of the natural world into market growth in particular, and from open-ended market growth to state budgets, or from 'people' (social movements or civil society) to shifts in the direction of states which, in turn, govern mar-kets and how the natural world is being transformed – nevertheless all these potential interactions between orders are also constrained.

One limit of how separate institutions have come to dominate each order thus arises from the greater complexity of society – or more pre-cisely, from differentiation. This differentiation allows for an absence of conflict: the lack of intersection between, say, the dominant institutions of the political and economic orders entails that how markets function within and between states is not the source of destabilizing political conflict between them. Or again, the way in which the transformation of nature rests on scientific foundations that are not subject to politi-cal or economic determinants allows for (politically or economically untainted) realism and pragmatism in pursuing and exercising the extensibility of our technological 'cage' (or exoskeleton). The constraints of this differentiation, however, also entail an increasing lack of control. This is best highlighted by noting that unlike in evolutionist or functionalist views of the operation of different subsystems of society, which sees them as increasingly interdependent, on the view presented here, the autonomy of markets, of the transformation of nature, and a state shaped by forces from below – each imposes a separate form of caging, decoupled from each other.[3]

A different way of highlighting the implications of this argument is to contrast it with the alternative (touched on in Chapter 1): primacy. Social theorists from Marx to Mann have argued that it is possible to identify primacy in the relation between different sources of power in determining social development. Weber and his followers have argued for 'multicausality', but this is either an evasion or it cannot be a progressive research programme unless causes are 'fixed' somewhere – and thus comparable – as being political or economic or cultural (or using other concepts or categories that are defined so that they build on how others define and distinguish between them). The alternative presented here is how a lack of primacy in the Age of Limits (or the non-overlap between orders or powers) is itself a key to understanding contemporary social change. One understanding of this mutual non-determination is that the dominant institutions cannot become de-differentiated without a regress in social development. Yet another is that this lack of primacy is simply a characteristic of how society has caged us, which includes different time-horizons and spatial extents of the mechanisms in different orders (to be discussed further below).

This decoupling can be seen from yet another perspective: what of 'agency'? It has been noted, for example, that the cultural drive for consumption, the push to extend social rights, and the open-ended and divisible nature of economic growth are all independent from each other: this isolates the impact of possible countervailing forces, while it also potentially allows them to emerge 'from the ground up' (from the environments); though, as we shall see in moment, the constraints in each case also apply to the interstices between different orders and their operations. At the same time, these countervailing forces are contained, in the first instance, within their respective orders: popular pressures can democratize the state further, but this will only translate into extending social rights (and the 'indivisible' resource benefits that spring from these); it will not bring about a direct mitigation of market inequalities. Similarly with curbing economic growth for the sake of pursuing greater stability in relation to the natural world: even if less spending on commodities can contribute to this aim, to have an effect, this lower demand would need to translate into fewer resources from the natural world being called upon. And finally, growth can be achieved in a way that sustains people's livelihoods via exchanges that ensure frictionless and effective material benefits throughout markets, but this will not per se bring about a redistribution of political control.

Put in a more abstract way, changes in how dominant institutions exercise power or control over their environments require translation for transmission, but this transmission is limited to indirect effects between orders. This thought can be taken to its conclusion immediately in pointing to the fact that how this shaping occurs – 'agency' – can take place in a more or less democratic way, in a way that targets science and technology more and less precisely, and such that markets allow more and less stable and sustained growth. Yet each of these ways of addressing contemporary challenges will address them mainly within the terms of reference of the dominant institution within one order, including their respective environments, and only via translation in the others: for example, stable and sustained growth in the economic order will be primarily achieved within financial markets via the regulation of financial instruments and credit (by central banks and bank coordinating bodies, among others) such that these maximize advantage for the actors involved on an ongoing basis (by means of ensuring liquidity, among other things, for continued profit). Or again, markets for consumer goods and services can be 'stabilized' vis-à-vis the natural world such that they ensure that profits are derived from a sufficient amount of demand.[4]

Second, whatever challenges are addressed this way, they ensure stable and sustained growth *within* the economic order, and only address, say, greater equity in terms of how resources are distributed (determined by the state) insofar as money (the means of economic exchange) can be translated into the benefits of social rights (say, the provision of medical care). Similarly with translation into technoscientific advance, where targeting of innovation towards a sustainable transformation of nature can come about when economic exchange is translated, via cost/benefit mechanisms, to a shift in direction in the transformation of nature. And similarly with the other two orders, where translation of authority and of valid knowledge is called for to affect the other orders. Note, again, that all these translations leave the dominant institutions and their environment intact, while in the interactions between the orders, the mechanisms or operations become re-appropriated or dissipated when one order passes into the other order(s).

Finally, the incongruity of dominant institutions within and between orders can be highlighted by noting a hierarchy between them which is relativized by the different timescales and geographies of their operations: the transformation of nature is facing limits, possibly becoming ever more irreversible, but the timescale of how this rebounding seriously affects economic growth (and possibly a less livable natural world) is decades in the future, and it is more invisible closer in time. Similarly with the limits to markets, which face a shifting of gears that is taking place within a somewhat shorter timeframe and which also consists of slow-moving but perceptible geographical shifts in the centres of economic power. Finally, the pressures that can be brought to bear on political change are closest to hand in time and mainly bounded by states, and simultaneously have the more dispersed economic forces and more distant transformation of the natural world as a more large-scale and more long-term horizon in the background.

These relationships can be visualized in Figures 9.1 and 9.2. Figure 9.1 (recalling Figure 1.1) shows the countervailing forces against limits within each macro-social order as solid arrows and counterforces against these limits as dashed arrows – dashed, because these counterforces become dissipated via translation. So more coherent and effective pressure from 'people' *could* lead to the state ensuring more financial stability and more evenly distributed and thus sustained growth. This pressure *could* also focus science towards a more sustainable transformation of nature. Markets *could* then provide more resources, as *could*

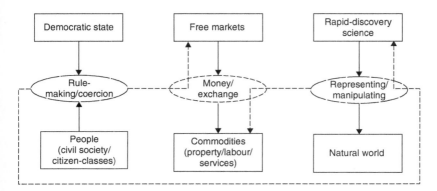

Figure 9.1   Social orders and counterforces against limits

innovations that are less resource intensive but produce more sustained economic growth (which could, in turn, support the deepening and extension of social citizenship). Note, however, that we have encountered limits to all these possibilities, even before taking into account the indirect workings of these counterforces, which become clearer in Figure 9.2.

Figure 9.2 shows both the different time horizons and different spatial scales of the forces interacting in the three orders, with solid arrows indicating limits and dashed arrows counterforces. This figure also shows their different degrees of boundedness or otherwise: the planet's resources in terms of the natural world are finite and so impose limits to the extent to which they can be transformed; markets are global but diffuse (and limits vary by region, though this is not visualized); and states are most closely bounded (and again, vary in terms of the severity of limits).

This hierarchy of limits and counterforces at different spatial scales and spans of time also puts the scope of 'agency' that has just been discussed, including how independently or otherwise 'agency' in one order affects that in another, into context. As we can see, the orthogonality of the orders prevents social theory from identifying a singular

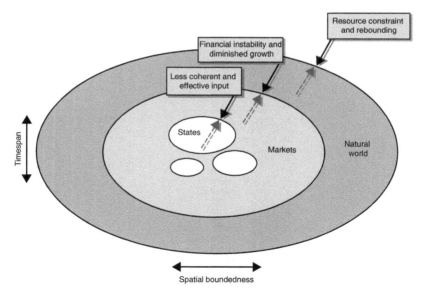

Figure 9.2   Spatial and temporal dimensions of orders, limits and counterforces

'agency' or primacy, even if it is possible to establish a chain of how the autonomies of orders impose longer- and shorter-term and more and less extensive constraints on each other – the intensive exploitation of natural resources, the changing geography and pace of growth, and forces pushing towards greater democratic political inclusion.

Thus the counterforces to limits also have different dynamics: politics, the most circumscribed form of power but also the most coherent (because authority is centralized), constitutes the most unambiguous counterforce. Perhaps, within the bounds of the limits of the other two social orders, this makes it more central to contemporary social change than the other two, such that 'people' and the state can (though 'indirectly') govern markets and science. But this difference is also a product of the different mechanisms in the three social orders: markets are not 'actors' in the way that states are; as we have seen, they only aggregate divisible exchanges. Thus they are more stable (by being more evenly distributed or curtailing financial volatility) and sustainable growth is primarily a product of patterns of markets that are more solidly grounded via stable consumption patterns and financial stability. Technoscience is 'blind' inasmuch as it moves only in the direction of cumulation, but it can be focused on a more sustainable transformation of the natural world by shifting technoscientific efforts towards this aim. How forceful these three processes are – and will be – within the constraints that have been identified remains to be seen: the key is to have pinpointed their scope, interdependence, and modes of operation.

In any event, it can be noticed how well this account of counterforces fits with their different horizons: for the transformation of nature, there is a longer and more spatially diffuse room for inaction, but the limits will also become more severe over time. The stabilization and enhancement of economic growth requires building solid long-term foundations, but this is (again) a diffuse process encountering the recalcitrance of existing patterns (for example, of consumption and how it is stratified). Political change, finally, depends on mobilization, but local and short-term mobilization must be sustained over time.

Finally, the autonomy or differentiation between the social orders entails that limits reinforce each other, but they are also de-coupled or non-overlapping. Put differently, these counterforces do not necessarily directly conflict with or go against each other. This creates an interstitial space for them: for example, since the rebounding from natural resource constraint is diffused across the planet and distant in time, market growth can in the meantime expand in a sustained and sustainable way. Or again, market growth, not bounded by nation-states, may provide more resources that provide scope for states to expand social rights. In short, the non-overlap or orthogonality of limits creates openings or options (more useful terms than 'agency', in my view), even if these limits can also reinforce or compound each other negatively (for example, the rebounding of natural resource constraints impacting on markets and states over the longer term, as we have seen). These limits and mutual shapings can now be pursued systematically, in turn.

The limits of markets

Markets, as we have seen, are characterized by divisible and atomized relations, and by diffuse power. However, the contrast between diffuse and authoritative power should be not be taken to imply that the latter is more constraining than the former: true, it is easier to choose one market transaction over another than to change one's statehood and the attendant rights. But engaging in market transactions (as a firm, a working person or a consumer) as such is not 'optional', and market behaviour imposes constraints throughout economic relations, including how these relations are aggregated in market dynamics.[5] We have also seen that markets are constrained via their coupling to how innovation (science and technology harnessed to growth) transforms the natural world, a coupling that is constrained in the face of the future of how natural resources are available for this transformation without rebounding (Chapter 6).

Another way to notice these limits is by means of further contrasts between market economies and the other two orders: the political and cultural orders are both dominated by monopolies – the monopoly of legitimate violence (the state) and of valid knowledge (science), but the economic order is specifically regulated to prevent monopolies – although the near-universal legitimacy of free markets could be seen as a monopoly of its own (but note again the lack of clear boundaries). To be sure, economic profits are sometimes a product of temporary monopolies of innovation (Chapters 4 and 5), and economic wealth and income are highly concentrated. However, even if the economic order is characterized by monopolizable peaks and resource concentrations, there are many of them. Further, there is a 'single-strandedness' to market relations which make them open-ended; namely, that all market exchanges consist of fungible and atomizable assets. This is ensured by the generalized medium of exchange; money. In this way, the market as such dominates – monopolizes – the economic order, but not (in contrast with the other two orders) as a single bounded or organizationally exclusive unit with a single hierarchy or apex.

On the other hand, how can there be limits to markets if they are 'free' (disembedded)? Economists' ideas about free markets and neoclassical economics are functionalist; that is, an optimum arises from the greatest openness within the system. In other words, functionalism by definition does not allow for systemic conflict. It is therefore difficult on this theory, and the one presented here (which argues for market 'autonomy'), to allow for systemic conflict or power asymmetries. I have also argued however (Chapters 3 and 4) that limits are re-introduced (though not in economic thought) via the inequalities created by how markets enable and constrain social citizenship and generate economic inequalities, and it is a constraint that these inequalities are not eliminable by markets as such in a general way (or at least not, to date, in the evenly spread way that trickle-down economic theory presupposes). Thus markets are limited insofar as they require supervening (extra-market) forces to shape resource allocation via social rights and political redistribution via taxes (Chapters 2 and 3), and this redistribution is effected by interests represented in the state. We can note again that this limit arises from the non-overlap between autonomous markets and states, which require a translation in order to be coupled (money into rights).

This brings us to the limits at the nexus between economics and politics. Even if classes-citizens and states are no longer shaped by the mode of production (insofar as it was ever so), new asymmetries are constantly being created. These inequalities can be linked to economic growth and performance, and there are highly technical debates about how to compare and improve these (how social science can intervene here with its knowledge is also subject to constraints, since economic expertise is only one input into economic policy). But the intersection of how economic growth and how political citizenship rights extend equality is also 'open': growth is divisible whereas political rights are indivisible (here we can think of taxes, which are not payments for particular services, but an obligation to pay for a package of them; see Martin et al. 2009: 3). In any event, the separateness of the economic and political orders is evident in relation to how the mechanisms in the two operate, though discussions of inequalities need to bridge this analytical and substantive separation (we will come back to this). Finally, in the Age of Limits, with the extension and deepening of social citizenship stalled, it is markets which produce and perpetuate inequalities, and perhaps ever more so – and again, on a different temporal and spatial scale – in the absence of states being unable to counteract these except through its limited (institutional and resource) means.

Markets are also limited at their highest level: if we consider the recent financial crisis (or financial markets generally), then, to be sure, states or international governing bodies may be able to impose regulations to avoid illegal or destabilizing practices. They may also be able use taxes (such as a Tobin tax) on financial transactions to create funds to mitigate future crises. However, financial markets have their own logic, and they have also grown to constitute a sizable superordinate market which is essential to the smooth functioning of 'subordinate' markets. Regulation or control have limited possibilities to interfere in these disembedded financial markets, and in any event regulate them to function more effectively *as markets.* These markets will therefore continue, if only by their size and influence, but also because they are transnational, to introduce uncontrollabilities (again, on different scales) into economies. Finally, it can be noted that this autonomy of markets comes not just with negative or destabilizing effects: the autonomy of financial markets from politics, for example, can help to ensure that a crisis like that in 2008 does not become a cause of geopolitical conflict.

The limits of culture, and of science and technology

Culture, as argued in Chapter 7, consists of three main constituent parts. The first limit to point to is that only one of these (science) plays an essential role: culture apart from science explains little, even though the study of (the non-science part of) culture has recently expanded enormously in the social sciences (viz. cultural studies). Yet this non-science part of culture, for which I have drawn here on anthropology and social history, has little intersection with the macro-structural shifts discussed here. Perhaps it can be separated from theories of social change at the macro level, and treated primarily within the frame of reference of everyday life and within the ambit of cultural history. Science, on the other hand, has recently come to be regarded by social scientists as playing no independent and significant role, and any hint of technological determinism is held to be inadmissable. Thus my analysis goes against the prevailing grain on both sides.

After science and technology, to which we shall come in a moment, the two other major components of culture are religion and consumption, which, as I argued in Chapter 7, play (respectively) a residual role and a role that is so embedded as to disappear into everyday economic life. Put differently, both these parts of culture are non-essential: religion, as argued in Chapter 7, still plays a role only if we miss the wood for the trees. The trees are continuing debates about how religion is shaping social issues or 'civilizational' differences, while the wood is how religion has increasingly become sequestered in everyday life in the global North. The wood also consists of the continuing divorce of religion from dominant institutions, so that, again, its role is residual (though not, in the cases discussed here, in India where religious and ethnic divisions are partly lodged in the state, a lack of differentiation that is an obstacle to a globalizing modernity; Chapter 8).

The role of consumption, on the other hand, though not diminished, runs up against the limits of sustainability (Chapter 6), so that even if it remains a deeply entrenched part of culture, it is perhaps most visible where it is running into buffers. Yet – and this is an oddly overlooked idea – the containment or diminution of levels of consumption would have no serious structural consequences. (An economist might say that weakening demand will hurt the economy, but this is unlikely due to the diffuse and divisible nature of economic life). Hence, too, how an 'autonomous' cultural change could effect a reduction in consumption remains to be seen – it would need to be translated into lower spending on one side, or ways of conserving natural resources on the other – and the same applies to political steering and movements relating to these changes, also within limits (as we saw in Chapter 7). After these two, by some way, the main role of culture is in marking national boundaries (not national 'character', as for Fischer 2010). However, in this case, although national culture continues to be solidified, it is also playing – again – a residual role, and that is because after the solidification brought about by nationalism (Gellner 1983), any assertion of national culture per se becomes 'ironic'.

What about other limits? Science is in principle unlimited, as is technology (though practical knowledge comes up against natural constraints, and the constraints of embedded systems). After all, there is no part of the physical world that is – again, in principle – too recalcitrant for representing and intervening, or refining and manipulating. In practice, however, technoscience in today's Age of Limits is constrained not just by the limits of the transformation of nature, but also because innovation is increasingly harnessed to goals – especially economic ones – with resources that can be foreseen to be no longer as unlimited as they appeared during the Golden Age (and far more resources will be needed in the future). We can think here emblematically of the space programme or of the race for nuclear weapons in the case of science, but also of the large technological infrastructures that are now mainly extended to new populations rather than being created anew or made more powerful in a way that radically departs from existing ones.

Still, science and technology provide a potential means of overcoming the limits to the transformation of nature, even if these means are themselves subject to constraints (as we saw in Chapter 7). The implications of these limits, which are also imposed by an ethical duty towards future generations – a 'duty of anticipation' (Partridge 2001: 386–7) – have not yet become widely known outside of expert circles. That is because there is yet another limit of science: which is that while it constrains belief within a narrow sphere in which expertise is essential, it is otherwise distant from everyday life. In the meantime (before the limits to transforming nature are more widely recognized or experienced as such), technoscience will continue to be yoked to consumption, continue to transform culture in the direction of an expanded cage/exoskeleton, and thus extend a more homogeneous diversification of consumer ways of life – or, to put it differently, making societies the same in providing more. Apart from this, the autonomy of science and technology entail that political or economic steering of the growth of scientific knowledge is not possible except via the extra-scientific mechanism of providing resources or regulation, but similarly science also informs the political and economic orders only within its limited scope: again, more targeted transformations of the natural world – the environment of technoscience – could, translated into economic exchange, contribute to more stable commodity growth (the dashed arrow in Figure 9.1) or perhaps more efficient governance by states. But such a steering of knowledge would need to become subject to economic divisibility or adapt to authoritative rules, and thus also constrict science and the technological manipulation of the natural world.

The limits of the state and politics

While the state before the Age of Limits was shaped by pressures from civil society (as described in Chapter 3), nowadays the expansion of social rights has increasingly narrowed not just by a weakening of these pressures, by also by how the relative decline in growth and economic instability translate into limited resources. Collins has summarized the rational-choice (or economic) view of democracy as follows: 'The winning politicians are those who make promises that attract more people than the promises of rival politicians' (1994b: 172). This view fits with the arguments put forward here insofar as the erstwhile 'moral projects' of the state (Perez Diaz 1993: 66–9), which were characteristic of the Age of Extremes, have been left behind in the democratic North. Put differently, the idea of the state as a moral project nowadays only applies to single-party nation-states with the claims of the party to represent 'the people' (as in China; Chapter 8). But pluralist states are states where different projects must compete and compromise, howsoever they are conceived. Yet there are no mainstream parties that can avoid legitimating themselves without a commitment to economic growth – if only to ensure continuing support for social rights – whatever else their aims may be. This, too, is a constraint on politics in the Age of Limits inasmuch as the state is frozen as a plural aggregation of interests, with the main variation among states being how well-organized or coordinated this pluralism is.

Gellner puts the same point differently when he says that the state has become 'desacralized' or 'instrumental' (1994: 142). For better or worse, this means that there is little attachment to the state, and America, with its anti-statism (Hall and Lindholm 1999: 112), or the EU, with an anaemic popular attachment to Brussels (Mann 1998), are not alone in this. And as we have seen, national cultures, though solidified, play a diffuse role. At the same time, the ideals of freedom and equality are nowadays trumped by democracy insofar as the drive for the incorporation of party (again, in a broad sense) interests, compromising both ideals, has been central to modern political development (as argued in Chapter 3). But if, furthermore, neither freedom nor equality are philosophically coherent on their own (as we shall see in a moment), then we need to ask: how deep is democracy – understood sociologically?

One limit here is that (nation-state-bounded) democracy does not shape or control supranational issues (the EU is only a partial exception). On the other hand, if democracy within national bounds should accurately reflect people's interests or preferences, then this expression should be evident in the type of market economy – or variety of capitalism – they prefer; inasmuch as this a question of politics rather than of markets. Yet as we have seen, there are limits here too because these aggregated interests (citizen-class or civil society interests promoted by parties), which once shaped states, no longer play the role they once did, after the 'end of the parabola' (Crouch 2004). This leaves political interests concerning distributional issues and how they are represented in states 'locked in', except insofar as opposition parties 'outside' states have an influence on – even if they do not control – implementation of political agendas.

What drivers of political change, then, remain in an Age of Limits? As we have seen, there are various forms of stratification across the

North: income and wealth, urban versus rural divides, excluded or sub-ordinate groups (though I have barely touched on these) versus elites. The limits of how they may become mobilized are apparent: these forms of stratified and aggregated interests cut across each other within civil society and in terms of rights. Further, inasmuch as economic and political powers are separated, these interests would only become driving forces if clear asymmetries induced conflict or mobilization – and then economic transfers, for example, would need to be translated into secure rights. There are also limits inasmuch as political authority is skewed by politically powerful economic groups ('incomplete' incorporation from 'below'), such that elites may still be more powerful than 'people' even if the state is counterbalanced by civil society. And, as we have seen, in India and China this 'incompleteness' is intertwined with the incomplete 'cultural' separation in the former case and authoritarian rule in the latter case. In this way elites also continue to set the agenda for the balance between states or markets and thus for the extension or otherwise of social citizenship rights. As we shall see in a moment, these rights can be conceived of in philosophy in certain ways, but it has been concluded here (Chapter 3) that there are limits to how the state, shaped by these various interests, is able to extend these rights, or distribute them more equally and deepen them (a requirement, as we shall see, for certain positions in political philosophy).

The differentiation of the economic and political orders thus complicates the analysis of stratification, which takes two separate forms; economic (market) inequalities versus rights which deepen from civil and political rights into social rights. Yet markets, as I have argued, are now difficult to shape and operate on a different scale, while the state's resources for deepening social rights and the pressures for this are weak. The two forms of social stratification are thus layered in different ways (or again, orthogonal): economic inequalities ('market chances', as Weber called them, taking into account skills) of wealth, income and mobility constitute a horizontal layer and they are also shaped by supra-national forces. Social rights are vertical in terms of the depth and reach to different parts of the 'people', but they are also particularistic versus universalistic in terms of inclusion and exclusion: a reaching 'down' into more or less of a bounded society. As we have seen, taxes and spending have been transmission belts between two forms of strati-fication and between the two orders, but with growing autonomy and a stalled extension and deepening of social rights, the possibility of trans-lation between non-divisible 'social *rights*' and transferable and divisible market exchanges are subject to different constraints. Stratification has thus become suspended between the two orders, and become frozen (or inequalities grown, via markets).

Against this backdrop, we can turn to how sociological knowledge informs philosophical questions. Before we do so, it can briefly be anticipated that there are connections between macro structures (or cages) and our choices as individual social actors. In the next section, I will draw on Sen's philosophical ideas about 'capabilities' as pre-requisites for human flourishing (2009). Sen argues that philosophical arguments about how we should live must be based on comparisons of the extent to which they provide capabilities for choosing the life we value, a 'substantive freedom' (2009: 19). If substantive freedoms are at issue, however, then the discussion must revolve around comparisons of the affordances and constraints of different cages, or the choices that dominant institutions enable or permit. Thus we will be asking to what extent markets provide the economic growth that is one basis for human flourishing, how well states allow for democratic input and self-determination, and to what extent science and technology give us enhanced control over the natural world and enabling both. In view of the discussion above and in previous chapters, there are limits to all three.

From comparative-historical sociology to political philosophy

Unlike left or radical social theorists (such as Walby 2009 and Mann 1999), who argue that political and economic rights are inseparable and that the incompleteness of the extension and deepening of both is central to contemporary social change, I have argued that there is a separa-tion between political and economic 'power' (or authority and market exchange, in my preferred terminology). This separation is substantive, arising from relatively diminishing rates of economic growth and from the stalled push by civil society interests for extending the capacity of states. Limits are thus being encountered in the extension to the depth and scope of social citizenship rights. But the separation is also substan-tive in the sense that the workings of markets (disembedded, with dif-fuse power and atomized relationships) and states (concentrated, with authoritative control over indivisible rights) have become more differ-entiated. The separation between the two orders entails that states have diminished control over the workings of economies and are, rather, constrained by them: they cannot incur open-ended further public debt or engage in open-ended Keynesian demand-side management. States are trapped between relatively slower growth and financial instability on the one hand and the lack of legitimacy for statist economic management on the other. If this seems an obvious point, it is not one that is made in the varieties of capitalism literature or by economists.

Against liberal social theorists, I have argued that state and market structures are both constraining. It may be that elites can learn to cope with societal challenges and that individuals can develop their skills and abilities to do the same (as liberals argue). Both, however, must be placed in the context of constraints: if there is no reason to hypostatize the optimal workings of markets and the endless possibilities of innovation, and if states also have limited room for manoeuvre externally and internally, then individual flourishing and elite power are likewise limited in practice, even if they are (mistakenly, in my view) 'open-ended' in liberal theory.[6] And against the liberal understanding of democracy whereby civil society or plural forces shape the state, growing inequalities in the four cases examined here (or at best stalled political and economic equality) mean that elite power is in an important sense becoming more concentrated.

As we have seen (Chapters 2 and 3), the liberal and radical interpretations of the relation between states and markets diverge. Yet curiously, they also overlap in seeing classes as the motor or as requiring stabilization via an open-ended enrichment of growing middle classes, with different roles for state elites in each case. I have argued that it is necessary to go beyond both: in the post-Cold War era, both states and markets are constrained. This is where the link between social theory and philosophy comes in. As we have seen, for both the liberal and radical interpretations, political development nowadays revolves around social citizenship rights or economic enablement, and these also remain at the centre of debate in political philosophy, which continues to be mainly concerned with the relation between freedom and equality. Before moving on to discuss these concepts, one further limit should be made clear: there is no necessary connection between social theory, motivated and driven by advancing knowledge (and constraining and enabling social structures), and political or philosophical norms, which must be chosen and voluntarily pursued in order to have value in the first place. We shall come back to this.

Sen (2009) has tried to square the circle of freedom versus equality by arguing for a capabilities approach, comparing how actual capabilities are realized in different societies. This approach can fit well with the analysis here (and with Walby [2009], who also draws on Sen). However, in view of the argument that has been made, it is also necessary to examine the constraints on the extension of capabilities. One such constraint is that it is necessary to distinguish between the (social citizenship-enabled) capabilities within the states of the North and different rights pertaining to the development of capabilities outside of stably institutionalized democracies.

In other words, to consider universal norms (indeed, norms should be universal), we can widen the scope for a moment to a globalizing modernity. To do this, we can consider an important argument that has been made by Singer (2002), from a utilitarian standpoint, and Pogge (2008) from a rights-based one, that more should be done globally to equalize wealth and thus maximize overall happiness or to secure human rights. However, Nagel (2005) and Sen have argued against this, pointing out that there are that no institutions to which such strong global (negative) rights and (positive) obligations can be attached.[7] An added problem is that people have misleading beliefs about existing conditions which would make progress of such rights and obligations difficult in any event. For example, Singer presents survey evidence that shows that people are misinformed and vastly overestimate the levels of aid that their countries give to others (2002: 180–5). There is a parallel here with how, in states in the North, for example in America, there is a belief that there is higher social mobility in the US than in Europe – which is in fact not the case (Baldwin 2009: 225). These misconceptions suggest that people should, if they were prepared to be consistent, favour more aid and more generous social citizenship, but also that their (false) beliefs might prevent them from doing so.

If we turn back to focus merely on social justice in the countries of the North, then in political philosophy, the fundamental debate has been about the relation between freedom and equality, which remains unresolved.[8] As Charvet has argued (1981), there is an irreconcilable tension between the two in the realm of ideas. To appreciate this argument, consider the value of the individual which is at the core of this debate: the individual must be valued for him- or herself – the unique ends or aims of the person – in order to constitute an object of value. This individual value, which must be given free expression, should then be valued equally for all persons. But this equal valuing must have something to value in the first place, and this can only be the free unfolding of the individual's ends or aims. At the level of philosophy, this circularity or stand-off between equality and freedom cannot be reconciled. The equal value of self-determining beings does not admit of resolution in favour of prioritizing '*equal* value' or '*free individual* self-determination', since they depend on each other.

Based on the arguments made here, it is possible to go further: before the idea of an 'end of history' (Fukuyama 1992), it was argued that freedom and equality represented competing ideologies; equality on the side of communism, freedom on the side of Western democracies. After the Cold War, with Northern societies now 'free' democracies (even if imperfectly), the two sides have continued to be identified with different societies; freedom with Anglo-American liberal societies, and equality with corporatist or Nordic social democracies. Yet as we have seen (in Chapters 2 and 3), this misleads insofar as, on the one side, social democratic states do not generally constrain freedom and have not until relatively recently generated higher equality than liberal Anglo societies do (though they do now); but nor do Anglo liberal societies *generally* permit more market freedoms than social democracies since states and markets operate separately in both (and the higher levels of taxation in Sweden as against the US, for example, can be decomposed into different types of state redistribution, which, as we saw in Chapter 2, are not as different in overall levels or effects as they may first appear). The rub therefore lies rather with social citizenship rights and their scope (universalistic or partial) as well as their scale (how irrevocable or secure, and how generous). These, however, are questions of social citizenship and thus of *politics*. The orientation of economies and markets towards maximizing growth (environmentalists who argue for limits to growth are the exception) has become a well-entrenched and separate feature of all market societies, including in the expertise devoted to and beliefs about economies. Markets have become more firmly disembedded, which is obscured in theories of 'political economy'.

Where does this leave freedom and equality? Not in the equal value of self-determining beings as an abstraction, but rather in pragmatic arguments about how to achieve the means to ensure the most extensive scale and scope of social citizenship (welfare) rights – deepening capabilities – against the backdrop of (or bounded by and coming up against the limits of) disembedded markets. Note the disconnect here between political philosophy and comparative sociology: the latter can focus on how individuals are supported on the basis of certain social conditions, whereas the former seeks to adjudicate on a general level between the norms (with politics and economics intertwined) of different societies. Yet social citizenship rights are bounded by nation-states, which chimes with the argument in political philosophy that we have just encountered by Nagel (2005) that justice beyond nation-states lacks recognizable institutions. Put the other way around, this boundedness stems from the fact that rights that are accorded within states – here focused on welfare or shared well-being (social citizenship as a 'political' right insofar as the state manages the distribution of economic resources for political purposes) – and are based on the membership in a shared nationally bounded society (Nagel 2005: 128). Contra Nagel, however, there is nothing to prevent social scientists from making comparisons between nations, and noting better and worse options in terms of justice. Further, comparisons are likely to become more pressing: as Milanovic points out,

> global inequality, or inequality among all citizens of the world . . . is the sum of . . . two inequalities, that of individuals and that among nations . . . it is a new topic because only with globalization have we become used to contrasting and comparing our own fortunes with the fortunes of individual people around the globe. Yet it is probably a type of inequality whose importance will, as the process of globalization unfolds, increase the most. (2011: x)

Still, global and transnational ideas about justice face limits. Singer and Pogge point us towards the goal of alleviating suffering among the least well off (as does Rawls [1971]); we can also recall Popper's ideas mentioned at the outset of this chapter. Sen adds substance to these ideas by arguing that justice must be about real capabilities and not just abstract rights, and that these should apply universally to *all* self-determining beings. If these ideas about justice can be grounded universally and not just within nation-states (even if they are applied based on obligations within nation-states, in accordance with Nagel's argument), then we nevertheless have a valid yardstick across societies, the deepening of a universal human right, which can be seen not just as applicable to the state's economic assistance and redistribution, but as a political ideal that could operate – again, as a yardstick – everywhere. Moreover, this political ideal can be informed by the theory of social development that has been put forward here (even if, again, there is no necessary connection between them): based on the extent to which this ideal has been realized in social development so far ('what is'), we can foresee options in different paths of social development in the future ('what should be').

This political ideal thus stands independently. As we have seen, the pressure from civil society to realize this ideal has weakened in recent decades.[9] Capabilities can be seen as a requirement for deepening and widening democracy and for full participation in society. More equalized capabilities provide an independent justification for holding states to account in promoting social citizenship universally, or providing an aspirational idea for all states (even if, again, it is restricted in practice, as Nagel argues, to nation-bounded societies). In the global North, it is this deepening of rights that is at stake; whereas in the South, for those worst off, rights to a basic subsistence are at stake, and developing societies like China and India are somewhere between – though, as we have seen, with different engagements between state and society. Both deepening and securing these rights are about how economic (extra-market) resources should be politically managed and distributed, and Sen's 'capabilities' covers both, but the capabilities in question are part of a continuum that nevertheless points to universalizable goals.

Markets, as we have seen, provide (often uneven) economic growth, and their powers are best analysed in terms of their separate disembedded workings. If these workings counteract or undermine capabilities, then it is the constraints they impose, and not the abstractions of economic freedoms, that should be focused upon. In the global North at least, this constraint has been created by the separation of markets, and thus capabilities (equal freedom) have become the province of the state. Seeing markets only in terms of freedom is misguided: Pogge talks of 'the massive persistence of severe poverty as a byproduct of a historical trend towards ever greater human-made harms being produced with ever less sense of wrongdoing' (2010: 210) and says this is a product of

> the uncoordinated activities of many influential players – each seeking its own advantage . . . an invisible hand, rather less benign than the one acclaimed by Adam Smith, ensures that the world, driven by these self-seeking efforts, equilibrates towards a mode of organization that gives the strong as much as possible while still allowing them to be in compliance with their moral norms. (2008: 6)

This indictment of markets by Pogge sits next to the fact that these same markets, combined with technoscience, and with only a supporting role played by states (which mainly redistribute economic resources, rather than generate them), are responsible for the increased levels of economic growth and thus of living standards enjoyed in the North. Free markets (and technoscience) are both enabling and constraining, and social science shows how this is so by indicating the directions of equality and inequality (towards greater equality, especially during the Golden Age, but now stalled or towards greater inequality in the Age of Limits for the countries examined here).

This way of taking ideas about freedom, equality and justice within and beyond the nation-state does not provide a practical resolution to the great global differences in human rights and economic inequalities, but it shifts the ground of the debates in political philosophy towards recognizing that the injustices of economic inequality must come from arguments about the universal right to develop individual capabilities (as Sen wants to do), which can only be done via states that are able to extend the scale and scope for doing this (as Nagel, and Mann and I from a sociological perspective, argue). In short, the argument centres ideas about freedom and equality squarely on the state. This is not an argument against global economic justice, but a radical argument to the effect that states should – universally – promote the capacities of all their citizens, and be measured by the shortcomings in how they do so. These arguments are starting to be promoted in ideas about measuring well-being across societies in development indexes. Instead of focusing exclusively on economic growth, however, which puts the onus on disembedded markets (which may be useful for other purposes), these indexes of well-being (or capabilities development) should assess and compare states in terms of how they measure up to promoting, for example, economic security. These measures should not just be of economic development in terms of growth rates, but of social development enabled by states.

This book has argued that social theory must, following Weber, remain value-neutral and strive for objectivity. This chapter has gone beyond facts to discuss values – freedom and equality. The contest between the two permeates fundamental debates in social science and it is deeper than right versus left. The debates about freedom and equality have recently (as mentioned in Chapter 1) been overtaken by new theoretical debates around 'agency' and 'rational choice'. This book has argued against both: the edifice that has been built been here consists of structures that interact, and the main task in relation to these is to show how much or how little scope there is for strain and change between them. These structures, however, foster freedom and equality (in philosophical, not sociological, terms) in different measure. This is not to do with a traditional way of thinking which might associate freedom with markets and states with equality. Instead, *as a mechanism* (though not in practice), markets are neutral between the two and now operate throughout the global North (where they do not, as in China and, in a different way in India, especially with the informal economy; this is a pathology or shortcoming of a globalizing modernity insofar as political elites gain from non-disembedded markets, or markets have been disembedded in such a way that they are skewed towards the gain of economic elites). Further, as states shape social citizenship, and thus freedom and equality, they do so not by promoting more or less agency or rational choice, but by fostering greater and lesser equal capabilities (superseding the opposition between the two competing concepts).

A different way to make this point is that the distinction between right versus left (as has often been pointed out) has lost its relevance in recent times. While regimes like Sweden and the US, for example, are still associated with the two poles, the key measure for this (levels of economic inequality and the depth and universality of social citizenship rights) is not so much about how these states have curbed or freed markets, but rather about the distributive efforts of the state, and specifically the universalism or particularism of these. At the same time, the parties in the two countries strain to realize the promise of equal capabilities with different interpretations – against the constraints of limited resources, the force of peoples' and supporters' beliefs (perhaps going against their own economic self-interests and values) that put the parties into power, and the strengths of prevailing beliefs about the role of the state. Politics is not primarily about different ideas about how markets function in these two and other countries. At the same time, political ideas or beliefs about redistribution and their translation into plural interests within the state are hemmed in by the diminished role of civil society on one side and by state resources on the other – so that even if the differences in the paths of these two states remain, these paths now both face limits, as they do elsewhere. Put differently, Sweden and the US have in the past both been models of social development. Yet, in view of the limits discussed here, it is time to ask where such 'models' of social development could go, except towards enhancing and deepening 'capabilities' in a more universal way. In any event, the ideas of limits and countervailing forces to these limits have indicated some options, and the narrowness of their scope.

Put differently, the state provides the cage of social citizenship whereas the cage of the market admits only atomistic exchanges. The limits of containing philosophy within the 'freedom versus equality' or 'left versus right' debate is that there is no recognition that markets and states are now separate but mutually constitutive cages in the sense that they constrain each other. This brings us to the other side of how the cage of the state constrains; in relation to freedom. Sociologists (and I) have often focused on how social rights enable equality. Yet in presenting us with different options, social theory should also address (equal) freedom. These freedoms, as we have seen (Chapter 3), consist in the first instance of civil and political rights, and these need to be stressed mainly in relation to countries like China where these rights are limited and countries that fall outside the scope of this book in the global South. In the global North, such restrictions are not the norm and differences – if we think, for example, of media systems (Hallin and Mancini 2004) – are limited. Or we can think of the different regimes and constraints on privacy, which should be secured for all individuals equally but where there are some important differences between states in the North (Rule 2007).

More importantly, and in a less conventional sociological but also more philosophical way, we can think of how the capabilities of free-dom, the individual's powers to develop in an unfettered or unrestricted way, fall short – and for whom. In sociological terms, even if the focus is on individual powers, it is the maximization of the aggregate equal capabilities of freedom – rather than those of individuals – that are at issue. So, for the nation-states that we have analysed here, we can ask: do they provide the means or the basis for individuals to lead the lives they shape and value (Sen 2009)? To be sure, all societies of the North do this compared to those of yesteryear. But if freedom means freedom from an overbearing state, or from a form of rule via democracy in which the constraints of the state do not apply equally, then there are important differences between states and their shortcomings, since the imbalances (following in the wake of struggles for citizenship rights) in how these constraints have been arrived at, and how democracy has served their removal, have followed different paths – now perhaps locked in rather than continuing to diverge.

Again, however, the removal of these constraints does not consist of strengthening market liberties (which are well-entrenched) but rather of strengthening state liberties – or eliminating how the state's authority misrepresents people in the sense of skewing the freedoms it provides for some at the expense of others. These skews might be on account of special interests within and outside of the private sector, or when states are unaccountable in the use of resources. Such sinecures or monopo-lized opportunities impose disproportionate constraint on those who do not enjoy them, and this too follows from the account that has been given here of the extension and expansion of rights – in this case against 'arbitrary' states. Criticizing this arbitrariness constitutes yet another way that a value-free social science, perhaps via expert knowl-edge in the public sphere, can inform how freedoms could be extended against an all-too-powerful state.

Thus a liberal interpretation of states and societies is not just about 'learning' or flexible adaptation (Chapter 3), but how also about how to further strengthen the power of 'the people' (civil society) against the authority of the state – not as a counterbalance via markets, but in terms of how widely this authority is anchored and how it can be expanded for all politically relevant groups and individuals. The state, even with minimal interests of its own (except maintaining Hobbesian order), should have no distorted or captured interests favouring particular individuals or groups. In this sense, there is no end of history for this expansion and deepening of equal capabilities – just as there is none to the extension of social citizenship.

'Capabilities' means that people can shape their own lives, without interference, and they should have growing resources to do this. How widely and effectively this equal freedom is distributed is the philosophical question that sociological analysis can be seen to have a bearing on. And again, this is not a question in relation to markets, but rather a political question related to how states support what is required for the capability to develop as a person. Given that 'education' (in quotes because in a broad sense) and with it the possibility for social mobility, as well as being cared for and health and financial security even in adverse circumstances, are all widely desired (again, in the widest terms derived from the discussion of capabilities, and thus going beyond particular understandings of welfare states), then these should be freedoms too – or 'freedom to'. Sociological realism can establish what reality has been given to these freedoms, not just in terms of how the state has enabled them, but also in relation to how the state is limited in providing them equally and how it can avoid distorting them in favour of some at the expense of others. On the level beyond the individual, this freedom should also entail a society vibrant or dynamic enough to ensure that aggregate interests (groups of political interests) can change and be part of being represented in and shaping the state. This is a liberal ideal, but with a wider and more sociological sense of 'learning' than that of the traditional liberal view (presented in Chapter 3).

These implications can be formulated differently: the corrective or steer that social theory can provide for political and social philosophy is away from the focus on economic justice or the preoccupation with economics in promoting freedom (as capabilities) and equality – and towards focusing on states and social rights. Rawls (1971), echoing Popper (as mentioned earlier), correctly focuses our attention on the least well-off; Singer and Pogge correctly remind us that well-being in advanced societies cannot be de-coupled from well-being among the least well-off outside of advanced societies (though Nagel notes the difficulties that must be overcome in the imperative to link them in practice beyond the silos of states) and Sen combines freedom and equality in the concept of capabilities. Yet all these thinkers put the emphasis on economic justice. In both parts of the world, however, markets and economic growth sit orthogonally in relation to well-being as enabled and constrained by states, and here we need to think – again – not of economic classes or stratification, but of how the range of options among advanced and other states can be interpreted in two ways: in terms of the polarization of rights within them, or of the coverage and depth of rights afforded to all. How this polarization can be overcome, or how this coverage can be deepened and extended – that is the 'What Is To Be Done?' in an Age of Limits. Put differently, societies are pursuing economic justice, democracy and freedom – but in fact, ensuring that the state has the capacity to enable equal capabilities is a single aim that encompasses all three – though with the autonomy of the economic order and of transforming nature both imposing bounds on these politics.

I have presented a theory of how society enables and constrains people, and the implications of this theory for political philosophy. It should be obvious that theory and philosophical implications are analytically separate: knowledge informs, but does not determine, ethical action and political options. Put the other way around: ethical and social or political imperatives about what we should do are exempt from the social forces – the determinants – that shape us. This point has been made by Gellner (1974: 184–8), following Kant, who argues that even if, from a scientific point of view, we know that there are causal forces that determine the way the world works – including social behaviour – this does not trump our status as moral beings who need to act as if we are free agents (for otherwise, we could not attach value to our selves and our behaviour, to recall the earlier discussion of freedom and equality). Despite this caveat – or exemption – it is important to infuse philosophical debates with a dose of sociological realism. This realism can provide us with the range of existing and likely social options – for example, that this range is narrower than but also different from how it is often conceived. Here we can think of what has been argued in relation to the state – the range of how it shapes and how it determines rights. This narrowing of focus, as we have seen, enables criticism. But we can also think of the constraints of free markets, with their instabilities and inability to translate into secure rights or a controllable resource future.

Perhaps counterintuitively, a concentration on narrower and more realistic options can also be more 'radical' than a radicalism based on imagined options (this follows from the view of science and knowledge presented in Chapter 5). Further, this realism can strip away some of the ideological baggage that has become attached to certain concepts, such as associating markets only with openness rather than also with constraints. Another example is 'freedom', which, as mentioned earlier, is often imported from arguments that made sense during the Cold War and in the context of geopolitics, whereas in relation to freedom and equality conceived as capabilities, it should properly be located in relation to individual states. Finally then, this realism may allow us to focus on comparing real capabilities, or how to live freely and equally within the limits that our age imposes on us.

Notes

1 From the Birth of the Modern World to the Age of Limits

1. This school of thought has been labelled the 'California school', see Goldstone (2006: 272–3).
2. Osterhammel's 19th century in fact reaches further back in time as well as beyond the First World War in certain respects.
3. It is not possible to date this period more accurately than the 1970s and 1980s since a longer-term economic downturn began in the 1970s but the end of the Cold War was only confirmed as a political break in the late 1980s. As we shall see in the concluding chapter, economies and political change – and the transformation of nature – all have different time horizons. Still, these breaks will become clearer with time.
4. This dependence on innovation is also implicit in ideas about 'post-industrial society', which depends on information and communication technologies as 'prime movers' for moving into a service- or knowledge-intensive society.
5. As Mann (1993: 26) has argued, only classes with organizational capabilities for change are of interest.
6. It can also be noted that although consumerism relies on technoscience or innovation – the first component of culture – this connection is at one remove: consumption rests on the transformation of the natural world, but consumer goods are exchanged via markets. This indirectness, that consumerism is driven by and drives economic forces, rather than being intrinsically linked to technoscience, is important for its 'dispensability'.
7. Weber sometimes used 'spheres' and at other times 'social orders'. The subtitle of the German original of Max Weber's *Economy and Society* (1978) was 'The Economy and the Social Orders and Powers [die Gesellschaftlichen Ordnungen und Maechte], but in his essay 'Religious Rejections of the World and their Directions' (1948: 323–359), he used 'spheres'. Fligstein and McAdam (2012) speak of 'meso-social orders'.
8. The specific points on which I differ from Mann will be discussed below, especially in Chapter 3 when I compare his 'radical' ideas with liberal ones. It is worth mentioning again that one reason that I am able to simplify his theory in this way is that I only deal with the modern period, approximately 200–250 years, whereas his theory covers the history of power from the beginning, more than 10,000 years. The same applies to the work of Gellner, Turner, Luhmann and Collins, whose work offers generalizations across human societies, past and present.
9. I use 'nature', 'natural world' and 'physical world' interchangeably. It would be better to use the more encompassing word 'environment', physical or natural, instead of 'world' here, but this might cause confusion with my use of 'environment' in the Luhmannian sense in Table 1.1. Nothing hangs on the difference.

10. Any claim about *general* primacy or mutual influence only constitutes a kind of re-description of social change in a different language ('the economy is cultural here' etc.) and so it is about language rather than substance, or otherwise it is vacuous. In Mann's theory of power, primacy is the ultimate determinant of how the four sources are interrelated – even if they are also intertwined. For systems theorists like Luhmann, systems have their own operations and structural couplings between them, though for Luhmann, communication also acts as a kind of meta-transmission belt between systems. These two approaches illustrate how the logical possibilities are exhaustive – as long as the three orders or powers or systems are not inextricable from the start (in which case there is some general primacy), then primacy whereby one determines the other, or a coupling that provides an account of how the translation of one into the other occurs, are the only possibilities. The theory presented here will accommodate both and conclude that both primacy and (limited) interaction of dominant institutions have their place (it can be noted in passing that Luhmann is sometimes regarded as a 'conservative' thinker, but as Moeller [2012] and King and Thornhill [2003: 201–25] have argued, he can equally be claimed for a left-leaning or radical theory). In any event, how orders affect each other in different periods must be shown via a substantive and empirical account, rather than via philosophical or theoretical a priori.

11. Mann distinguishes spatially between extensive and intensive power: 'Extensive power refers to the ability to organize large numbers of people over far-flung territories and to engage in minimally stable cooperation', while 'intensive power refers to the ability to organize tightly and organize a high level of mobilization and commitment from the participants, whether the area and numbers covered are large or small' (Mann 1986: 7). The distinction is a useful one and is adapted to my purposes in Table 1.1: power vis-á-vis nature, where I use the label 'intensive', as against the 'extensive' ordering in market exchanges. It can be added that the spatial limit of technoscience to the planet is necessary because natural resources from beyond the planet have not actively been harnessed for social purposes in a significant way.

12. Mann (2013) also argues against such a 'world society'.

13. The main exception to the nation-state as a unit is the European Union, but this has been added to – rather than superseding – nation-states.

2   Convergence and Divergence

1. A different approach would be to compare the 'most similar cases'; see Archer (2007) for the political trajectory of the US and Australia; and Sejersted's (2011) comparison of Sweden's and Norway's social democracy.

2. Steinmo compares not just Sweden and the US, but also Japan (2010) and Britain (1993).

3. Swenson (2002: 5) argues that the origins of the welfare state in Sweden are later, in the 1950s, whereas in the US Roosevelt's welfare reforms had already emerged in the 1930s, which supports his focus on employer rather than worker strategies. As Mann (2012) argues, however, Swenson's focus on employers does not rule out other explanations.

4. Hall and Lindholm (1999: 54–8) note that a similar 'peasant-worker alliance' could have emerged during the Depression in the US, but it was prevented by religious and ethnic cleavages and also by the unusually high levels of violence against workers (see Archer 2007).
5. For the earlier roots of the 'folkhem' idea at the beginning of the 20th century, including in community centres and libraries for workers, see Bjorck (2008).
6. Pontusson (2005: 99) gives the following figures for union density: Sweden in 1980, 80 per cent (80 per cent covered by collective bargaining) and in 2000, 79 per cent (90 per cent); versus the US in 1980, 22 per cent (26 per cent) and in 2000, 13 per cent (14 per cent).
7. Health care provides another example: we can think of the diverse interests shaping American health care reform, in contrast to the comparatively monolithic Swedish health care system.
8. The average for the OECD in both cases lies between the two; figures come from Tanzi and Schuhknecht (2000: 141) based on OECD data; see also Steinmo 2010: 38–40.
9. Steinmo (1993) argues that attitudes towards taxation are not so different in Sweden and the US, but that it is elites that have been responsible for creating different tax regimes. It is also not clear how attitudes to taxation translate into policy: Bartels (2008), for example, found that Americans voted for the tax cuts of President George W. Bush even when it was not in their best economic interest to do so.
10. A good summary of the literature about 'small states in world markets' can be found in Campbell and Hall (2006).
11. Separable here does not mean separate 'to the same extent' or 'in the same way': as we have seen, the state in the US is also more exposed, for example, to private economic actors, the Swedish one to union power.
12. The question of the extent to which American culture has been influenced by Sweden can be left to one side here, or perhaps to Minnesota local historians.
13. Steinmo (2010: 202, see Table 4.8) notes that 'the US has a much worse level of inequality than other developed societies, including Sweden: for example, the share of income or consumption of the richest 10% to the poorest 10% (in 2000) in Sweden was 6.2, in the US it was 15.9'. Gender and ethnic inequalities fall outside of the scope of the argument made here (but see Walby 2009: esp. 250–76).

3 Paths towards Pluralist Democracy: Liberal versus Radical Interpretations

1. Mann, the exception to this statement, will be discussed shortly. Fukuyama (2011) makes the same complaint.
2. 'Liberal' is used here in the British-English or John Stuart Mill sense, not in the American-English usage of a left-wing political inclination.
3. Arguably, as mentioned in Chapters 1 and 2, for *contemporary* advanced states, these 'outside-in' forces only play a critical role where they impose a fiscal burden on the declining hegemon; the US. This is Mann's argument (2013) about the American empire.

4. The fact that civil and political rights do not discriminate between pluralist democracies should not be taken to diminish the importance of their being achieved in the first place; in this respect the former communist states of Eastern Europe and the Soviet Union, for example, have come further than China.

5. Hall puts it differently (2006: 33): hope must not come before analysis. The political views of the three thinkers discussed here will be left to one side. Suffice it to say that Hall (2006; 2010) labels both Mann and Gellner 'social democrats' even though Gellner is often thought of as a liberal, while Hall's own work has often been concerned with Denmark and its social democratic tradition (Campbell and Hall 2006) as well as a study defending 'Liberalism' (1987).

6. There is a separate story that concerns the role that states play in promoting economic growth and what kind of economic policies they pursue. That topic is secondary here.

7. In Chapters 6 and 7, we shall come across technological infrastructures, including transport, energy and communications, but these are different from infrastructures aimed at supporting social rights (again, education, health and public services).

8. The set of countries to which the figures taken from Tanzi and Schuknecht refer vary somewhat from one set of tables to the next, but the differences are not great. This can be checked by going to the source of the citation.

9. On Habermas versus Luhmann in relation to the public sphere, see Schroeder (2007: 74–98).

10. Top incomes have risen in recent decades: according to Atkinson et al. (2010), the share of the top incomes (the top 1 per cent and 0.1 per cent) fell in Sweden and the United States between the two World Wars, and fell but then rose in the post-war period (there are other countries which are 'flat' in the post-war period, including Germany, France, Japan and the Netherlands). Looking ahead to Chapter 8, the same goes for India and China, which saw a post-war fall and then rise in the share of top incomes.

11. This point would need to be developed at length, but telling evidence comes from Mann (2012), who points out that in the US the bases of support for the Democratic and Republican parties are split more along an urban/rural divide than other divides such as economic or religious ones.

12. To be fair, Mann (2013) has a chapter on the looming environmental crisis, but this chapter is not well-integrated in his history of power and in his account of the four sources of power, which do not include science and technology.

4   Free and Unfree Markets

1. 'Modernity' is potentially a fourth term (in addition to capitalism, industrial revolution or markets) which could be held responsible for the rise of industrial society rather than the other way around, but this term only works if the focus is on *modern* capitalism. In that case, perhaps modern capitalism shaped industrial society rather than vice versa? But this argument is suspect: for example, as Dandeker argues, 'no matter how much the technical

and organizational attributes of industrialism can be shown to have been originally the products of the capitalist enterprise system, they are relatively autonomous from it: they can be adapted for use in quite different institutional contexts' (1990: 204). This argument was necessary at the time of the Cold War because the implication was that industrial society could be adapted not just to capitalist economic systems but also to others, such as communist systems. But nowadays there are no serious alternatives to capitalism in that even the last large remaining communist society, China, is moving towards a capitalist market economy (Chapter 8). Hence it is preferable to avoid 'modernity' as a prime mover, but it can spelled out specifically *how* the economy became modern, as outlined below, and see Chapter 1.

2. It is important to add: on a *mass* basis; long-distance exchange in luxury goods came earlier. But the pattern of bimodal trade (local versus long-distance) was only overcome in the 19th century when economies became more integrated for manufactured goods; see, for example, Dicken (1992: 11).

3. The 'hidden' premise of this argument can be made explicit: this break with the past entails the differentiation of the economic order and is thus part of a neo-evolutionist approach to history – but it is 'neo-' because there is no telos of this part of society, nor, as we shall see, to the logic within it – thus avoiding the common criticisms normally levelled at this type of argument (again, see Chapter 1).

4. One of the 'levels' or limits in this sentence will be revisited in Chapters 5 and 6. It can be noted that other sociologists make the same point about supply and demand: for example, Centeno and Cohen say 'markets allocate the flow of goods and payments according to the intrinsic logic of a balance between needs and offers' (2010: 13). Further, as argued, this 'logic' is central to market organization: 'The *market logic* can be understood as a form of social organization premised on materialism, individualism, and rational utility-maximization' (ibid.: 23).

5. I am ignoring for the moment 'rational choice' approaches to politics and religion, for example, but these can be left to one side here as they are treated in other chapters as dominant institutions with different mechanisms. It can be noted that 'choice' seems an odd way to describe 'rationality' (for a non-economist), since rational-actor models postulate that all actors must behave the same way in the same situation (Morgan 2012: 357–9).

6. Even the proposed 'Tobin' or 'Robin Hood' tax on financial transactions is aimed not at exercising political control over financial markets, but at stabilizing them.

7. Another set of markets which are embedded but also interact with global markets are economies that are dominated by particular resources such as the oil-producing states, but these economies fall outside the scope of the focus in this book on the developed North.

8. Here it can be added parenthetically that the state has shaped the economy in various ways, but deliberate and professional economic policy is a recent phenomenon. Skidelsky points out, for example, that economic planning in the West had its origins in the 'Economic Section' in Britain during the Second World War (2003: 643).

9. Here it is worth mentioning Vogel's argument that regulation should not be seen in seen in zero-sum, more or less, terms: rather, he says, markets

have in recent decades been reformed by being 're-regulated', and 'states themselves, even more than political interest groups, have driven the reform process' (1996: 4). He further notes that 'governments ... have converged most in that they have all liberalized: they have opened markets to more competition' (1996: 261), although *how* this has happened in the countries he examined has varied, leaving room for different policy options.

10. On the problematic nature of 'rational' models of actors in economics, see Morgan (2012: 136–64). She points out that maximizing actors and an equilibrium are interdependent in economic thought and have become dominant in the 20th century (Morgan 2012: 394). Hence I have opted to use 'maximizing' (without 'utility') rather than 'rationality', and similarly used 'equilibrium' in a non-technical sense.

5   The Paradoxes of Science, Technology and Social Change

1. An earlier version of this chapter can be found in Schroeder (2011a).
2. I am indebted to Michael Mann for urging this point on me. However, it is hard to gauge how much this concentration in the service of other social powers matters: after all, other sciences have also been ongoing at the same time as these three 'peaks', and economic and political factors do not affect the validity of science. There is a larger point here, which is that science and technology do not start from a 'blank slate', ab novo, except insofar as they transform nature directly, but rather often build on how nature *has already been transformed* by technoscience. This is the main reason why techno-science is intertwined with economic and political forces, and this is also why re-orienting technoscience is difficult, and tackling the rebounding of nature (Chapter 6), in view of the constraints of the natural world, confronts locked-in processes.
3. The extent to which these increasing communications lead to more similar values among countries with high levels of ICT uses – or fail to do so – is documented by Norris and Inglehart (2009).
4. See Headrick (2010) for the role of technology in colonialism, an example of military technology with implications beyond nation-states. Nuclear weapons are another example.

6   The Limits to Transforming the Environment

1. An earlier version of this chapter was published as Schroeder (2010).
2. All these approaches are reviewed in Hulme (2009), Speth (2008) and Yearley (2005), where further references can be found.
3. 'Nature' and the 'physical world' will be used interchangeably here; the latter includes nature beyond the earth. For the idea that the physical or natural worlds are separate from, but transformed by, scientific knowledge and technological manipulation, see Chapter 5 and Schroeder (2007: 8–13). Here it can also be noted the term 'environment' should always be understood in this chapter as conjoined with the adjective 'natural'. It can be recalled that

that there is a potential confusion with the use of 'environment' in Chapter 1 to indicate the different 'environments' for each of the three social orders (but the environment that 'belongs to' the technoscientific order is always the *natural* environment).

4. As with modern science and technology, this discontinuity is distinctively 'modern', to take issue with Latour (1993).
5. In fact, there are two main limits and ways that the environment is rebounding: the limits imposed by resource use, and the limits of harms done to the environment via pollution and the like. This chapter can focus on the former because future constraints are more clear-cut in the case of resource use, and particularly energy uses. Still, the argument potentially has much wider implications, and so we will need to return to how energy uses are only one part of 'limits' in the conclusion.
6. Rockstroem et al. (2009) argue that there is a 'safe operating space' within which burdens can be placed on the resilience of different parts of the natural environment, several of them already exceeded and with more that can be foreseen. 'Realistic' assessments of limits can thus be undertaken not just for energy, but for other uses of natural resources.
7. Thus Wilson and Dowlatabadi argue that, in research, 'the main integrative challenge is to resolve this assumption of individual agency (in economics, technology diffusion, and social psychology) with sociological findings on the structuring of behaviour by sociotechnical systems' (2007: 191), which is the perspective of this chapter.
8. Bauer and Gaskell elaborate the model for biotechnology, but in my view it fits environmentalism equally well.
9. Crone has pointed out that the cost of industrialized society, as opposed to traditional (pre-modern) society, is intrinsic instability (1989: 196–7).
10. Scientists are already undertaking such analyses; see Rockstroem et al. (2009).
11. It will be evident that this theoretical frame is both functionalist but also based on conflict theory, a combination that is inescapable for the relation between technology and social change, to come back to the discussion in Chapter 1, and as argued elsewhere (Schroeder 2007: esp. pp. 127–8).
12. Priestland (2012: 254) points out that even if 'limits to growth in the developed world' are achieved via 'a greater role of the state', 'low growth hits the poor, and without much more substantial redistributions of wealth, zero growth will lead to even wider inequalities'.

7 Three Cultures

1. An earlier version of this chapter has been published as Schroeder (2011b).
2. On this point, see DiMaggio (1994: 45–6) and Fischer (2010: 59–94), and esp. p. 74: 'economists cannot easily dismiss or define away the notion of overbuying; people do distinguish need from luxury and act accordingly'.
3. To be sure, there is a part of the economy that is devoted to cultural goods and services (see Swedberg 2003: 249–57; see also DiMaggio 1994); yet this should be counted among economic rather than cultural forces.

4. In Chapter 1, Bayly (2004: 480) was cited as arguing that the very notion of religion only became separated in the 19th century.
5. Why no 'clash' of civilizations (Huntington 1996)? But why should they clash, except for dominance? The three cultures described here are too diffuse to compete for dominance, and to clash, Islam, the only political religion, would need an enemy (which American foreign policy may provide). Science does not need to compete; its dominance is pervasive because of its success, and it has an institutional base.

8   Modernization and the Politics of Development

1. This paragraph is based on Naughton (2007: 427–46).
2. See also Guthrie (2006: 48–50), and the paper by Walder, Luo and Wang (2010), which distinguishes between industrial assets, real estate, and agricultural property and the quite different processes of a transition from state to private ownership in each case.
3. There is an important debate on these questions in the review by Andreas (2010) of Huang's book (2008), and Huang's reply (2010). Tsai (2007) documents different 'models' of development in China's turn to capitalism, and how these models cope with different political constraints in various Chinese regions.
4. This is not to say that Confucianism may not be a political ideal that is worth pursuing. Indeed, there are many scholars who seek to show that Confucian political ideas are compatible with Western democratic, liberal and egalitarian ideals (Chan 2002), or that they are more suitable to the Chinese context (Bell 2008). We will return to this in the concluding chapter.
5. Davis and Wang say, for example, that 'between the mid-1980s and 2000, the share of owner-occupied units rose from about 10% to over 75% . . . but because the primary routes to ownership were sales of publicly owned flats to sitting tenants, home ownership initially reset the clock of wealth distribution and equalized rather than polarized household wealth . . . more recently, as the real estate market matured, new inequalities have clearly emerged in terms of resale value' (2009: 12).
6. A more nuanced picture is possible in relation to the political legacy of colonialism, since there was great variation in the extent to which, in parts of India, local kings retained their autonomy: it has been argued that 'the more directly ruled regions of India currently have higher levels of development than the more indirectly ruled regions' (Lange 2009: 176). In other words, the regions where the colonial state was stronger – Lange's main measure is the extent to which a centralized legal-administrative apparatus supplanted local authority relations – have fared better since Independence (although caution is advised for this correlation: Lange himself refers to the limits of his mixed methods analysis). Different regions or states are in any event ruled with varying degrees of success, as discussed below (see Kohli 2012).
7. Cf. Misra (2008: 392–8) on the causes of liberalization. It can be noted that even with liberalization, much of the economy is still part of the state: 'In the last two decades the private corporate sector has thrived, even though in

the formal sector state-owned companies still account for about 40% of total sales' (Bardhan 2010: 78), though the formal sector, as we shall see, is only one part of the economy.

8. The question of the emergence of an emerging class consciousness among Indian workers continues to be subject to debate (see Mann 2005: 309).

9. Mann has argued along similar lines that although ethnic violence has escalated in recent decades, unlike in other parts of the world it has also been held in check because India's 'secular, liberal, socialist, and especially its caste institutions survive, and its state still channels development funds to backward tribal areas' (Mann 2005: 490).

10. Gupta says that 'among urban Indians, caste plays a minor role, if any at all, outside the personal sphere' (2009: xv). Still, as Quigley notes, 'for hundreds of millions of people these concepts' – of caste – 'are the primary means by which they identify themselves and others' (1999: 98). See also Bayly (1999), who relates caste to the politics of the colonial and post-independence state.

11. David Gellner (2009) has argued that apart from activists, parties which represent ethnic and economically disadvantaged groups should be included in civil society in India. Yet, as I have argued in Chapter 3, the concept of civil society should not include parties since this concept should be restricted to non-state (including parties in power) and non-market forces, though Gellner is right to point to the extensive party-mobilization on behalf of these groups: perhaps, insofar as groups with a narrow agenda come into power, this points to incomplete differentiation or modernization.

12. The problem of wealth and economic opportunities being captured by political elites is, of course, characteristic of many developing societies, such as Africa's 'gatekeeper' states (Cooper 2002).

13. It is worth mentioning parenthetically that the underlying functionalism of the idea of differentiation of the theory being put forward here is exposed at this point: full marketization (disembedding of markets) would entail that there are no distortions of the market by political embedding of favouring religious/ethnic groups in India or party members and their aims in China. And vice versa: these economic distortions continue to cause problems for the extension of neutrally administered and universal political rights. However, this functionalism does not predetermine social evolution: it is conceivable that incomplete institutionalization of modern states and markets or incomplete differentiation between the political and economic orders could take the two countries in a different direction from the global North. Put differently, there is no inevitable friction between the two orders if they remain undifferentiated, nor an inevitable trajectory towards stable institutionalization. However, there is also no necessary departure from these.

9   Social Theory in the Face of the Future

1. 'Usefulness' is one criterion, 'testable' is another. For usefulness, theoretical ideas should also – again, in the manner of science as interpreted here – exercise some degree of control over the social environment insofar as they provide more powerful ways to capture it. In relation to testability, the patterns identified here should be assessed in the light of the record of

historical or social change, and subject to refutation. I have also ventured some prognoses (prediction is too strong) and will make a few more in this chapter, also open to refutation. In any event, the key, as Gellner pointed out, is not to put forward a refutation-evading 'package deal'.

2. If it seems obvious that state spending is constrained by a relative economic downturn, this constraint also works in the other direction: economic demand has come to be constrained by an end to states stimulating consumerism.

3. As mentioned, differentiation or the increasing separation of orders has advantages and disadvantages. Yet it can be noted that any argument that 'evolution' or increasing 'functional interdependence' leads to greater efficiency has been avoided here: although a larger volume of commodified material is exchanged, technoscience has expanded its control over the natural world, and citizen-classes have become more incorporated within the state – there are constraints in respect to all of these, as we have seen. Further, the argument has been applied to states with different population sizes, to avoid another type of evolutionary argument.

4. We can note that this kind of change involves both the dominant institutions (coordinating bodies for financial institutions, self-organization of firms providing goods and services) and their environments (borrowers and customers for financial instruments, or consumers and their aggregate demand for goods and services), but the mechanisms translate between and re-embed exchanges within the respective orders.

5. It can be mentioned immediately that apart from the coercive power of states, technoscience is also constraining: this is not only because of the limits of the physical world, but also because of the institutions of science and technology, such as peer review and openness, or the systemic nature of many technologies (Chapter 5).

6. Hall recognizes the constraint on liberal 'open-endedness' when he says that we are 'learning how to control and understand the roles that we have been, and continue to be, forced to play' (1987: 92).

7. To clarify: Nagel and Sen would agree that there are certain global or universal human (negative) rights, but not the strong ones for securing economically grounded well-being that Pogge is seeking.

8. The debate about freedom and equality does, of course, apply beyond the North. But in linking normative theory to the substantive argument here, other questions such as deepening or enabling democracy are more relevant to India, China and beyond.

9. Pressure must be conceived here in terms of the organization of political interests, not merely beliefs, since values indicate that support for state intervention in markets is steady or growing: there are 'steady levels of support for liberal economic values', with Sweden and America 'remarkably similar', and a 'gradual trend in economic values towards more *collectivist* or leftist values . . . even [in] the United States' (Norris and Inglehart 2009: 275).

References

Abdelal, Rawi (2007) *Capital Rules: The Construction of Global Finance* (Cambridge, MA: Harvard University Press).

Abercrombie, Nicholas, Stephen Hill and Bryan Turner (1980) *The Dominant Ideology Thesis* (London: George Allen & Unwin).

Acemoglu, Daron and James A. Robinson (2006) *Economic Origins of Dictatorship and Democracy* (Cambridge: Cambridge University Press).

Adeney, Katharine and Andrew Wyatt (2010) *Contemporary India* (Basingstoke: Palgrave Macmillan).

Alesina, Alberto and Edward Glaeser (2004) *Fighting Poverty in the US and Europe: A World of Difference* (Oxford: Oxford University Press).

Alm, Martin (2009) 'Bilden av Amerika' [The View of America], in Jacob Christensson (ed.), *Signums svenska kulturhistoria: 1900-talet* (Stockholm: Bokforlaget Signum), pp. 179–197.

Archer, Robin (2007) *Why Is There No Labor Party in the United States?* (Princeton: Princeton University Press).

Anderson, Perry (1974) *Lineages of the Absolutist State* (London: Verso).

Anderson, Perry (2010) 'Two Revolutions', *New Left Review*, vol. 61, pp. 59–96.

Andreas, Joel (2008) 'Changing Colours in China', *New Left Review*, vol. 54, pp. 123–42.

Andreas, Joel (2009) *Rise of the Red Engineers. The Cultural Revolution and the Origins of China's New Class* (Stanford: Stanford University Press).

Andreas, Joel (2010) 'A Shanghai Model? On Capitalism with Chinese Characteristics', *New Left Review*, vol. 65, pp. 63–85.

Atkinson, A. B., Thomas Piketty and Emmanuel Saez (2010) 'Top Incomes in the Long Run of History', in A. B. Atkinson and Thomas Piketty (eds), *Top Incomes: A Global Perspective* (Oxford: Oxford University Press), pp. 664–740.

Baldwin, Peter (2009) *The Narcissism of Minor Differences: How America and Europe are Alike* (Oxford: Oxford University Press).

Banerjee, Mukulika (2010) 'Elections as Communitas', *Social Research*, vol. 78, no. 1, pp. 75–98.

Bardhan, Pranab (2010) *Awakening Giants, Feet of Clay: Assessing the Economic Rise of India and China* (Princeton: Princeton University Press).

Bartels, Larry (2008) *Unequal Democracy: The Political Economy of the New Gilded Age* (Princeton: Princeton University Press).

Baron, Naomi (2008) *Always On: Language in an Online and Mobile World* (Oxford: Oxford University Press).

Bauer, Martin and George Gaskell (2002) 'The Biotechnology Movement', in Martin Bauer and George Gaskell (eds), *Biotechnology: The Making of a Global Controversy* (Cambridge: Cambridge University Press), pp. 379–404.

Bauman, Zygmunt (2007) *Liquid Times* (Cambridge: Polity Press).

Bayat, Asef (2007) *Making Islam Democratic: Social Movements and the Post-Islamist Turn* (Stanford: Stanford University Press).

Bayly, Christopher Alan (2004) *The Birth of the Modern World 1780–1914* (Oxford: Blackwell).

Bayly, Susan (1999) *Caste, Society and Politics in India from the Eighteenth Century to the Modern Age* (Cambridge: Cambridge University Press).

Bayly, Susan (2007) *Asian Voices in a Postcolonial Age: Vietnam, India and Beyond* (Cambridge: Cambridge University Press).

Beck, Ulrich (1992) *Risk Society: Towards a New Modernity* (London: Sage).

Beck, Ulrich (2010) 'Remapping Social Inequalities in an Age of Climate Change: for a Cosmopolitan Renewal of Sociology', *Global Networks*, vol. 10, no. 2, pp. 165–81.

Beckert, Jens (2009) 'The Social Order of Markets', *Theory and Society*, vol. 38, no. 3, pp. 245–69.

Bell, Daniel A. (2008) *China's New Confucianism: Politics and Everyday Life in a Changing Society* (Princeton: Princeton University Press).

Beniger, James (1986) *The Control Revolution: Technological and Economic Origins of the Information Society* (Cambridge, MA: Harvard University Press).

Berggren, Henrik and Lars Trägårdh (2006) *Är svensken människan? [Are Swedes Humans?]* (Stockholm: Norstedts).

Bjorck, Henrik (2008) *Folkhemsbyggare [Builders of the People's Home]* (Stockholm: Atlantis).

Block, Fred and Margaret Somers (1984) 'Beyond the Economistic Fallacy: The Holistic Social Science of Karl Polanyi', in Theda Skocpol (ed.), *Vision and Method in Historical Sociology* (Cambridge: Cambridge University Press), pp. 47–84.

Blyth, Mark (2002) *Great Transformations: Economic Ideas and Institutional Change in the Twentieth Century* (Cambridge: Cambridge University Press).

Bowles, Samuel (1986) 'The Production Process in the Competitive Economy: Walrasian, Neo-Hobbesian, and Marxian Models', in Louis Putterman (ed.), *The Economic Nature of the Firm: A Reader* (Cambridge: Cambridge University Press).

Boykoff, Maxell (2011) *Who Speaks for the Climate? Making Sense of Media Reporting of Climate Change* (Cambridge: Cambridge University Press).

Boykoff, Max, Adam Bumpus and Diana Liverman (2009) 'Theorizing the Carbon Economy: Introduction to the Special Issue', *Environment and Planning A*, vol. 41, pp. 2299–304.

Boykoff, Max and Jules Boykoff (2004) 'Balance as Bias: Global Warming and the US Prestige Press', *Global Environmental* Change, vol. 14, no. 2, pp. 125–36.

Braun, Ingo (1994) 'The Technology–Culture Spiral: Three Examples of Technological Developments in Everyday Life', *Research in Philosophy and Technology*, vol. 14 ('Technology and Everyday Life'), pp. 93–118.

Breuer, Stefan (1998) 'The Concept of Democracy in Weber's Political Sociology', in Ralph Schroeder (ed.), *Max Weber, Democracy and Modernization* (Basingstoke: Macmillan), pp. 1–13.

Bryant, Joseph (2006) 'The West and the Rest Revisited: Debating Capitalist Origins, European Colonialism, and the Advent of Modernity', *Canadian Journal of Sociology*, vol. 31, no. 4, pp. 403–44.

Campbell, Colin (1987) *The Romantic Ethic and the Spirit of Consumerism* (Oxford: Basil Blackwell).

Campbell, John and John Hall (2006) 'Introduction: The State of Denmark', in John Campbell, John Hall and Ove Pedersen (eds), *National Identity and the*

Varieties of Capitalism: The Danish Experience (Montreal and Kingston: McGill-Queens University Press), pp. 3–49.

Castells, Manuel (2000) 'Materials for an Exploratory Theory of the Network Society', *British Journal of Sociology*, vol. 51, no. 1, pp. 5–24.

Centeno, Miguel and Joseph Cohen (2010) *Global Capitalism* (Cambridge: Polity Press).

Chan, Anita, Richard Madsen and Jonathan Unger (2009) *Chen Village: Revolution to Globalization* (Berkeley: University of California Press).

Chan, Joseph (2002) 'Moral Autonomy, Civil Liberties, and Confucianism', *Philosophy East and West*, vol. 52, no. 3, pp. 281–310.

Chang, Ha-Joon (2002) *Kicking Away the Ladder: Development Strategy in Historical Perspective* (London: Anthem Press).

Charvet, John (1981) *A Critique of Freedom and Equality* (Cambridge: Cambridge University Press).

Chaves, Mark and Philip Gorski (2001) 'Religious Pluralism and Religious Participation', *Annual Review of Sociology*, vol. 27, pp. 261–81.

Christian, David (2004) *Maps of Time: An Introduction to Big History* (Berkeley: University of California Press).

Collier, Paul (2007) *The Bottom Billion. Why the Poorest Countries Are Failing and What Can Be Done about It* (Oxford: Oxford University Press).

Collins, Randall (1975) *Conflict Sociology: Toward an Explanatory Science* (New York: Academic Press).

Collins, Randall (1986) *Weberian Sociological Theory* (Cambridge: Cambridge University Press).

Collins, Randall (1993a) 'Ethical Controversies of Science and Society: A Relation Between Two Spheres of Social Conflict', in Thomas Brante, Steve Fuller and William Lynch (eds), *Controversial Science: From Content to Contention* (Albany: State University of New York Press), pp. 301–17.

Collins, Randall (1993b) 'Liberals and Conservatives, Religious and Political: A Conjuncture of Modern History', *Sociology of Religion*, vol. 54, no. 2, pp. 127–46.

Collins, Randall (1994a) 'Why the Social Sciences Won't Become High-consensus, Rapid-discovery Science', *Sociological Forum*, vol. 9, no. 2, pp. 155–77.

Collins, Randall (1994b) *Four Sociological Traditions* (Oxford: Oxford University Press).

Collins, Randall (1998) *The Sociology of Philosophies: A Global Theory of Intellectual Change* (Cambridge MA.: Harvard University Press).

Collins, Randall (1999a) *Macrohistory: Essays in the Sociology of the Long Run* (Stanford: Stanford University Press).

Collins, Randall (1999b) 'The European Sociological Tradition and Twenty-first-century World Sociology', in Janet Abu Lughod (ed.), *Sociology for the Twenty-first Century: Continuities and Cutting Edges* (Chicago: University of Chicago Press), pp. 26–42.

Collins, Randall (2000) 'Situational Stratification: A Micro-macro Theory of Inequality', *Sociological Theory*, vol. 18, no. 1, pp. 17–43.

Collins, Randall (2004) *Interaction Ritual Chains* (Princeton: Princeton University Press).

Collins, Randall (2006) 'Mann's Transformation of the Classical Sociological Traditions', in John A. Hall and Ralph Schroeder (eds), *An Anatomy of*

Power: The Social Theory of Michael Mann (Cambridge: Cambridge University Press), pp. 19–32.

Cooper, Fred (2002) *Africa Since 1940: The Past of the Present* (Cambridge: Cambridge University Press).

Corbridge, Stuart and John Harriss (2000) *Reinventing India: Liberalization, Hindu Nationalism and Popular Democracy* (Cambridge: Polity Press).

Coyle, Diane (2007) *The Soulful Science: What Economists Really Do and Why It Matters* (Princeton: Princeton University Press).

Crone, Patricia (1989) *Pre-industrial Societies* (Oxford: Blackwell).

Crouch, Colin (2004) *Post-Democracy* (Cambridge: Polity Press).

Dabringhaus, Sabine (2009) *Geschichte Chinas im 20. Jahrhundert* (München: C. H. Beck).

Dahl, Robert A. (1998) *On Democracy* (New Haven: Yale University Press).

Dandeker, Christopher (1990) *Surveillance, Power and Modernity* (Cambridge: Polity Press).

Dasgupta, Partha (2009) 'Nature's Role in Sustaining Economic Development', *Philosophical Transactions of the Royal Society B*, vol. 365, pp. 5–11.

Davis, Deborah and Feng Wang (2009) 'Poverty and Wealth in Postsocialist China: An Overview', in Deborah Davis and Wang Feng (eds), *Creating Wealth and Poverty in Postsocialist China* (Stanford: Stanford University Press), pp. 3–19.

De Grazia, Victoria (2005) *Irresistible Empire: America's Advance through 20th-century Europe* (Cambridge, MA: Harvard University Press).

Deere-Birkbeck, Carolyn (2009) 'Global Governance in the Context of Climate Change: The Challenges of Increasingly Complex Risk Parameters', *International Affairs*, vol. 85, no. 6, pp. 1173–94.

Dicken, Peter (1992) *Global Shift: The Internationalization of Economic Activity*, 2nd ed. (London: Paul Chapman Publishing).

DiMaggio, Paul and Walter Powell (1983) 'The Iron Cage Revisited: Institutional Isomorphism and Collective Rationality in Organizational Fields', *American Sociological Review*, vol. 48, no. 2, pp. 147–60.

DiMaggio, Paul (1994) 'Culture and the Economy', in Neil Smelser and Richard Swedberg (eds), *The Handbook of Economic Sociology* (Princeton: Princeton University Press), pp. 27–57.

Drori, Gili, John Meyer, Francisco Ramirez and Evan Schofer (2003) *Science in the Modern World Polity: Institutionalization and Globalization* (Stanford: Stanford University Press).

Dumont, Louis (1970) *Homo Hierarchicus: The Caste System and Its Implications* (Chicago: University of Chicago Press).

Dumont, Louis (1977) *From Mandeville to Marx: The Genesis and Triumph of Modern Ideology* (Chicago: University of Chicago Press).

Economy, Elizabeth (2004) *The River Runs Black: The Environmental Challenge to China's Future* (Ithaca: Cornell University Press).

Edgerton, David (2006) *The Shock of the Old: A Global History of Twentieth Century Technology* (London: Profile Books).

Eisenstadt, Schmuel (2000) 'Multiple Modernities', *Daedalus*, vol. 129, no. 1, pp. 1–29.

Esping-Andersen, Gosta (1990) *The Three Worlds of Welfare Capitalism* (Cambridge: Polity Press).

Evans, Peter and James Rauch (1999), 'Bureaucracy and Growth: a Cross-national Analysis of the Effects of "Weberian" State Structures on Economic Growth', *American Sociological Review*, vol. 64, no. 4, pp. 748–65.

Fewsmith, Joseph (2008) *China since Tiananmen: From Deng Xiaoping to Hu Jintao*, 2nd ed. (Cambridge: Cambridge University Press).

Fischer, Claude S. (2010) *Made in America: A Social History of American Culture and Character* (Chicago: University of Chicago Press).

Fischer, Claude and Michael Hout (2006) *Century of Difference: How America Changed in the Last One Hundred Years* (New York: Russell Sage Foundation).

Fligstein, Neil (2001) *The Architecture of Markets: An Economic Sociology of Twenty-first-century Capitalist Societies* (Princeton: Princeton University Press).

Fligstein, Neil and Doug McAdam (2012) *A Theory of Fields* (Oxford: Oxford University Press).

Frank, David John and Jay Gabler (2006) *Reconstructing the University: Worldwide Shifts in Academia in the 20th Century* (Stanford: Stanford University Press).

Friedman, Benjamin (2005) *The Moral Consequences of Economic Growth* (New York: Random House).

Frykman, Jonas and Orvar Löfgen (1987) *Culture Builders: A Historical Anthropology of Middle-class Life* (New Brunswick: Rutgers University Press).

Fuchs, Stephan (1992) *The Professional Quest for Truth: A Social Theory of Science and Knowledge* (Albany: State University of New York Press).

Fuchs, Stephan (2001) *Against Essentialism: A Theory of Culture and Society* (Cambridge, MA: Harvard University Press).

Fuchs, Stephan (2002) 'What Makes Sciences Scientific?', in Jonathan Turner (ed.), *Handbook of Sociological Theory* (New York: Kluwer Academic/Plenum Publishers), pp. 21–35.

Fukuyama, Francis (1992) *The End of History and the Last Man* (London: Hamish Hamilton).

Fukuyama, Francis (2011) *The Origins of Political Order. From Prehuman Times to the French Revolution* (New York: Farrar, Straus and Giroux).

Fuller, C. J. (2004) *The Camphor Flame: Popular Hinduism and Society in India*, 2nd ed. (Princeton: Princeton University Press).

Fuller, C. J. and John Harriss (2001) 'For an Anthropology of the Modern Indian State', in C. J. Fuller and Veronique Benei (eds), *The Everyday State and Society in Modern India* (London: C. Hurst and Company), pp. 1–30.

Fuller, C. J. and John Harriss (2005) 'Globalizing Hinduism: A "Traditional" Guru and Modern Businessmen in Chennai', in Jackie Assayag and Chris Fuller (eds), *Globalizing India: Perspectives from Below* (London: Anthem Press), pp. 211–36.

Galison, Peter and Bruce Hevly (eds) (1992) *Big Science: The Growth of Large-scale Research* (Stanford: Stanford University Press).

Gans, Herbert (1974) *Popular Culture and High Culture: An Analysis and Evaluation of Taste* (New York: Basic Books).

Garfinkel, Irwin, Lee Rainwater and Timothy Smeeding (2010) *Wealth and Welfare States: Is America a Laggard or Leader?* (Oxford: Oxford University Press).

Gellner, David (2009) 'Introduction: How Civil Are "Communal" and Ethno-nationalist Movements?', in David Gellner (ed.), *Ethnic Activism and Civil Society in South Asia* (New Delhi: Sage Publications), pp. 1–24.

Gellner, Ernest (1974) *Legitimation of Belief* (Cambridge: Cambridge University Press).

Gellner, Ernest (1979) 'A Social Contract in Search of an Idiom: The Demise of the Danegeld State', in Ernest Gellner, *Spectacles and Predicaments: Essays in Social Theory* (Cambridge: Cambridge University Press), pp. 277–306.

Gellner, Ernest (1983) *Nations and Nationalism* (Oxford: Basil Blackwell).

Gellner, Ernest (1987) *Culture, Identity and Politics* (Cambridge: Cambridge University Press).

Gellner, Ernest (1992) *Postmodernism, Reason and Religion* (London: Routledge).

Gellner, Ernest (1994) *Conditions of Liberty: Civil Society and Its Rivals* (London: Hamish Hamilton).

Gellner, Ernest (1988) *Plough, Sword and Book: The Structure of Human History* (London: Collins Harvill).

Gereffi, Gary (1994) 'The International Economy', in Neil Smelser and Richard Swedberg (eds), *The Handbook of Economic Sociology* (Princeton: Princeton University Press), pp. 206–33.

Gerth, Karl (2010) *As China Goes, So Goes the World* (New York: Hill and Wang).

Giddens, Anthony (1985) *The Nation-state and Violence* (Cambridge: Polity Press).

Giddens, Anthony (1990) *The Consequences of Modernity* (Cambridge: Polity Press).

Glaeser, Jochen (2006) *Wissenschaftliche Produktionsgemeinschaften: Die Soziale Ordnung der Forschung* (Frankfurt am Main: Campus).

Goldman, Merle (2005) *From Comrade to Citizen: The Struggle for Political Rights in China* (Cambridge, MA: Harvard University Press).

Goldstone, Jack (2006) 'A Historical, Not Comparative Method: Breakthroughs and Limitations in the Theory and Methodology of Michael Mann's Analysis of Power', in John A. Hall and Ralph Schroeder (eds), *An Anatomy of Power: The Social Theory of Michael Mann* (Cambridge: Cambridge University Press), pp. 263–82.

Gorski, Philip and Ates Altinordu (2008) 'After Secularization?', *Annual Review of Sociology*, vol. 34, pp. 55–85.

Goossaert, Vincent and David Palmer (2011) *The Religious Question in Modern China* (Chicago: University of Chicago Press).

Granovetter, Mark (1985) 'Economic Action and Social Structure: The Problem of Embeddeness', *American Journal of Sociology*, vol. 91, no. 3, pp. 481–510.

Guha, Ramachandra (2007) *India after Gandhi: The History of the World's Largest Democracy* (Basingstoke: Pan Macmillan).

Guillen, Mauro (2001) 'Is Globalization Civilizing, Destructive or Feeble? A Critique of Five Key Debates in the Social Science Literature', *Annual Review of Sociology*, vol. 21, pp. 235–60.

Guthrie, Doug (1999) *Dragon in a Three-Piece Suit: The Emergence of Capitalism in China* (Princeton: Princeton University Press).

Guthrie, Doug (2006) *China and Globalization* (Abingdon: Routledge).

Gupta, Dipankar (2009) *The Caged Phoenix: Can India Fly?* (Stanford: Stanford University Press).

Haas, Peter (1992) 'Introduction: Epistemic Communities and International Policy Coordination', *International Organization*, vol. 46, no. 1, pp. 1–35.

Hacking, Ian (1983) *Representing and Intervening* (Cambridge: Cambridge University Press).

Haddon, Leslie (2004) *Information and Communication Technologies in Everyday Life* (Oxford: Berg).

Hall, John (1986) *Powers and Liberties: The Causes and Consequences of the Rise of the West* (Harmondsworth: Penguin Books).

Hall, John (1987) *Liberalism: Politics, Ideology and the Market* (London: Paladin Grafton).

Hall, John (1988) 'Classes and Elites, Wars and Social Evolution: A Comment on Mann', *Sociology*, vol. 22, no. 3, pp. 385–91.

Hall, John (2006) 'Political Questions', in John A. Hall and Ralph Schroeder (eds), *An Anatomy of Power: The Social Theory of Michael Mann* (Cambridge: Cambridge University Press), pp. 33–55.

Hall, John (2013) *The Importance of Being Civil: The Struggle for Political Decency* (Princeton: Princeton University Press).

Hall, John A. (2010) *Ernest Gellner: An Intellectual Biography* (London: Verso).

Hall, John A. and Charles Lindholm (1999) *Is America Breaking Apart?* (Princeton: Princeton University Press).

Hall, John A. and Frank Trentmann (2005) 'Contests over Civil Society: Introductory Perspectives', in Hall and Trentmann (eds), *Civil Society: A Reader in History, Theory and Global Politics* (Basingstoke: Palgrave Macmillan), pp. 1–25.

Hall, Peter and David Soskice (2001) 'An Introduction to Varieties of Capitalism', in *Varieties of Capitalism: The Institutional Foundations of Comparative Advantage* (Oxford: Oxford University Press), pp. 1–68.

Halle, David (1993) *Inside Culture: Art and Class in the American Home* (Chicago: University of Chicago Press).

Hallin, Daniel and Paolo Mancini (2004) *Comparing Media Systems: Three Models of Media and Politics* (Cambridge: Cambridge University Press).

Hamilton, Gary (1994) 'Civilizations and the Organizations of Economies', in Neil Smelser and Richard Swedberg (eds), *The Handbook of Economic Sociology* (Princeton: Princeton University Press), pp. 183–205.

Hamilton, Gary and Robert Feenstra (1998) 'The Organization of Economies', in Mary Brinton and Victor Nee (eds), *The New Institutionalism in Sociology* (New York: Russell Sage Foundation), pp. 153–80.

Harriss-White, Barbara (2003) *India Working: Essays on Economy and Society* (Cambridge: Cambridge University Press).

Headrick, Daniel (2010) *Power over Peoples: Technology, Environments, and Western Imperialism, 1400 to the Present* (Princeton: Princeton University Press).

Heilbron, Johan (2005) 'Taking Stock: Towards a Historical Sociology of Financial Regimes', *Economic Sociology: European Electronic Newsletter*, vol. 7, no. 1, October.

Hess, David (1997) *Science Studies: An Advanced Introduction* (New York: New York University Press).

Hicks, Alexander (1999) *Social Democracy and Welfare Capitalism: A Century of Income Security Politics* (Ithaca: Cornell University Press).

Hobsbawm, Eric (1994) *Age of Extremes: The Short Twentieth Century, 1914–1991* (London: Michael Joseph).

Hobson, John (2003) 'Disappearing Taxes or a "Race to the Middle"? Fiscal Policy in the OECD', in Linda Weiss (ed.), *States in the Global Economy: Bringing Domestic Institutions Back In* (Cambridge: Cambridge University Press), pp. 37–57.

Hobson, John and Leonard Seabrooke (2007) 'Everyday IPE: Revealing Everyday Forms of Change in the World Economy', in John Hobson and Leonard

Seabrooke (eds), *Everyday Politics of the World Economy* (Cambridge: Cambridge University Press), pp. 1–23.

Hodgson, Marshall (1993) *Rethinking World History: Essays on Europe, Islam and World History* (ed. by Edmund Burke III) (Cambridge: Cambridge University Press).

Hounshell, David A. (1984) *From the American System to Mass Production, 1800–1932* (Baltimore: Johns Hopkins University Press).

Huang, Yasheng (2008) *Capitalism with Chinese Characteristics: Entrepreneurship and the State* (Cambridge: Cambridge University Press).

Huang, Yasheng (2010) 'The Politics of China's Path: A Reply to Joel Andreas', *New Left Review*, vol. 65, pp. 87–91.

Hughes, Thomas (1987) 'The Evolution of Large Technological Systems', in Wiebe Bijker, Thomas Hughes and Trevor Pinch (eds), *The Social Construction of Technological Systems* (Cambridge, MA: MIT Press), pp. 51–82.

Hughes, Thomas (1989) *American Genesis: A Century of Invention and Technological Enthusiasm* (Harmondsworth: Penguin).

Hughes, Thomas (1994) 'Technological Momentum', in Leo Marx and Merritt Roe Smith (eds), *Does Technology Drive History? The Dilemma of Technological Determinism* (Cambridge, MA: MIT Press), pp. 101–13.

Hulme, Mike (2009) *Why We Disagree About Climate Change: Understanding Controversy, Inaction and Opportunity* (Cambridge: Cambridge University Press).

Huntington, Samuel (1996) *The Clash of Civilizations and the Remaking of the World Order* (New York: Simon and Schuster).

Ingham, Geoffrey (2004) *The Nature of Money* (Cambridge: Polity Press).

Inglehart, Ronald (1990) *Culture Shift in Advanced Industrial Societies* (Princeton: Princeton University Press).

Jaffrelot, Christophe (2011) *Religion, Caste and Politics in India* (London: C. Hurst and Co.).

Josephson, Paul (2004) *Resources Under Regimes: Technology, Environment and the State* (Cambridge, MA: Harvard University Press).

Katz, James and Mark Aakhus (eds) (2002) *Perpetual Contact: Mobile Communication, Private Talk, Public Performance* (Cambridge: Cambridge University Press).

Katz, James (2008) 'Mainstreamed Mobiles in Daily Life: Perspectives and Prospects', in James Katz (ed.), *Handbook of Mobile Communication* (Cambridge, MA: MIT Press), pp. 433–45.

Katzenstein, Mary, Sumitu Kothari and Uday Mehta (2001) 'Social Movement Politics in India: Institutions, Interests, and Identities', in Atul Kohli (ed.), *The Success of India's Democracy* (Cambridge: Cambridge University Press), pp. 242–69.

Keck, Margaret and Kathryn Sikkink (1998) *Activists Beyond Borders: Advocacy Networks in International Politics* (Ithaca: Cornell University Press).

Kent, Neil (2000) *The Soul of the North: A Social, Architectural and Cultural History of the Nordic Countries* (London: Reaktion Books).

King, Michael and Chris Thornhill (2003) *Niklas Luhmann's Theory of Politics and Law* (Basingstoke: Palgrave Macmillan).

Kohli, Atul (2004) *State-directed Development: Political Power and Industrialization in the Global Periphery* (Cambridge: Cambridge University Press).

Kohli, Atul (2012) *Poverty amid Plenty in the New India* (Cambridge: Cambridge University Press).

Krippner, Greta (2011) *Capitalizing on Crisis: The Political Origins of the Rise of Finance* (Cambridge, MA: Harvard University Press).

Krippner, Greta (2005) 'The Financialization of the American Economy', *Socio-Economic Review*, vol. 3, no. 2, pp. 173–208.

Krippner, Greta, Mark Granovetter, Fred Block et al. (2004) 'Polanyi Symposium: a Conversation about Embeddedness', *Socioeconomic Review*, vol. 2, no. 1, pp. 109–35.

Kuper, A. (1999) *Culture: The Anthropologists' Account* (Cambridge, MA.: Harvard University Press).

Lange, Matthew (2009) *Lineages of Despotism and Development: British Colonialism and State Power* (Chicago: University of Chicago Press).

Latour, Bruno (1993) *We Have Never Been Modern* (Hemel Hempstead: Harvester Wheatsheaf).

Lee, Ching Kwan (2007) *Against the Law: Labor Protest in China's Rustbelt and Sunbelt* (Berkeley: University of California Press).

Li, Jieli (1993) 'Geopolitics of the Chinese Communist Party in the Twentieth Century', *Sociological Perspectives*, vol. 36, no. 4, pp. 315–33.

Lindbom, Anders (2008) 'The Swedish Conservative Party and the Welfare State: Institutional Change and Adapting Preferences', *Government and Opposition*, vol. 43, no. 4, pp. 539–60.

Lindert, Peter (2004) *Growing Public. Social Spending and Economic Growth since the Eighteenth Century* (Cambridge: Cambridge University Press).

Löfgren, Orvar (1995) 'Consuming Interests', in Jonathan Friedman (ed.), *Consumption and Identity* (Chur: Harwood Academic Publishers), pp. 47–70.

Lipset, Seymour Martin (1996) *American Exceptionalism: A Double-edged Sword* (New York: W. W. Norton).

Lomborg, Bjorn (2001) *The Skeptical Environmentalist* (Cambridge: Cambridge University Press).

Lomborg, Bjorn (ed.) (2004) *Global Crises, Global Solutions* (Cambridge: Cambridge University Press).

Luce, Edward (2011) *In Spite of the Gods. The Strange Rise of Modern India*, 2nd ed. (London: Abacus).

Luhmann, Niklas (1977) *Die Funktion der Religion* (Frankfurt am Main: Suhrkamp).

Lupher, Mark (1996) *Power Restructuring in China and Russia* (Boulder: Westview Press).

Lyon, David (2000) *Jesus in Disneyland: Religion in Postmodern Times* (Cambridge: Polity Press).

MacKay, David (2009) *Sustainable Energy: Without the Hot Air* (Cambridge: UIT Cambridge).

Maddison, Angus (2001) *The World Economy: A Millennial Perspective* (Paris: OECD).

Maddison, Angus (2007) *Contours of the World Economy, 1–2030 AD* (Oxford: Oxford University Press).

Magee, Bryan (1973) *Popper* (London: Fontana).

Malešević, Siniša (2010) *The Sociology of War and Violence* (Cambridge: Cambridge University Press).

Mann, Michael (1986) *The Sources of Social Power, Volume I: A History of Power from the Beginning to 1760 AD* (Cambridge: Cambridge University Press).

Mann, Michael (1988a) 'The Autonomous Power of the State: Its Origins, Mechanisms, and Results', in Michael Mann, *States, War and Capitalism* (Oxford: Basil Blackwell), pp. 1–32.

Mann, Michael (1988b) 'Ruling Class Strategies and Citizenship', in Mann, *States, War and Capitalism*, pp. 188–209.

Mann, Michael (1993) *The Sources of Social Power, Volume II: The Rise of Classes and Nation-states* (Cambridge: Cambridge University Press).

Mann, Michael (1996) 'Nation-states in Europe and Other Continents: Diversifying, Developing, Not Dying', in Gopal Balakrishnan (ed.), *Mapping the Nation* (London: Verso), pp. 295–316.

Mann, Michael (1995) 'Sources of Variation in Working-class Movements in Twentieth-century Europe', *New Left Review*, vol. 212, pp. 14–54.

Mann, Michael (1998) 'Is There a Society Called Euro?', in Roland Axtmann (ed.), *Globalization and Europe: Theoretical and Empirical Investigations* (London: Pinter), pp. 184–207.

Mann, Michael (1999) 'Has Globalization Ended the Rise and Rise of the Nation-state?', in T. V. Paul and John A. Hall (eds), *International Order and the Future of World Politics* (Cambridge: Cambridge University Press), pp. 237–51.

Mann, Michael (2001) 'Globalization as Violence', unpublished essay, retrieved 29 September 2010, at: www.sscnet.ucla.edu/soc/faculty/mann/globasviol%5B1%5D.pdf).

Mann, Michael (2005) *The Dark Side of Democracy: Explaining Ethnic Cleansing* (Cambridge: Cambridge University Press).

Mann, Michael (2005) *Geschichte Indiens: Vom 18. bis zum 21. Jahrhundert [The History of India: From the 18th to the 21st Century]* (Paderborn: Schoeningh).

Mann, Michael (2006) 'The Sources of Social Power Revisited: A Response to Criticism', in John A. Hall and Ralph Schroeder (eds), *An Anatomy of Power: The Social Theory of Michael Mann* (Cambridge: Cambridge University Press), pp. 343–96.

Mann, Michael (2011) *Power in the 21st Century* (Cambridge: Polity Press).

Mann, Michael (2012) *The Sources of Social Power, vol. 3: Global Empires and Revolution, 1890–1945* (Cambridge: Cambridge University Press).

Mann, Michael (2013) *The Sources of Social Power, vol. 4: Globalizations, 1945–2011* (Cambridge: Cambridge University Press).

Mann, Michael and Dylan Riley (2007) 'Explaining Macro-regional Trends in Global Income Inequalities', *Socio-Economic Review*, vol. 5, no. 1, pp. 81–115.

Manor, James (1996) "Ethnicity" and Politics in India, *International Affairs*, vol. 72, no. 3, pp. 459–75.

Marshall, Thomas H. (1950) *Citizenship and Social Class, and Other Essays* (Cambridge: Cambridge University Press).

Martell, Luke (2010) *The Sociology of Globalization* (Cambridge: Polity Press).

Martin, David (1974) *A General Theory of Secularization* (Oxford: Basil Blackwell).

Martin, Isaac William, Ajay Mehrotra and Monica Prasad (2009) 'The Thunder of History: The Origins and Development of the New Fiscal Sociology'; Isaac Martin et al. (eds), *The New Fiscal Sociology: Taxation in Historical and Comparative Perspective* (Cambridge: Cambridge University Press), pp. 1–27.

McGregor, Richard (2010) *The Party: The Secret World of China's Communist Rulers* (London: Allen Lane).

McNeill, John R. (2000) *Something New Under the Sun: An Environmental History of the Twentieth-century World* (New York: W. W. Norton).

Merton, Robert (1942) 'The Normative Structure of Science', in Robert Merton, *The Sociology of Science* (Chicago: University of Chicago Press [1973]), pp. 267–78.

Metcalf, Barbara and Thomas Metcalf (2002) *A Concise History of India* (Cambridge: Cambridge University Press).

Meyer, John, John Boli, George Thomas and Francisco Ramirez (1997) 'World Society and the Nation-State', *American Journal of Sociology*, vol. 103, no. 1, pp. 144–81.

Milanovic, Branko (2011) *The Haves and the Have-nots: A Brief and Idiosyncratic Guide to Global Inequality* (New York: Basic Books).

Misra, Maria (2008) *Vishnu's Crowded Temple: India since the Great Rebellion* (London: Penguin Books).

Mitter, Rana (2004) *A Bitter Revolution: China's Struggle with the Modern World* (Oxford: Oxford University Press).

Mokyr, Joel (1990) *The Lever of Riches – Technological Creativity and Economic Progress* (Oxford: Oxford University Press).

Moeller, Hans-Georg (2012) *The Radical Luhmann* (New York: Columbia University Press).

Morgan, Mary (2012) *The World in the Model: How Economists Work and Think* (Cambridge: Cambridge University Press).

Nagel, Thomas (2005) 'The Problem of Global Justice', *Philosophy and Public Affairs*, vol. 33, no. 2, pp. 113–47.

Naughton, Barry (2007) *The Chinese Economy: Transitions and Growth* (Cambridge, MA: MIT Press).

Norris, Pippa and Ronald Inglehart (2004) *Sacred and Secular: Religion and Politics Worldwide* (Cambridge: Cambridge University Press).

Norris, Pippa and Ronald Inglehart (2009) *Cosmopolitan Communication: Cultural Diversity in a Globalized World* (Cambridge: Cambridge University Press).

Nye, David (1998) *Consuming Power: A Social History of American Energies* (Cambridge, MA: MIT Press).

O'Dell, Tom (1997) *Culture Unbound: Americanization and Everyday Life in Sweden* (Lund: Nordic Academic Press).

O'Rourke, Kevin and Jeffrey Williamson (1999) *Globalization and History: The Evolution of a Nineteenth Century Atlantic Economy* (Cambridge, MA: MIT Press).

Orfali, Kristina (1991) 'The Rise and Fall of the Swedish Model', in Antoine Prost and Gerard Vincent (eds), *A History of Private Life: Riddles of Identity in Modern Times* (Cambridge, MA: Harvard University Press), pp. 417–49.

Osterhammel, Juergen (1989) *China und die Weltgesellschaft. Vom 18. Jahrhundert bis in unsere Zeit* (München: C. H. Beck).

Osterhammel, Juergen (2009) *Die Verwandlung der Welt. Eine Geschichte des 19. Jahrhunderts* (München: C. H. Beck).

Osterhammel, Juergen and Niels Petersson (2003) *Geschichte der Globalisierung: Dimensionen, Prozesse, Epochen* (München: C. H. Beck).

Partridge, Ernest (2001) 'Future Generations', in Dale Jamieson (ed.), *A Companion to Environmental Philosophy* (Oxford: Blackwell), pp. 377–89.

Perez-Diaz, Victor (1993) *The Return of Civil Society: The Emergence of Democratic Spain* (Cambridge, MA: Harvard University Press).

Perkin, Harold (1996) *The Third Revolution: Professional Elites in the Modern World* (London: Routledge).

Perrow, Charles (2002) *Organizing America: Wealth, Power, and the Origins of Corporate Capitalism* (Princeton: Princeton University Press).

Perry, Elizabeth (2011) 'From Mass Campaigns to Managed Campaigns: "Constructing a New Socialist Countryside"', in Sebastian Heilman and Elizabeth Perry (eds), *Mao's Invisible Hand: The Political Foundations of Adaptive Governance in China* (Cambridge, MA: Harvard University Press), pp. 30–61.

Pieke, Frank (2009) *The Good Communist: Elite Training and State Building in Today's China* (Cambridge: Cambridge University Press).

Pielke, Roger Jr., Tom Wigley and Christopher Green (2008) 'Dangerous Assumptions', *Nature*, vol. 452, no. 3, pp. 531–2.

Pogge, Thomas (2008) *World Poverty and Human Rights*, 2nd ed. (Cambridge: Polity Press).

Pogge, Thomas (2010) 'Responses to the Critics', in Alison Jaggar (ed.), *Thomas Pogge and his Critics* (Cambridge: Polity Press), pp. 175–250.

Pomeranz. Kenneth (2000) *The Great Divergence: China, Europe, and the Making of the Modern World Economy* (Princeton: Princeton University Press).

Pomeranz, Kenneth (2009a) 'Introduction: World History and Environmental History', in Edmund Burke III and Kenneth Pomeranz (eds), *The Environment and World History* (Berkeley: University of California Press), pp. 3–32.

Pomeranz, Kenneth (2009b) 'The Transformation of China's Environment, 1500–2000', in Edmund Burke III and Kenneth Pomeranz (eds), *The Environment and World History* (Berkeley: University of California Press), pp. 118–64.

Pomeranz, Kenneth and Steven Topik (1999) *The World that Trade Created* (Armonk: M. E. Sharpe).

Pontusson, Jonas (2005) *Inequality and Prosperity: Social Europe vs. Liberal America* (Ithaca: Cornell University Press).

Priestland, David (2012) *Merchant, Soldier, Sage: A New History of Power* (London: Allen Lane).

Putnam, Robert (2000) *Bowling Alone: the Collapse and Revival of American Community* (New York: Simon and Schuster).

Quigley, Declan (1999) *The Interpretation of Caste* (New Delhi: Oxford University Press).

Radkau, Joachim (2008) *Nature and Power: A Global History of the Environment* (Cambridge: Cambridge University Press).

Radkau, Joachim (2011) *Die Aera der Oekologie: Eine Weltgeschichte* (München: C. H. Beck).

Rantanen, Terhi (2005) *The Media and Globalization* (London: Sage).

Rawls, John (1971) *A Theory of Justice* (Cambridge, MA: Harvard University Press).

Rudolph, Lloyd and Susan Hoeber Rudolph (1987) *In Pursuit of Lakshmi: The Political Economy of the Indian State* (Chicago: University of Chicago Press).

Rule, James (2002) 'From Mass Society to Perpetual Contact: Models of Communication Technologies in Social Context', in James Katz and Mark Aakhus (eds), *Perpetual Contact: Mobile Communication, Private Talk, Public Performance* (Cambridge: Cambridge University Press), pp. 242–54.

Rule, James (2007) *Privacy in Peril* (Oxford: Oxford University Press).

Rueschemeyer, Dietrich, Evelyne Huber Stephens and John D. Stephens (1992) *Capitalist Democracy and Development* (Cambridge: Polity Press).

Roberts, J. Timmons and Bradley Parks (2007) *A Climate of Injustice: Global Inequality, North-South Politics, and Climate Policy* (Cambridge, MA: MIT Press).

Rockstroem, Johan et al. (2009) 'A Safe Operating Space for Humanity', *Nature*, vol. 461, pp. 472–5.

Schroeder, Ralph (1992) *Max Weber and the Sociology of Culture* (London: Sage).

Schroeder, Ralph (1998) 'From Weber's Political Sociology to Contemporary Liberal Democracy', in Ralph Schroeder (ed.), *Max Weber, Democracy and Modernization* (Basingstoke: Palgrave Macmillan), pp. 79–92.

Schroeder, Ralph (2007) *Rethinking Science, Technology and Social Change* (Stanford: Stanford University Press).

Schroeder, Ralph (2010) 'The Limits to Transforming the Environment and the Limits to Sociological Knowledge', *Sustainability*, vol. 2, no. 8, pp. 2483–98.

Schroeder, Ralph (2011a) 'Science, Technology and Globalization', in Tilman Mayer, Robert Meyer, Lazaros Miliopouloss and Hans-Peter Ohly (eds), *Globalisierung Im Fokus von Politik, Wirtschaft, Gesellschaft: Eine Bestandsaufnahme* (Wiesbaden: Verlag fuer Sozialwissenschaften), pp. 283–97.

Schroeder, Ralph (2011b) 'The Three Cultures of Post-industrial Societies', *Sociological Focus*, vol. 44, no. 1, pp. 1–17.

Schulze, G. (2005) *Die Erlebnisgesellschaft: Kultursoziologie der Gegenwart*, 2nd ed. (Frankfurt am Main: Campus Verlag).

Sen, Amartya (2009) *The Idea of Justice* (London: Allen Lane).

Sejersted, Francis (2011) *The Age of Social Democracy: Norway and Sweden in the Twentieth Century* (Princeton: Princeton University Press).

Shambaugh, David (2008) *China's Communist Party: Atrophy and Adaptation* (Berkeley: University of California Press).

Shapin, Steven (2008) 'Science and the Modern World', in Edward Hackett, Olga Amsterdamska, Michael Lynch and Judy Wajcman (eds), *Handbook of Science and Technology Studies* (Cambridge, MA: MIT Press), pp. 433–48.

Shinn, Terry (2007) *Research-technology and Cultural Change: Instrumentation, Genericity, Transversality* (Oxford: The Bardwell Press).

Shristava, Lara (2008) 'The Mobile Makes Its Mark', in James Katz (ed.), *Handbook of Mobile Communication* (Cambridge, MA: MIT Press), pp. 15–27.

Shue, Vivienne (2010) 'Legitimacy Crisis in China?', in Peter Hays Gries and Stanley Rosen (eds), *Chinese Politics: State, Society and the Market* (Abingdon: Routledge), pp. 41–68.

Silver, Beverly (2003) *Forces of Labor: Worker's Movements and Globalization since 1870* (Cambridge: Cambridge University Press).

Singer, Peter (2002) *One World: The Ethics of Globalization* (New Haven: Yale University Press).

Skidelsky, Robert (2003) *John Maynard Keynes 1883–1946: Economist, Philosopher, Statesman* (London: Macmillan).

Slater, Dan (2010) *Ordering Power: Contentious Politics and Authoritarian Leviathans in Southeast Asia* (Cambridge: Cambridge University Press).

Slaughter, Ann-Marie (2004) *A New World Order* (Princeton: Princeton University Press).

Snyder, Jack (2000) *From Voting to Violence: Democratization and Nationalist Conflict* (New York: W. W. Norton).

Snyder, Jack (2006) 'Networks and Ideologies: The Fusion of "Is" and "Ought" as a Means to Social Power', in John A. Hall and Ralph Schroeder (eds), *An Anatomy of Power: The Social Theory of Michael Mann* (Cambridge: Cambridge University Press), pp. 306–27.

Speth, James Gustave (2008) *The Bridge at the End of the World* (New Haven: Yale University Press).

Steinmo, Sven (1993) *Taxation and Democracy: Swedish, British and American Approaches to Financing the Modern State* (New Haven: Yale University Press).

Steinmo, Sven (2010) *The Evolution of Modern States: Sweden, Japan and the United States* (Cambridge: Cambridge University Press).

Stearns, Peter (2001) *Consumerism in World History: The Global Transformation of Desire* (London: Routledge).

Stearns, Peter (2005) *Global Outrage: The Impact of World Opinion on Contemporary History* (Oxford: Oneworld Publications).

Stern, Nicholas (2007) *The Economics of Climate Change: The Stern Review* (Cambridge: Cambridge University Press).

Stern, Nicholas (2010) 'The Economics of Climate Change', in Stephen Gardiner, Simon Caney, Dale Jamieson and Henry Shue (eds), *Climate Ethics: Essential Readings* (Oxford, Oxford University Press), pp. 39–76.

Stinchcombe, Arthur (1983) *Economic Sociology* (Orlando: Academic Press).

Strange, Susan (1986) *Casino Capitalism* (Oxford: Basil Blackwell).

Swedberg, Richard (1990) 'Introduction', in Richard Swedberg, *Economics and Sociology – Redefining their Boundaries: Conversations with Economists and Sociologists* (Princeton: Princeton University Press), pp. 5–23.

Swedberg, Richard (1994) 'Markets as Social Structures', in Neil Smelser and Richard Swedberg (eds), *The Handbook of Economic Sociology* (Princeton: Princeton University Press), pp. 255–82.

Swedberg, Richard (2003) *Principles of Economic Sociology* (Princeton: Princeton University Press).

Swedberg, Richard (2005) 'The Economic Sociology of Capitalism: An Introduction and an Agenda', in Victor Nee and Richard Swedberg (eds), *The Economic Sociology of Capitalism* (Princeton: Princeton University Press), pp. 3–40.

Swenson, Peter (2002) *Capitalists against Markets: The Making of Labor Markets and Welfare States in the United States and Sweden* (New York: Oxford University Press).

Tanzi, Vito and Ludger Schuhknecht (2000) *Public Spending in the Twentieth Century: A Global Perspective* (Cambridge: Cambridge University Press).

Thomas, Keith (1983) *Man and the Natural World* (London: Allen Lane).

Tilly, Charles (1990) *Coercion, Capital, and European States* (Oxford: Blackwell).

Tilly, Chris and Charles Tilly (1994) 'Capitalist Work and Labor Markets', in Neil Smelser and Richard Swedberg (eds), *The Handbook of Economic Sociology* (Princeton: Princeton University Press), pp. 282–312.

Tilly, Chris and Charles Tilly (1998) *Work under Capitalism* (Boulder: Westview Press).

Tomlinson, B. R. (1993) *The Economic History of India 1860–1970* (Cambridge: Cambridge University Press).

Tomlinson, John (1999) *Globalization and Culture* (Cambridge: Polity Press).

Tragardh, Lars (2010) 'Rethinking the Nordic Welfare State through A Neo-Hegelian Theory of State and Civil Society', *Journal of Political Ideologies*, vol. 15, no. 3, pp. 227–39.

Tsai, Kellee (2007) *Capitalism without Democracy: The Private Sector in Contemporary China* (Ithaca: Cornell University Press).

Tsang, Steve (2009) 'Consultative Leninism: China's New Political Framework', *Journal of Contemporary China*, vol. 18, no. 62, pp. 865–80.

Turner, Bryan (1986) *Citizenship and Capitalism* (London: Allen and Unwin).

Turner, Jonathan (1995) *Macrodynamics: Towards a Theory on the Organization of Human Populations* (New Brunswick: Rutgers University Press).

Turner, Jonathan (1997) *The Institutional Order* (New York: Addison Wesley Longman).

van Creveld, Martin (2008) *The Changing Face of War* (New York: Ballantine Books).

van der Wee, Herman (1987) *Prosperity and Upheaval: The World Economy 1945–80* (Harmondsworth: Penguin Books).

Varenne, Hervé (1977) *Americans Together: Structured Diversity in an American Town* (New York: Teachers College Press).

Varshney, Ashutosh (2000) 'Is India Becoming More Democratic?', *The Journal of Asian Studies*, vol. 59, no. 1, pp. 3–25.

Varshney, Ashutosh (2001) 'Ethnic Conflict and Civil Society: India and Beyond', *World Politics*, vol. 53, no. 3, pp. 362–98.

Vogel, Steven (1996) *Freer Markets, More Rules: Regulatory Reform in Advanced Industrial Countries* (Ithaca: Cornell University Press).

Walby, Sylvia (2009) *Globalization and Inequalities: Complexity and Contested Modernities* (London: Sage).

Walder, Andrew, Tianjue Luo and Dan Wang (2010) 'The Property Revolution: Asset Conversion and Social Change in Transitional Economies', paper presented in the Sociology Department at UCLA, 28 April: at:www.soc.ucla.edu/event/colloquia-calendar

Wasserstrom, Jeffrey (2010) *China in the 21st Century: What Everyone Needs to Know* (Oxford: Oxford University Press).

Weber, Max (1948) *From Max Weber: Essays in Sociology* (London: Routledge and Kegan Paul).

Weber, Max (1978) *Economy and Society: An Outline of Interpretive Sociology*, ed. by Guenther Roth and Claus Wittich (Berkeley: University of California Press).

Weiss, Linda and John Hobson (1995) *States and Economic Development: A Comparative Historical Analysis* (Cambridge: Polity Press).

Weiss, Linda (2003) 'Introduction: Bringing Domestic Institutions Back In', in Linda Weiss (ed.), *States in the Global Economy: Bringing Domestic Institutions Back In* (Cambridge: Cambridge University Press), pp. 1–33.

Westad, Odd Arne (2005) *The Global Cold War* (Cambridge: Cambridge University Press).

White, Harrison C. (1981) 'Where Do Markets Come From?', *American Journal of Sociology*, vol. 87, no. 3, pp. 54–47.

Whitley, R. (1999) *Divergent Capitalisms. The Social Structuring and Change of Business Systems* (Oxford: Oxford University Press).

Whyte, Martin King (2009) 'Paradoxes of China's Economic Boom', *Annual Review of Sociology*, vol. 35, pp. 371–92.

Whyte, Martin King (2010) *Myth of the Social Volcano: Perceptions of Inequality and Distributive Injustice in Contemporary China* (Stanford: Stanford University Press).

Wilson, Charlie and Hadi Dowlatabadi (2007) 'Models of Decision Making and Energy Use', *Annual Review of Environment and Resources*, vol. 32, pp. 169–203.

Wong, R. Bin (1997) *China Transformed: Historical Change and the Limits of European Experience* (Ithaca: Cornell University Press).

World Bank (2008) *Global Economic Prospects: Technology Diffusion in the Developing World* (Washington, DC: World Bank).

World Internet Project (WIP) Report (2009), available at: www.worldinternetproject.net

Yates, JoAnne (1989) *Control through Communication: The Rise of System in American Management* (Baltimore: Johns Hopkins University Press).

Yearley, Steven (2005) 'The Sociology of the Environment and of Nature', in Craig Calhoun, Chris Rojek and Bryan Turner (eds), *The Sage Handbook of Sociology* (London and Thousand Oaks: Sage), pp. 315–26.

Yongming, Zhou (2006) *Historicizing Online Politics: Telegraphy, the Internet, and Political Participation in China* (Stanford: Stanford University Press).

Index

Italic page numbers indicate tables; bold indicate figures.